pLANET OF THE APES

REVISITED

Joe Russo and Larry Landsman with Edward Gross

FOREWORD BY CHARLTON HESTON

The Behind-the-Scenes Story
of the Classic Science Fiction Saga

 THOMAS DUNNE BOOKS / ST. MARTIN'S GRIFFIN ✒ NEW YORK

pLANET
OF THE
APES

↓

REVISITED

Thomas Dunne Books.

An imprint of St. Martin's Press.

www.stmartins.com

Book design by James Sinclair

Library of Congress Cataloging-in-Publication Data

Russo, Joe

    Planet of the Apes revisited : the behind-the-scenes story of the classic science fiction saga / Joe Russo and Larry Landsman with Edward Gross ; foreword by Charlton Heston—1st ed.

    p. cm.

Includes index.

ISBN 0-312-25239-0

    1. Planet of the Apes films. I. Landsman, Larry. II. Gross, Edward. III. Title.

PN1995.9.P495 R87 2001

791.43'75—dc21

2001020254

First Edition: August 2001

10 9 8 7 6 5 4 3 2 1

Arthur P. Jacobs kept the original Lawgiver statue in his backyard as a monument to his beloved series.

The authors would like to dedicate this book to the memory of two men whose talent, devotion, and contributions to the *Planet of the Apes* phenomenon are positively immeasurable . . .

Arthur P. Jacobs
(March 7, 1922–June 27, 1973),
whose tenacity and vision made *Planet of the Apes* a cinematic reality, and who helped change the way science fiction films were made and accepted.

Roddy McDowall
(September 17, 1928–October 3, 1998),
whose warm, generous spirit as an actor and a human being gave life to the wonderful characterizations he created throughout the *Planet of the Apes* film and television series.

CONTENTS

ACKNOWLEDGMENTS

An undertaking of this size and scope requires the cooperation of many individuals and we owe them all a debt of enormous gratitude. *Planet of the Apes Revisited* simply could not have been written without the generous support of Natalie Trundy Jacobs who allowed us exclusive access to the personal archives of Arthur P. Jacobs/ APJAC Productions. She also offered us tremendous encouragement throughout the years we were peddling our book all over New York from publisher to publisher.

We would particularly like to offer a very special thanks to Charlton Heston for his loyalty to this project, and for being a fine actor and an extraordinary man. His significant contributions to the project, as well as to the *Planet of the Apes* legacy, cannot be overstated.

For consenting to be interviewed and for

graciously opening their homes to us throughout the years in both New York and Los Angeles, we would like to thank the following (in alphabetical order): Mort Abrahams, Claude Akins, Eric Braeden, Frank Capra, Jr., John Chambers, Joyce Hooper Corrington, Severn Darden, James Franciscus, James Gregory, Linda Harrison, Charlton Heston, Herbert Hirschman, Kim Hunter, Natalie Trundy Jacobs, Buck Kartalian, Andy Knight, Roddy McDowall, Don Murray, Ted Post, Carol Serling, Don Taylor, J. Lee Thompson, Lou Wagner, and Richard Zanuck.

A great debt is owed to our agent, Christopher Schelling, as well as our editors at St. Martin's Press, Peter Wolverton, Emily Hopkins, and particularly Barry Neville, for being the first one to take a chance on us and believing that *Apes* could really "talk." A big thank you to Liz McNamara, who guided us through all the legal issues.

A special thanks to the following individuals whose contributions to and support of *Planet of the Apes Revisited* were indispensable: Carol Lanning, for passing along all our faxes and for helping us to spell the word "foreword" correctly; Lydia Heston, Lou Wagner, and Linda Harrison, for use of their personal photography; as well as Joseph Choate, Carol Serling, Guy Dehn, Jimmy Bernard, Hazel Court, and Sally Walsh, for collaborating with us on the estates of Roddy McDowall, Rod Serling, Paul Dehn, and Don Taylor, respectively.

For their additional contributions to the manuscript and/or invaluable assistance, we would like to thank John Mathews (aka "the News Hound"), Roger Alford from "The Forbidden Zone" website, Rory Monteith, Chris Davies, Terry Hoknes from "Ape Chronicles," Jeff Krueger, Kevin Burns at Foxstar Productions, Lynn Weiss at AMC, Jeff Bond for his insights into the music of *Planet of the Apes*, John L. Flynn for his valuable point of view on Pierre Boulle's novel, and especially Abbie Bernstein for her inspiration and enthusiasm, as well as her ongoing guidance through the unfilmed sequences of the series. For their early advice and for pointing us in the right direction, we want to thank authors Brian Lowry, Gregory William Mank, Marc Scott Zicree, and Steve Rubin. A fellow author is invaluable during a time of crisis.

And last, but not least, on a personal note we want to thank Angela, Alyson, Jared, Eileen, Teddy, Dennis, and Kevin—our families and significant others—for their love and support—especially for putting up with our long hours of misanthropic behavior. We also want to express our love to our parents for always being supportive of us, especially throughout our obsessive adolescent years. As we used to remark, "Who's to say what's normal?"

A big thanks to each and every one of you. It's certainly been a long haul.

FOREWORD

Planet of the Apes turned out to be one of my most successful films, though it drifted around the studios for a couple of years like a stray dog looking for a home. Arthur Jacobs owned the property and spent his time peddling it around town, being laughed at by every studio he pitched it to: "Talking monkeys! Rocket ships! You outta your *mind*? Get out!!"

Arthur, however, was convinced he had a wonderful film, if only someone would make it. I read the book, which didn't impress me very much . . . but the *idea* did. Frank Schaffner agreed, we told Arthur we'd like to do it, if he could get the several million it would require to film.

By this time we had a wonderful Rod Serling screenplay. More importantly, we had Dick Zanuck's interest. He was running Fox at the time. "I'll put up fifty thousand to develop the makeups," he said, "then we show it to the board. If nobody laughs, you've got a go film."

And so we did. We shot for several months through the summer, and I, half naked most of the time, was sprayed with firehoses, caught in nets, and stoned (yes, even rubber rocks hurt).

Apes was really the first of the Space Operas, all still popular. It's a very fine film, and I'm proud to be in it. It's amazing how many people still write me about it. I'd say that film has the best ending of any movie I've ever seen. Before word got around, audiences would stand stunned when I stood below the ruins of the Statue of Liberty screaming, "They finally, really did it! You maniacs! You blew it up! God damn you . . . God damn you all to hell!"

—Charlton Heston

INTRODUCTION

A labor of love.

It's a phrase used to describe something to other people who think that your efforts are foolhardy at best, pointless at worst. And yet, you believe. You have to. You're the keeper of a dream that no one else can see, and you just know that you're right.

This is what producer Arthur P. Jacobs felt when he first came across Pierre Boulle's *Planet of the Apes* in 1963, and optioned it as a feature film. It all came down to the fact that he believed. Jacobs believed that a world in which intelligent apes ruled over beastlike humans could be brought to life, he believed that a man and an ape could have an intelligent conversation on screen and not get laughs from the audience, and he believed that he held a modern cinematic classic in his hands. Jacobs was three for three.

Planet of the Apes was indeed a modern classic, mixing sci-fi concepts with a powerful allegory to create one of the most satisfying genre films ever offered and a sci-fi epic that touched a generation. Beyond that—and it's important to remember that this was in the days before *Star Wars*—it gave birth to four theatrical sequels (1970's *Beneath the Planet of the Apes*, 1971's *Escape from the Planet of the Apes*, 1972's *Conquest of the Planet of the Apes*, and 1973's *Battle for the Planet of the Apes*), two television series, and an unprecedented amount of merchandise tie-ins.

Not bad for a labor of love!

While it took Jacobs five years to bring the original *Planet of the Apes* to life, that was nothing in comparison to the seventeen years it's taken to bring this book on the making of the *Apes* saga—a genuine labor of love for authors Joe Russo, Larry Landsman, and Edward Gross—to fruition.

Long before Tim Burton elected to "reimagine" the original film, or, for that matter, Fox deciding to relaunch the series, this book was in development. And, with the exception of Dale Winogura's fascinating early-'70s article on the making of the films in the pages of *Cinefantastique*, this is the first serious, in-depth, behind-the-scenes examination of those films.

The roots to this project can be traced back to 1968, when the original film was about to hit theaters. As author Joe Russo explains it, "My first introduction to *Planet of the Apes* was the actual pre-release TV spots which declared, '*Planet of the Apes* . . . beyond your wildest dreams.' I was immediately fascinated, despite my young age. I begged my mother to take me to see the film. My grandmother was a bookkeeper at a local theater (the Central in Passaic, New Jersey) so I got to see each of the *Apes* films first-run as often as I wanted. This was clearly how my life-long infatuation with 'show biz' began. I'd accompany my grandmother to the theater on Saturdays and just watch all these great films all day. I did this almost weekly until 1974, when the neighborhood changed and the format moved away from family entertainment.

"But *Planet* absolutely blew my mind," he continues. "Totally blew my young, little imagination away. All the neighborhood kids eventually saw it and throughout childhood it would be a constant source of thrills and enjoyment. By the time *Beneath the Planet of the Apes* came out in 1970, I was a bit older and got into that film even more than the original. To me, it was even more outrageous an experience. And when the film ended its run, I asked the manager for the theater poster and pressbook, which began the start of my *POTA* collection. For the following films I would go with groups of my friends and they were all major highlights growing up."

So strong did his fascination over the films grow, that Russo took to writing many of the cast and crew members, eventually receiving a reply from actress Kim Hunter, who had portrayed the talking chimpanzee Zira in the first three films of the series. "Her note came on 'psychedelic' stationary," he reflects, "and I was thrilled. She wrote, 'I'm glad you enjoyed the Apes films so enthusiastically.'"

When he was in the fifth grade, Russo also decided to create what was undoubtedly the first "making of" book devoted to *Planet of the Apes*. "I wrote and illustrated a hand-stitched and plastic-covered book which I called *From Man to Ape*," he explains. "It was a brief overview of the creation and application of the *Apes* makeup. I was already a pretty good artist at that age. This was for an art project in school, so technically I 'wrote' my first *POTA* book in the mid-seventies."

He also wrote to *Famous Monsters of Filmland* magazine, looking to contact other *Apes* fans. His name and address appeared in an issue, and as a result he was flooded with mail from dozens of other *Apes* fans across the country. "Through these fans," Russo points out, "I was able to start collecting photos and other memorabilia, and share my enthusiasm. Around this time I was reading the Sunday edition of the local paper when I saw an article about a local *Apes* fan who had acquired one of Roddy McDowall's appliances and was making himself up as an ape and doing in-store promo appearances at a local mall."

That "*Apes* fan" was actually coauthor Larry Landsman, whose life had been impacted by *Planet of the Apes* just as strongly as Russo's.

"For me," explains Landsman, "it really all started close to three decades ago, in the summer of '72, with the release of the fourth film, *Conquest of the Planet of the Apes*. Prior to that time, I recall catching *Beneath* and *Escape* in the theaters and being mesmerized by them, but it wasn't until my grandmother took me to see *Conquest* that I truly became hooked. I became an avid *Apes* fanatic that summer.

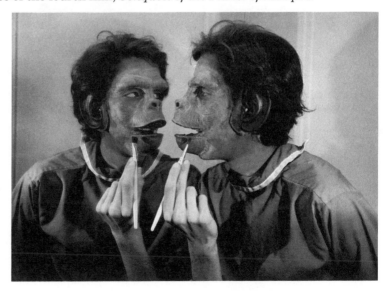

"Reflecting back on those thirty years," he continues, "I realize now that it was a time more important to my coming of age than I ever imagined. I was fifteen years old and about to enter high school." Landsman admits he could have been labeled a typical sci-fi geek back then, as he was somewhat of a loner, shy, and unassuming. "I turned to the world of science fiction for adventure, heroics, and intellectual stimulation. The *Apes* saga was not only the biggest continuing science-fiction canvas on the screen at that time, but there was nothing like it before. Moreover, I was enthralled with the Academy Award–winning makeup, and some of the ideas the films espoused were important to me—the warning to Man, where we are headed as a species, the profound implication of atomic war, and the concept that when mankind falls, another species will take over."

At the same time, Landsman points out, he was also a *Star Trek* fan (which he still is), and his love for both franchises would fill his life for the next few years. "Later on," he says, "it would be cooler to be a *Star Trek* fan than an *Apes* fan, so during college I became a 'closet' *Apes* fan." But of all those universes, it was *Apes* that captured his imagination most in the summer of '72.

As a result, he began collecting anything and everything imaginable that was based on the series, from models to garbage cans, from lobby cards to toys. Laugh-

ing, he adds, "I even went so far as to dive into actual garbage bins at the National Screen Service building (which happened to be located near my hometown) to scrounge for *Apes* posters that were thrown away. That was how obsessed I had become. My room eventually was covered from ceiling to floor with *Apes* memorabilia. I even rented a print of *Planet* from Films Incorporated, and watched it, by my own reckoning, eighteen times in a row!"

Landsman, like Russo, began finding *Apes* pen pals, and through a newfound Los Angeles–based friend, Landsman was able to obtain a set of prosthetic makeup pieces that had been sculpted for series star Roddy McDowall. In fact, he even wore the makeup on the flight back home to New Jersey. "At the airport," he says, "I was escorted onto the plane by security guards and was afforded deferential treatment on the ride home. I had no problem getting people interested in my hobby, and, obviously, I was a ham deep down inside."

Once his parents got over the shock of picking up the chimpanzee that had been their son, Landsman obtained permission to walk the local mall in ape makeup to help promote the live-action series. That stunt landed him in the local paper and caught Russo's attention.

"When I read about Larry," Russo explains, "I called his house. His mom answered and I left a message. Later that day, Larry called me and we began a friendship that continues to this day. Since he was quite older, he was way ahead of me. I remember the first time I went to his house I was in awe of his collection."

When the idea of writing a book occurred to Russo in late-1983/early-1984, he mentioned the concept to Landsman who was ironically thinking along the same lines. They decided to work together on the project and *Planet of the Apes Revisited* finally got underway in earnest in 1984. Russo and Landsman began writing to every significant cast and crewmember of the entire series to request interviews. The vast majority of everyone contacted was delighted to speak and share their experiences, because the films had represented such a unique and fondly remembered part of their respective careers.

That summer, the duo flew out to California, where they were invited to stay at the mansion of Natalie Trundy, Arthur P. Jacobs's widow and frequent costar of the film series. Trundy allowed Russo and Landsman to use her home as their headquarters as they dove into unprecedented research regarding the films. "Natalie Trundy gave us complete and total access to her late husband's entire production archives, covering the entire series from its earliest days," Landsman notes. "By her doing so, our ambition of being 'authorized' became reality and the credibility and integrity of the project was immediately established."

"We were granted complete access to the files and material of APJAC Productions," Russo elaborates, "including letters, scripts, photos, studio cast and call sheets, interoffice memos, sketches, film footage, and all other kinds of behind-the-scenes information. Roddy McDowall was generous enough to come to *us* at Natalie's house. It was there we did our in-person interview. We also met, interviewed, and watched the respective films of directors Don Taylor (who directed *Escape*) and Ted Post (director of *Beneath*). Then we met with actor Lou Wagner, director J. Lee Thompson, actor Severn Darden, and *Apes* makeup creator John

Chambers—all in one incredible trip!" Many more interviews would be conducted on the phone and in person at different locations over the next couple of years.

Another highlight for the duo was the discovery of the original 1966 makeup test film that starred Charlton Heston and Edward G. Robinson, and which served an integral role in Twentieth Century Fox going forward with the project. Only two prints of this test were still in existence, the other having been given "under the table" to Robinson. Amazingly, Russo discovered the makeup test sitting half-unspooled on a manual film rewinder in Jacobs's projection room.

In order to help interest a publisher, Russo and Landsman came up with the concept of something *extra* that would hopefully attract attention. "We wanted people to take the project seriously and not look at it as just a fan-type thing," says Russo. "I created/designed an eight-page presentation booklet that was heavily illustrated, complete with a full-color cover and printed on heavy-coated stock. This booklet so impressed people (Roddy McDowall in particular, who referred to it as 'elegant') that it definitely helped them to trust our intentions."

the Planet of the Apes (1972) chronicling the apes' uprising, and finally **Battle for the Planet of the Apes** (1973) which ties the loose ends together and brings the saga to a close.

Shortly before his death in 1973, producer Arthur P. Jacobs relinquished his interests in the "Apes" series to 20th Century-Fox, who in turn sold the films to CBS for their television premieres. The astronomical ratings garnered by the telecasts convinced the network to install **Planet of the Apes** as a weekly TV series ('74-75 season) which was able to explore many new ideas that had only been glimpsed at in the motion pictures. Actor Roddy McDowall, whose name had become synonymous with the "Apes" films, invariably returned to continue his simian portrayal. The apes' successful transition to television prompted even further adventures in the form of a Saturday morning animated series **Return to the Planet of the Apes** on NBC.

Today, 'Planet of the Apes' enjoys a large following of devoted enthusiasts who recognize it as the precursor to current sci-fi/fantasy/adventure film sagas such as **Star Wars** and **Star Trek**. The popularity of these film sagas today is in itself a tribute to producer Arthur P. Jacobs and the many talented directors, actors and technicians who are part of this trendsetting motion picture series.

The current popularity of the "Apes" films is illustrated by their recent performance on the ABC affiliate in Chicago. FOR FIVE CONSECUTIVE DAYS (NOVEMBER 28-DECEMBER 2, 1983) PLANET OF THE APES AND ITS FOUR SEQUELS RATED #1 IN THEIR TIME PERIOD!!

Both Russo and Landsman pressed forward with an incredible amount of research already under their belts. They now began the painstaking challenge of taking all of that research and turning it into a book. This is when Edward Gross entered the picture.

Desiring to be a writer from the time he was a child, Gross began his writing "career" penning original fan fiction, including stories taking place in the *Dark Shadows* universe and one particularly bizarre story called "Superman and Batman on the *Planet of the Apes*" (the title of which says it all). "As a child," he explains, "I absolutely loved *Planet of the Apes*. I can't tell you the sheer number of people I either bored, impressed, or infuriated with my memorization and constant reciting of Caesar's speech from the conclusion of *Conquest of the Planet of the Apes*. In fact, while I was writing this book, my sons came into the living room as I was watching one of the *Apes* films. They asked me what I was watching and I told them, adding that as important as *Star Wars* is to them today, *that's* how important *Planet of the Apes* had been to me when I was a kid. It was then that I realized how significant this project really was to me."

At the beginning of 1986, Gross decided that he would like to write a retrospective on the *Apes* films for *Starlog,* then the bestselling genre magazine on the newsstands, and proceeded to contact the films' directors. Both Ted Post (*Beneath*) and Don Taylor (*Escape*) told him about the book being written by Russo and Landsman, and suggested that he get in touch with them about some sort of collaboration. He did so, and the three hit it off fairly quickly, realizing that each of them had the desire to write a definitive account on the making of the *Apes* series. Fortuitously, they were also able to complement each other in the sense that most of the research for the book had been completed by Russo and Landsman, and Gross was another writer who could collaborate with them in molding that research into a manuscript.

After agreeing to work together, the trio went back to *Starlog* to see if they would be interested in an excerpt from the book in development. They were, and a behind-the-scenes article on *Beneath* appeared in issue #106 (published in 1986). For the authors, this was great news because it would serve as the perfect calling card for publishers.

Surprisingly, though, nothing happened. Five years later—in 1991—the premiere issue *Sci-Fi Universe* ran another excerpt, this one focusing on the project's early days. Again, the authors began contacting virtually every publisher in existence, both big and small, and the answer was, unfortunately, always the same.

The articles which appeared in *Starlog* and *Sci-Fi Universe* were written to help the authors sell their behind-the-scenes *Apes* book to a publisher, and the truth was that *no one* was interested. Ironically, it reminded them of the situation that Arthur P. Jacobs faced when he attempted to get a studio interested in the first *Planet of the Apes.* "Arthur kept pressing forward in spite of all the rejection he received," says Russo. "That was *exactly* the case with this book. But it's important to note that every time the book got rejected or derailed for one reason or another, we would say to ourselves, 'This book *is* going to come out some day; there will be interest again in *Planet of the Apes.*'"

While they waited, the three authors went about establishing their respective careers. Throughout the '90s and right up until the present, Russo has enjoyed a successful career as a musician/entertainer. He performs constantly and has appeared in over twelve countries. He recently cowrote and produced an album of original music with former Rascals drummer Dino Danelli. He has also written several articles, CD liner notes, and has self-published two books.

Landsman would complete his education at Hofstra University, and achieve success in the field of entertainment public relations. Throughout the last sixteen years, he conceived and executed national publicity campaigns for celebrity clientele, as well as for premium cable programming. Most recently, he served as corporate communications director at Showtime Networks, where, as fate would have it, he would encounter Charlton Heston, who had shot an episode of the network's *The Outer Limits*. On approaching the legendary actor, Landsman reminded him of the book (for which he had been interviewed several years earlier) and asked if Heston would be interested in writing the foreword, which he agreed to do.

"Charlton Heston's cooperation and loyalty to the project fueled us with renewed enthusiasm to see this book through to the end," says Russo. "At the same time, it gave us added credibility during our research." Landsman continues, "Mr. Heston's help and cooperation was immeasurably important to this project's success, and the fact that he agreed to write the foreword meant more than we could ever say."

During this time period, Gross moved on to write articles for a variety of magazines, among them *Cinefantastique*, *Fangoria*, *Comics Scene*, *Total TV*, and *Premiere*, while authoring numerous nonfiction books, including *Captains' Logs: The Complete Trek Voyages*, *X-Files: Confidential*, and *The Alien Nation Companion*.

Over the past ten years, rumors have run rampant that Twentieth Century Fox was attempting to relaunch the series. One name after another would become attached to the project and ultimately fall away, among them producer/director Oliver Stone, actor Arnold Schwarzenegger, and directors Chris Columbus and James Cameron. During this period of fits and starts, St. Martin's Press became convinced that a market for *Planet of the Apes Revisited* definitely existed, and they took the project on.

Then, to the benefit of *Apes* fans all over the world, as well as everyone who believed in this book project, the official word finally came from Fox: Tim Burton would be directing a brand new take on the material, and the all-new *Planet of the Apes* would reach theaters in July 2001. Suddenly, *Planet of the Apes Revisited* had real *legitimacy*. It would become the *only* "voice" on bookshelves chronicling the entire story. As such, it offers readers an intimate behind-the-scenes look that others devoted to the subject could never hope to achieve.

The results of all of those years of labor are in your hands. For the first time anywhere, the complete saga of the *Planet of the Apes*—from the day Arthur P. Jacobs first discovered Pierre Boulle's novel to the release of Tim Burton's new version—has finally been told. The journey, at last, has come to an end, and the results—the authors feel—are something special.

Labors of love usually are.

Planet of the Apes caricature by author Joe Russo.

The Road to the
PLANET OF THE APES

1

As 1998 was nearing a close, the science fiction world in general, and the World Wide Web in particular, was abuzz.

George Lucas had just gone on-line with the teaser trailer for *Star Wars Episode I: The Phantom Menace,* the first entry in that film series to be produced in sixteen years; Paramount Pictures was about to release the ninth *Star Trek* feature film, *Insurrection;* and Twentieth Century Fox was busy celebrating the thirtieth anniversary of *Planet of the Apes.*

It was all pretty heady stuff, particularly when one considers that back at the time of *Planet*'s release in 1968, sci-fi was a four-letter word that no studio executive in his right mind would willingly embrace. The genre was pretty much dismissed, its primary audience considered to be children who couldn't handle a sophisticated or philosophical approach. Certainly there had been exceptions along the way—among them *Forbidden Planet* and *The Day the Earth Stood Still*—but as far as mainstream Hollywood was concerned, sci-fi was best epitomized by television's *Lost in Space*. Indeed, even the original *Star Trek* was struggling ratings-wise on NBC at the time. But one man—producer Arthur P. Jacobs—believed when no one else would.

"It started in Paris in 1963," the late Jacobs had recalled to the press. "I was looking for material, and I would meet with various literary agents. [They] asked me what I was looking for and I said, 'I wish *King Kong* hadn't been made so I could make it.' I [also] said, 'What I would like to find is something like *King Kong.*' I didn't want to make *King Kong,* because you can't do that. About six months later, I was in Paris and a literary agent called me, came over and said he had a new novel by Francoise Saigan. I read it and wasn't too fascinated. Then he said, 'Speaking of *King Kong,* I've got a thing here, and it's so far out I don't think you can make it. It can't be filmed. How can you make talking apes believable?' He told me the story and I said, 'I'll buy it—gotta buy it.' He said, 'I think you're crazy, but okay.' So I bought it and that's how it came about."

In 1971, he summarized the early years of *Planet of the Apes*' development: "I spent about three and a half years of everyone refusing to make the movie. First, I had sketches made, and went through six sets of artists to get the concept, but none of them were right. Finally, I hit on a seventh one and said, 'That's how it should look.' Then, I showed the sketches to the studios and they said, 'No way.' Then I got Rod Serling to do the screenplay and went to everybody again—absolute turndown. I even went to J. Arthur Rank in England, and Samuel Bronston in Spain. Everyone said no. Then I figured I needed a top director to sell the package. Blake Edwards took it to J. L. Warner and they were both crazy about it. But then they got into a fight, and when Warner saw the high budget, he said, 'Forget about the apes.' So then I figured, maybe if I got an actor involved. I sent the script to Marlon Brando, who said he didn't understand it. Then I sent it to Charlton Heston who, in one hour, said yes. Then Heston suggested Franklin Schaffner as director, and he also said yes. Now I have Heston, Schaffner, a screenplay, and all the sketches. I go right back to everybody and they throw me out again.

"I went to Richard Zanuck at Fox," Jacobs elaborated, "and he turned it down, saying, 'Nobody will believe Charlton Heston talking to an ape.' I finally convinced [him] to let me make a test, and I got Heston and Edward G. Robinson, with Schaffner directing it. I showed it to Zanuck, who really got excited over it. Rod Serling wrote a long, nine-page scene, a conversation between Taylor and Dr. Zaius, which was condensed in the final film. Everyone still thought that no one would believe an ape talking to a man, and I said, 'I will prove it to you that they will believe it.' We packed the screening room with everyone we could get a hold of, and Zanuck said, 'If they start laughing, forget it.' Nobody laughed, they sat there tense, and he said, 'Make the picture.'"

Despite the fact that Jacobs made the creation of *Planet of the Apes* sound like an exercise in simplicity, the truth is that it took several very long and arduous years before Zanuck uttered the words, "Okay, go."

In the Beginning

Planet of the Apes' origin can probably be traced back to Irish satirist and poet Jonathan Swift (1667–1745), whose literary works included *Travels into Several Remote Nations of the World by Lemuel Gulliver* (1726), imagining a world not dissimilar to the one that Pierre Boulle had imagined. Popularly known as *Gulliver's Travels* (collected and revised in 1735), this four-book epic went about marooning its central character in a number of alien cultures, each of which contrasted sharply with Gulliver's world. In this way, Swift was able to address what he believed to be the absurdities of the eighteenth-century British society from which he came.

Swift's most biting parody—and the one which Boulle must have borrowed as a basis for his novel—was *Book IV: "A Voyage to the Houyhnhnms."* Gulliver finds himself stranded in a society of intelligent horses, who do not (for example) understand human concepts such as war, the telling of lies, or sexual passion. In fact, humans are commonly referred to as Yahoos by the Houyhnhnms, and are shunned by the graceful creatures. When Gulliver's ship is wrecked and he first washes ashore, he is mistaken as a Yahoo by the Houyhnhnms. As a result, he is caged and marked for extermination. Gradually, though, his intelligent actions reveal Gulliver to be "civilized." He is adopted by one of the Houyhnhnms, and quickly learns much about their advanced but emotionally sterile society. The Houyhnhnms (like *Star Trek*'s Vulcans several centuries later) have purged all emotions from their society, and structured lives devoted to pure reason. While Gulliver may admire the horses for their intellect, he finds them soulless; and yet he has nothing in common with the bestial humans. By the end of the story, the ship's captain is ready to return to his less-than-perfect English society. Swift reminds us that no matter how bad we may find some of the political or cultural aspects of our society, ironically, it is still *our* society.

Similarly, the great English novelist, Aldous Huxley (1894–1963) wrote about another dystopia, set in 2108 after an atomic and bacteriological war has devastated most of the world and apes now rule in place of man. Written in 1948 as an original screenplay (later published in book form), *Ape and Essence* follows the attempts of a human biologist to make sense out of the topsy-turvy world he is in. When a group of researchers from New Zealand—the last bastion of human society untouched by the final war—arrive in postholocaust Los Angeles, Alfred "Stagnant" Poole is captured by ruthless, de-evolved humans. He discovers their society has gone savagely wrong, with science being replaced by a type of devil worship. A baboon culture, on the other hand, living concurrently with the humans, is far more civilized, and has replaced man's society with one modeled after Hollywood's golden age. The baboons are contemptuous of the savage humans, and take steps to limit their reproduction by introducing the new creed of Belial, which preaches sexual abstinence (for all but two days out of the year). Poole is shocked by all he sees, and returns by his schooner to New Zealand with news that America is beyond hope of salvation.

The pessimism of Huxley's book is unalleviated, and its presentation, as the work of a misanthropic screenwriter, pokes fun not only at human folly but also the Hollywood system. His work nicely anticipates the kind of struggle that Arthur P. Jacobs would eventually go through to turn Boulle's novel into a film.

Monkey Planet

La planete des Singes, a witty, philosophical novel that fits in nicely with Karel Capek and other social satirists of the day, was first published in 1963. The idea of a world where apes had evolved into an intelligent society and where humans were hunted or enslaved was hardly a new one, but Boulle's ironic yet compassionate message, pinpointing many of the problems he saw in the world, struck a raw nerve. His novel was translated by Xan Fielding into English, and released in Great Britain as *Monkey Planet*; later retitled *Planet of the Apes* for its American release. Few realized at the time the kind of impact the novel would have upon Arthur P. Jacobs and the Hollywood establishment, but Boulle, for his part, simply regarded it as one of his minor works.

Pierre Boulle was born in Avignon, France, on February 20, 1912. Trained as an electrical engineer, he spent eight years in Malaysia as a planter and a soldier. He wrote both *William Conrad,* his first novel, and his best-known work, *The Bridge*

Producer Arthur P. Jacobs with Pierre Boulle, French author of *Monkey Planet,* the novel on which *Planet of the Apes* was based.

Over the River Kwai, while he was stationed there. When he returned home a disillusioned ex-patriot, he began writing moral fables to contrast his profound experience in Asia with those absurdities of life in France. Three of his books—*Contest de L'Absurde* (1953), *E=MC2* (1957), and *Garden on the Moon* (1965)—took to task his distress about science and man's overdependency on machines. While the press had classified them as works of science fiction, Boulle rejected that label, preferring to call his work social fantasy.

When he wrote the novel that became *Planet of the Apes,* Boulle was inspired by a visit to the zoo where he watched gorillas. "I was impressed by their humanlike expressions," he told the press. "It led me to dwell upon and imagine the relationships between humans and apes." Sketching out the novel over a period of six months, Boulle called upon several familiar devices—almost cliches—to tell his story. He wasn't interested in writing a science fiction novel, but in order to get his characters from the earth to his imaginary world, he relied on space travel and Einstein's theory of relativity.

Monkey Planet, structured in many ways like Swift's *Gulliver's Travels* and other incredible literary journeys from the eighteenth and nineteenth centuries, begins within a story frame. Jinn and Phyllis, a wealthy couple of leisure, are rocketing around the cosmos on holiday when they discover a message in a bottle. Written in some ancient dialect that Jinn thinks might have originated on a forgotten green world known as Earth, the multilingual space traveler translates for his wife.

The novel tells of the exploits of a trio of earth astronauts who come to a distant planet inhabited by intelligent apes, while humans are savages. One of these astronauts—Ulysses Merou, a journalist by trade—finds himself in a society that is very much earthlike, with cities, automobiles, planes, and so on; a society that has no use for humans and to which he must defend his kind. In the interim, he falls in love with a savage woman, Nova, to whom he teaches language and who becomes pregnant with his child. It is only through the efforts of chimpanzees Cornelius and Zira that Merou escapes from orangutan leader Dr. Zaius's murderous plans for him. Ultimately the man and his "family" make it aboard his orbiting space vessel and head back to earth, ignoring the fact that nearly eight centuries will have passed since he left. In the end, he is stunned to learn that in his absence the same evolution has occurred—apes have become the dominant species, man the lower life-form. Returning to the framing story, the final moment reveals that Jinn and Phyllis are chimpanzees.

To readers, the ending was quite a shock, seeming the perfect conclusion to a tale that had so successfully captured the imagination. At the time—in an age long before computer-generated imagery (CGI)—no one imagined that such a vision could be brought to the motion picture screen.

Well, almost no one.

Hollywood Goes Ape . . . Eventually

Arthur P. Jacobs was born on March 7, 1922, and in some ways had life stacked against him. Yet as chronicled in many a Hollywood saga, he managed to rise above the obstacles thrown in his path.

Destiny chose to make him an orphan, his father dying in a car accident and his mother losing a bout with cancer, but Arthur Jacobs chose not to allow himself to drown in emotional pain. Instead, he put himself through school and college, attending the University of Southern California. From there he took a job in the MGM mailroom, having fallen in love with Hollywood and grown determined to somehow be involved in the industry. Within two years he worked his way in to the publicity department of both MGM and Warner Bros., before setting up his own public relations firm that he ran from 1947 to 1962. That firm, known today as Rogers & Cowan, was originally called Rogers, Cowan & Jacobs, and had amassed such clients as the Principality of Monaco, American Airlines, David O. Selznick, Judy Garland, Rock Hudson, Richard Burton, Gregory Peck, James Stewart, and

Marilyn Monroe. "Arthur knew *everybody*," exclaims Mort Abrahams, who would eventually become Associate Producer of Arthur P. Jacobs (APJAC) Productions. "At one time or another, he represented just about anyone you could think of. He was a fantastic publicist."

Frank Capra, Jr., who would also serve as associate producer at APJAC, notes, "The company was one of the premier entertainment publicity firms in the country."

That being the case, it was,

Prior to becoming a film producer, Arthur Jacobs was one of Hollywood's top publicists. Clients included Marilyn Monroe (pictured here with husband Arthur Miller), Rock Hudson, and Ronald Reagan.

to say the least, risky for Jacobs to leave that secure position and venture into the highly volatile world of motion picture producing, but he refused to be deterred from his dream.

Andy Knight, a friend of Jacobs's for many years, offers, "Arthur treated failure and success equally. He enjoyed success, obviously. It's human nature. But public relations, as you know, is a lucrative business, especially if you have name clients like Marilyn Monroe, Frank Sinatra, Cary Grant, and people like that. He had very good literary people, too, like Ernest Hemingway. Obviously when you leave a lucrative business like that to embark on a rather precarious producing kind of business, you're taking a chance. As a producer, you don't know whether you're going to make any money or not, because there you are a captive audience as far as your public is concerned. If the picture takes off, you make a mint. With the most artistic picture, if the public doesn't go to see it, it' s not worth the film it's printed on, is it? It may win an Oscar or whatever, but it still doesn't put any butter on your bread, right? It may not even put any bread in you! So, obviously, in the time that it took—preproduction, talking stages—until a picture was made, it was always tough."

Director J. Lee Thompson, perhaps best known as the helmer of *The Guns of Naverone* and who would eventually helm the fourth and fifth entries in the *Apes* film series, met and became instant friends with Jacobs in 1959. "He hadn't been a producer at all," the soft-spoken Englishman smiles. "He came in one morning at breakfast and gave me a little card and said, 'Would this appeal to you?' And it said, 'Marilyn Monroe in *What a Way to Go!,* with Paul Newman, Grace Kelly, and a lot of other people.' I ended up directing that film, which Arthur made his debut on as producer."

In attempting to encapsulate the nature of Arthur P. Jacobs, Thompson explains that Marilyn Monroe committed suicide before she commenced work on the 1964 comedy. "Arthur was the first person who told me she was dead," he notes. "He rang me early one morning and said, 'Marilyn has committed suicide.' I was, you know, naturally shocked. And there was a pause on the telephone before Arthur said, 'What about Elizabeth Taylor?' Which sums up the delightful Arthur who I enjoyed. He just lived films and nothing was going to get in his way to do films and become a producer."

Natalie Trundy, destined to become Jacobs's only wife, is a perfect example of the producer's tenacity; a physical reinforcement of the fact that when he found something he wanted, he would go after it until he had achieved his goal.

Trundy began her career as a model at the age of eleven, and then starred in a live television adaptation of *Little Red Riding Hood*. At fourteen she managed to score roles in several plays, which led to producer Sam Taylor noticing her and ultimately deciding to cast Trundy in *The Monte Carlo Story*. It was during the making of this film—while she was still only fifteen—that Trundy met Arthur Jacobs.

"At the time," she says, "he wasn't a producer, he was the film's publicist. Because he was twenty-five years older than me, he said to my mother, 'When she grows up, I'm going to marry her.' And he did. He kept track of me all through my youth, and so now here I am living in London with a friend, Vanessa. She worked for my [future] husband. There was one night in London when the Playboy Club opened in 1965 or 1966. He was sitting at the bar alone having a drink and she said to him, 'Well, what's wrong with you?' And he said, 'I'm very lonely.' And she said to him, 'Well, what's your name?' He said, 'My name is Arthur P. Jacobs,' and she said, 'Oh, I work in your office.' He told her that he was in love with one person and Vanessa asked who it was. He said, 'Natalie Trundy. She's the only one I ever wanted to marry.' So now Vanessa comes home to our flat. She woke me up and said, 'Natalie, you will never believe who I ran into this evening. Arthur P. Jacobs has said that you're the only one he wants to marry.' And I said, 'Great, can I go back to sleep now?' The next morning the telephone rings. 'Ms. Trundy? Mr. Arthur Jacobs is on the telephone.' And so I said, 'Hello.' He said, 'I'm in love with you, we're going to get married.' I said, 'I don't think so. First of all, I'm just a kid, you're about twenty-five or twenty-four years older than me.' And he said, 'I will take care of you for the rest of your life.' I said, 'Arthur Jacobs, you're a wonderful man, I assume, howsoever, I'm not ready to get married to anyone. I live here with Vanessa and her child, James, and we have a very nice life here.' And he said, 'Oh well, we will take care of that.' Then Vanessa comes home, because she worked for him, and said, 'You stupid idiot, he's so in love with you!' I said, 'So what, you think I care?' Anyway, we did end up together and of course we ended up getting married [in 1968]."

Jack Hirshberg, a journalist and publicist who would be given the title of vice president of APJAC Productions, remembers Jacobs fondly. "He was a lovely man and a very unusual man," says Hirshberg, who handled publicity on all five *Apes* films. "He was a man who, I think, was very underrated in the movie business. The great thing about working with him, aside from the personal relationship and my fondness for him, was that he believed in doing things right. He was a great movie fan and he made movies from the point of view of a movie fan. Like a lot of other people, he wasn't self-indulgent and figured he wouldn't do something very arty-schmarty and so forth to glorify his own name. We didn't do anything dirty. There wasn't a single dirty word in anything that we did. There wasn't even a dirty plot. I suppose the closest we ever came to it was in *Play it Again, Sam,* and that was a really great comedy. There wasn't anything the whole family couldn't go to see. And that was his whole approach to movies—he had great respect for movies as the old-fashioned moviemakers made them, and whatever we did we really did it right. I think the box office results of the pictures that APJAC made testify to that. He had a great feel for what the public would accept and would buy."

According to Natalie Trundy, Jacobs's objective all along was to produce family-oriented product, such as *Doctor Dolittle* and, later on, the *Apes* films, *Tom Sawyer* and *Huckleberry Finn.* So serious was he in this intent, that he even relinquished the rights he owned to the first X-rated Hollywood film, *Midnight Cowboy* (ultimately an Oscar-winner starring Dustin Hoffman and Jon Voight).

"If Arthur had made that film, I would be six million dollars richer," says Trundy matter-of-factly, "but he wouldn't do it because of the subject matter. If you couldn't take the whole family to see it, then he wouldn't do it. He was really a family man and loved children. All he ever wanted was to have children, so we would borrow our friends' kids when they'd go away for the weekend."

Jacobs's friend Andy Knight recalls the *Midnight Cowboy* situation a little bit differently. "One Saturday morning a friend and associate of his by the name of Jerry Hellerman came in with a script and he and Arthur went for a walk," he says. "When Arthur came back, he was enraged. And he said, 'How dare Jerry even suggest for me to make a faggot picture?' He turned Jerry and *Midnight Cowboy* down. And Arthur told this story to *everybody*. You know, 'That day I could have been a multimillionaire over night and I threw him out.' It simply wasn't his bag. The moment the picture was a success, he would always tell that story. In many ways, Arthur was very straight-laced and old-fashioned. He would have to have two or three drinks before he would use any swear words."

As noted earlier, Jacobs had made his producing debut on 1964's *What a Way to Go!*, a black comedy starring a who's who of Hollywood, including Shirley MacLaine, Paul Newman, Gene Kelly, and Dean Martin. So enamored was Fox with the production—even before its extremely successful release—that Jacobs could *almost* write his own ticket. According to Mort Abrahams, he first tried to cash in that ticket on *Doctor Dolittle* and then *Planet of the Apes*.

"In 1963," Abrahams explains, "Arthur had gone to France and met with Allain Bernheim, who was a literary agent in Paris—and he was a friend of Arthur's, and he gave him the Pierre Boulle novel. Arthur read it and was immediately struck by it—called [Twentieth Century Fox chieftan] Richard Zanuck, who was, I believe, in London at the time. Arthur called him from Paris and gave him a kind of two-sentence description on the phone, and Zanuck said, 'I'll buy it for you.' And he did—he [optioned the rights] for Arthur. Zanuck was so intrigued with this thirty-second synopsis on the phone that he never really stopped to consider the problem of actually turning the book into a film."

Jacobs was immediately convinced that Boulle's *Monkey Planet* had all the markings of a high-concept film that would attract mass movie audiences. Together with J. Lee Thompson he began pursuing the idea of adapting the novel to the screen. To this end, he requested that Bernheim forward him several copies of the novel, which he passed on to, among others, MGM, Paramount Pictures, and—amazingly—Marlon Brando. Having scored so successfully in *A Streetcar Named Desire* and *On the Waterfront,* it was felt that Brando's interest would be all the clout necessary to get the film a green light.

Wrote Jacobs to the legendary actor, "J. Lee Thompson and I have acquired the rights to make this film, and we think it is one of the most exciting projects and certainly the most unusual in many, many years . . . Due to the unusual and unique aspects of this film, it was our thought that prior to consummating a distribution deal, we first submit it to you for your reaction. You are, of course, the first actor to whom this property has been submitted, and Lee and I feel you will share our enthusiasm for what we think can be one of the most exciting films ever made . . . Our thought is that if the material excites you as it does us, it could then be put together in any manner which would best suit your needs . . . As the book is coming out shortly, we want to effect an immediate distribution arrangement, so if you have any interest whatsoever, I would greatly appreciate if you would cable me."

At about the same time, Jacobs contracted Warner Bros. artist Mentor Huebner to do some conceptual artwork on the proposed film, which he forwarded to Brando on October 15, while still awaiting a response on the written material. Unfortunately, his dream of having Brando star never came to fruition.

Looking elsewhere, Jacobs turned his attention to Paul Newman, who was starring in APJAC's *What a Way to Go!* He wrote a telegram to Bernheim, noting, "Newman greatly interested in *Apes* . . . Believe that within next week deal may be possible to conclude . . . Will cable or write you all details by Monday and am sure will have a deal with or without Newman shortly."

This was good news for Bernheim, who had grown concerned by the lack of response from Brando. In a letter dated November 20, 1963, he mentioned to Jacobs that he had seen a review of the book that appeared in *Time* magazine, which he felt would be helpful in the negotiations. He also emphasized the point that, as they had agreed, he had not discussed Boulle's novel with anyone else. Still, he warned, there was a limit to how long he could keep things exclusive to Jacobs. "I must be able by the end of the month to present them with something concrete," he wrote.

Jacobs and Thompson intensified their efforts, writing a proposal that summarized their expectations for the project. It is actually a significant document as it offers an inside-look at the early stages of the project.

The *Planet of the Apes* is a rip-roaring horror story—a classic thriller utilizing the best elements of *King Kong, Frankenstein, Dr. Jekyll and Mr. Hyde, Things to Come, The Birds,* and other film classics," the duo wrote to potential interested parties. "The sole object in doing this is to entertain and thrill and nothing more. We see this not as just a film but rather as an attraction which will appeal to all ages and all audiences. It should be talked about on a worldwide basis as the most unusual movie ever made . . . The picture will be created firstly and mainly as the horror-adventure film of all time. It is important to note, however, that we feel there is great comedy inherent in this project as well as wonderful pathos which will develop from the characters. We must not underestimate the humor as well as the shock, which can come from these situations. Aimed for spring or early summer 1964, I believe we will have an edge over two other large-scale productions, *Brave New World* and *The Martian Chronicles* [neither of which were produced, incidentally], which are somewhat in the same vein and scope as *The Planet of the Apes.*

. . . In the initial thinking, it is suggested that the ending be given a more visual shock treatment—that perhaps instead of seeing an airport official and discovering he is an ape, instead we land at one of the jetways (such as Los Angeles International Airport) and upon opening the door of the plane we see not one ape attendant, but rather the interior of the airport lobby peopled with nothing but apes.

In regard to the physical appearance of the ape people, sketches have been

prepared which vividly illustrate how this will be effected. The more massive gorilla types will be used for such characters as the hunters, the policemen while they are pursuing our hero, etc., while the more humanlike apes will be used for the majority of the sequences. We have had considerable discussion with top makeup artists and there is no problem envisioned in getting the results we have indicated in our sketches.

The landscape of the planet is exactly like the landscape on Earth, as are the buildings, the wardrobe which is seen, and the automobiles. The animal-human race people wear the scantiest of clothing, while the apes are dressed exactly as our earth humans are today.

In regard to the language of the simians, we feel we have come up with a method of handling this which is completely plausible and further which is a bonanza in regard to the world market. When we first hear the apes, they speak in a deep gutteral language which would somewhat resemble a combination of Russian, Polish, and German. We of course do not understand what they are saying, nor does our hero. Then, little by little, as Ulysses is able to speak certain words such as proper names, i.e. Zira, our hero's over-screen narration finally tells us that he has been able to master enough of the language to converse with them. He then has his initial conversation with Zira, but as he is able to understand their language, therefore our audience is able to understand the language as the language becomes English at this point. Obviously, this is a great asset for us in Japan, the language then becomes Japanese, in Spain, Spanish, etc.

While the picture itself is the star and we plan to use good character actors for the principal parts, it is our conviction that utilizing a star for the part of Ulysses would greatly enhance the picture, lifting it above and beyond what conceivably might be thought of as an exploitation special. Our initial thinking is that Marlon Brando or Paul Newman or Burt Lancaster would be ideally suited for the role of Ulysses. There are several newer stars such as Steve McQueen, George Peppard, Rod Taylor, etc., who could probably do it, but we do not feel they would give it the prestige the picture should have. In regard to the casting of Nova, ideally this could be portrayed by Ursula Andress or possibly we would unleash an international search (as there is no language barrier) for the most fantastic beauty to be discovered for films.

Needless to say, we feel *The Planet of the Apes* can be the most exploitable, exciting and most talked-about motion picture of our time—a box office bonanza!

Unfortunately, no one else shared their enthusiasm. Besides contacting MGM and Paramount, APJAC had gone to United Artists for a possible distribution deal, but that didn't pan out either. Things seemed a little brighter in December, as negotiations commenced in earnest with Fox. Jacobs truly believed that they would eventually have a deal with the studio. On Christmas Eve, he presented company exec Richard Zanuck with a proposed below-the-line budget for *Planet of the Apes,* which came to a total of $1,710,700, a fee which undoubtedly did not send the executive into fits of ecstasy, as one can well imagine when you talk about 1963 dollars. In addition, they were talking about a science fiction film—a genre which had not yet come into its own, or gone far beyond Earth's battles with flying saucers or giant prehistoric behemoths on the rampage.

"At this point," Mort Abrahams notes, "Fox decided that they would give Arthur a crack at doing it elsewhere. [It] went into turnaround. They said, 'We're not in a position to do the picture at this moment, and if you can set it up elsewhere, we'll allow you to do it. All we want is our money back.'"

As 1964 rolled in, Bernheim was once again growing concerned. Jacobs, apparently tap dancing around the situation as best he could so as to not upset the agent or Boulle himself, noted that things were still going well with Fox, and that there was some renewed interest from Paramount. By January 22, Jacobs realized he had no choice but to be more honest with less-than-encouraging news. Fox, he told Bernheim, would not commit to the film unless it could be produced for one million dollars; Paramount had originally agreed to a tentative budget of $2,800,000 and then reduced it to $1,500,000 and finally lost all interest; and David Picker pushed as hard as he could to get United Artists behind the project, but company executive Bob Benjamin felt that it would be impossible to translate the novel to the screen, and the meeting ended in a "complete deadlock."

". . . It seems there is tremendous resistance because it's so different," Jacobs wrote. "In view of this lack of imagination that seems to be prevalent with the studios and/or company heads, it seems to us that we should stop everything and reevaluate the entire *Apes* situation. Up until this week we had decided that our savior was the fact we could make it for $1,500,000 as opposed to $2,500,000. Today, we are not certain and are beginning to doubt it will do the trick. More important than the money now, we believe, is the fact of who is going to direct and write it and how much weight they have. For example, we believe that if we had gone to UA or Fox or Paramount and said, 'Tony Richardson is directing the picture and John Osborne is writing it and Paul Newman wants to do it and it costs $2,500,000,' we would have had a meeting and probably a deal. In other words, we believe that if Tony Richardson or Blake Edwards would say that this is their next picture, the studios would go along with them. Even this may be wrong, but at least it's an approach."

He went on to explain that Lee Thompson, despite the fact he loved the material, would not be available for approximately two years and would have to move on for the time being.

"What happened," Thompson explains, "is that we'd formed a company and did *What a Way to Go!* And then had, as far as I remember, *Planet of the Apes,* which we were going to do. We were also going to do *Doctor Dolittle.* But Arthur had enormous difficulty in putting together the *Apes* film. After that, I had gone off to do other films. A producer can have ten different projects going, but I'm not a producer, I'm a director. Of course, when I saw the success of the film, I rued the day I left. But, really, I didn't have a choice."

Other potential directors were explored, including Mervyn Leroy and Fritz Lang, who was reportedly "ecstatic about it and would like to direct it," according to Jacobs. "An interesting idea, but we don't know if he's financeable." Also approached were Stewart Sheen and Paddy Chayefsky to write the screenplay, and he noted that it might be better from a financial standpoint to shoot in England, and suggested Terence Fisher, well known for his work at Hammer Films.

He concluded that the approach could not be rushed, for doing so would jeopardize the possibility of a deal anywhere and that the material needed to be available exclusively to them until May 31 so that they could try and put a package together. Bernheim ultimately agreed to this.

On February 12, Jacobs issued another letter to Bernheim in which he stated that Blake (*The Great Race, The Pink Panther*) Edwards had agreed to direct the film, and that with Edwards in tow he was confident that he would be able to set up a deal at either Warner Bros. or Twentieth Century Fox. "I think it's very exciting that we finally have a director set who is the best and the hottest," he wrote, "and I am certain we'll have everything in order very quickly."

The involvement of Edwards excited Bernheim, who wrote back the next day, "I think your choice is excellent and he will certainly see all the various facets of the humorous, satirical, and serious sides of *Apes*."

Jacobs's plan to put together a package to interest a studio apparently paid off. Shortly after Edwards agreed to make the film—on February 27, to be precise— Warner Bros. agreed to produce *Planet of the Apes*. On March 11, Jacobs sent a letter of rejoice to Bernheim, stating, "It was a tough battle, but we made it! We have not let one word out to the trades or to anyone and I hope you will keep it quiet over there as we are trying to work out a startling way to announce this via Telstar, which will take about two weeks if we can do it. If it comes off properly, it should break every newspaper in the world, with the sketches being beamed from Telstar—so please, please say nothing. I am sure that Pierre Boulle will be happy, as you will, to know that Rod Serling is going to do the screenplay and will start this week; but that is also secret until we make our initial announcement. We are planning to go into production in late January and for your *confidential* information, Shirley MacLaine is very excited about playing Zira . . ." MacLaine, of course, did not star in the film.

Rod Serling was considered a major coup for the production. Creator of *The Twilight Zone* and later, *Night Gallery,* Serling had been born on Christmas day, 1924, in Syracuse, New York. An army paratrooper in the second World War, he later studied at Antioch College under the G.I. Bill. In 1948, he went to New York as a fledgling writer. Freelancing in radio and then television, he wrote ninety scripts before signing a contract with CBS. He worked as a teleplay writer for *Kraft Theater, Playhouse 90,* and *The Hallmark Hall of Fame,* from which came his Emmy-

Kim Hunter, screenwriter Rod Serling, and Arthur P. Jacobs.

winning scripts *Patterns* (1955), *Requiem for a Heavyweight* (1956), and *The Comedian* (1957). In 1959, he created the science fiction anthology series *The Twilight Zone,* and won a Peabody Award, two Sylvania awards, and four Writer's Guild awards for his work. Soon after, he turned to writing motion picture scripts, adapting two of his winning teleplays and the screenplay for John Frankenheimer's *Seven Days in May* (1964). Serling was considered one of the finest talents in the industry and the ideal writer to cleverly adapt Boulle's novel.

Said Serling shortly before his death in 1975—although this bit of information has never come up anywhere else, "I first became involved with *Planet of the Apes* about ten years ago. I was approached by an outfit called the King Brothers, who did mostly Indian-elephant pictures shot for about $1.80. [They] had a notion about doing the Pierre Boulle book as a nickel-and-dime picture. I was convinced that it could be done at the time, as I recall. I did a whole treatment for them, a scene-by-scene breakdown of how he would lick the problem. They ultimately discarded it because of the ape population. I never heard any more about it, until I got a call from Blake Edwards, who was the next individual to get into it and who was going to . . . direct it. I was told by Blake to go, not to worry about money. It was going to be a big one."

Meanwhile, on April 8, Warner Bros. executive Reine Serviss shot off a note to Jacobs in which he mentioned that he had finished reading *Planet of the Apes* and was pretty blown away by it. Considering what he thought Jacobs would bring to the project in terms of having the story restructured for a cinematic point of view, he was very confident that the finished product would strike a chord with the audience. He wrapped things up by congratulating Jacobs on his courage in trying something out of the ordinary. "Producers are so quick to follow the successful leader," he wrote, "forgetting it is the 'new' and the 'different' that brings people into the theater. . . ."

In Serling's adaptation, Ulysses became Thomas, with the writer managing to streamline Boulle's overblown parody into a harrowing, bizarre, and masterful story, but the first few drafts of the screenplay are less than perfect. The action is reduced to a few key sequences that move the story along at a far greater pace than the original novel. From the astronauts' landing and their first contact with the primitive humans to the torturous hunt and Thomas's eventual capture, Serling's plot moves at breakneck speed. Regrettably, the story slows down considerably (as in the novel) in the second act, while the veteran *Twilight Zone* scripter indulged in his own brand of sermonizing. Also, far too much time is wasted moving Thomas from his cage to the congressional chambers and, finally, into the public sector. The menace of Dr. Zaius is made secondary and the overall tone of the piece becomes comedic (following Thomas from one simian function to the next).

By the third act, all the tension of the opening scenes has been lost, and Serling has to rebuild that sense of anxiety and terror with an entirely new threat. He also waits until the later scenes to introduce Cornelius, Zira's fiancé, then assigns him far too many duties. In fact, his expedition almost seems like an afterthought in order to provide Serling with an excuse to introduce a lost film on the atomic bomb. By this time, the ending of the motion picture is no longer a surprise. We recognize that the planet is Earth, and his surprise revelation is not particularly effective. Any person who has seen an episode of *The Twilight Zone* is well aware of Serling's fondness for twist endings, but he telegraphed this one all along.

On April 10, Jacobs wrote a confidential memo to Blake Edwards in which he discussed the script pages that had thus far been turned in by Serling, summing up his feelings by stating, "Overall, I believe we are going to have a fantastic script, but [something] disturbs me at this point: The lack of seriousness of the entire beginning and, in my personal opinion, therefore the lack of believability in the characters, dialogue, and actions. Take for example *King Kong,* which in my opinion today is still a classic. There was a tremendously long buildup, which was broken into several parts: (a) the trip to Skull Island, (b) once on Skull Island, the building tension in regard to what was behind the wall. This was played straight and was believable, and is believable today. I feel that, before seeing the 'people' and then the apes, the picture must have greater tension-building as to what is on the other side of the forest, and must be done in a spirit of high adventure and impending terror, which seems to be totally lacking in this first section."

Apparently Serling sensed that his draft wasn't quite right. To this end, he penned a memo to Jacobs on the twenty-seventh that said, "I'm sending a copy of this note to Blake. I've diddled around with the opening to simplify and take out a great deal of the small talk. You and Blake may both want even deeper cuts into this. I personally feel that the inclusion of at least some lightness might take it off a single level and give us a little relief. But again, this is first draft stuff and not engraved in any kind of rock. I've had occasion to look over the script in its entirety and I'm not at all satisfied with the last thirty or forty pages. I think the direction is probably right, but it's going to take a great deal of overhaul, tightening, and improving. One thing that does strike me with force is that I think it's important that we withhold the suspicion on the part of Zaius that there was a prior civilization. I think this should be discovered at the diggings. Zaius may have had an inkling of something based on a prior discovery, but it must be only an inkling."

Apparently during this period, which on the surface would seem to signal some sort of trouble between writer and producer, there was some good humor being generated. Jacobs praised Serling's script, and the writer asked for a crate of bananas as "payment." That's exactly what Jacobs gave him—four crates, to be precise.

"The bananas are delicious," Serling wrote on May 20. "Normally, when hanging from the rafter just above my typewriter, the blood rushes to my head and I suffer migraines as a result. But having the bananas at hand does much to assuage the pain. I've always been rather fond of bananas. But there is one small inconvenience that has shown itself since starting this project. I thought in broaching it to you, you might have a suggestion or two: What am I going to do about this fucking tail that I'm growing?"

In the 1970s, Serling described his early efforts, emphasizing a significant shortcoming of it. "My earliest version of the script featured an ape city much like New York. The ape society was not in limbo as it was in the film. It wasn't carved-out rocks with caves on the side of a hill, it was an altogether twentieth-century technology; a metropolis. *Everything* related to anthropoid. The automobiles, the buildings, the elevators, the rooms, the furniture. Of course that was too expensive to do.

"The script was very long," he added, "and I think the estimate of the production people was that if they had shot that script, it would've cost no less than a hundred million dollars—y'know, by the time they created an ape population, clothed it, and built a city for them to live in. I think the major [problem] was to make apes speak and not get a laugh. The whole thing was to make an audience believe it and take it seriously. Mine was a very free adaptation of the original material. Actually, it was not an adaptation. It was 'based on' the book by Boulle. There's quite a distinction . . . The problem with the novel is that as talented and creative a man as Boulle is, he does not have the deftness of a science fiction writer. Boulle's book was not a parody, but rather a prolonged allegory about morality, more than it was a stunning science fiction piece. But it contained within its structure a walloping science fiction idea. One reason it was so long in reaching fruition was the fact that the apes are intelligent and civilized. They wear clothes and speak English. Now as soon as you put a shirt and tie on an orangutan, you invite laughter—but our story is serious satire. We had to find a way to handle this properly."

On August 5, Jacobs discussed *Planet of the Apes* with the press, enthusiastically espousing his background in PR and how it aided in his becoming a producer. "In all fairness," he said, "I've represented and know the people I'm dealing with. I find a story and then the writers and directors who'll want to do it. I've been exposed to them and they to me. When I got the rights to *Planet of the Apes* from Pierre Boulle, who wrote *River Kwai,* I knew Blake Edwards was a natural to direct. We'll be coproducing it after Blake finishes *The Great Race.* Rod Serling has made some changes in his adaptation. All I can tell you is that it will look unlike any movie ever made. Three or four astronauts are given a mission to explore this planet and what they find is the reverse of us. Apes run it, while the people have regressed to animals—some in cages, others trained for slave tasks. There are three kinds of apes: the chimps, who are the lowest class; gorillas, the hunters; and orangutans, these being the teachers and philosophers. They'll be played by people—naturally. And you'd be surprised how many actors want to play apes.

"The picture will be deadly serious," he continued, "but we know an audience will begin to laugh when it first sees dressed-up gorillas hunting down men. How to get around this? When our first astronaut comes upon this scene, he will laugh, too. But right after, a gorilla shoots him in the throat. This should shock the audience and make the transition possible."

In a letter to Blake Edwards dated September 4, 1964, Jacobs noted that should Paul Newman choose not to do the film, the William Morris Agency had suggested Jack Lemmon in the role of the lead astronaut, and rumor had it that Rock Hudson was interested as well.

On October 14, Jacobs issued yet another letter to Edwards, explaining that Rod Serling would be delivering the second draft of the script on November 16 that would deal with some of their script problems. Additionally, Serling was "100 percent sold" on the new "Rosebud" ending.

"Rosebud," of course, was actually a code name for the new ending which they had come up with, where a mysterious statue in the script is actually the remains of the Statue of Liberty. This planet of apes—at the very last moment of the film— turns out to be Earth itself! It was a conclusion right out of Serling's *The Twilight Zone*. In fact, that series' episode *I Shot an Arrow Into the Sky* has an extremely similar situation, where a trio of astronauts survive a crash on a desertlike planet. One of them kills the others for their food and water rations, and then makes the horrifying discovery that they never left Earth. Surprisingly, Serling would rather have gone with Boulle's conclusion, in which the astronaut returns to Earth only to find that the evolutionary change has happened there as well.

Of the new ending, Jacobs recalled, "I was having lunch with Blake Edwards. I said to him at the time, 'It [the ending] doesn't work. It's too predictable.' Then I said, 'What if he was on the Earth the whole time and doesn't know and the audience doesn't know?' Blake said, 'That's terrific. Let's get ahold of Rod.' As we walked out . . . we looked up and there's this big Statue of Liberty on the wall of the delicatessen. We both looked at each other and said, 'Rosebud.' If we never had lunch in that delicatessen, I doubt that we would have had the Statue of Liberty as the end of the picture."

Mort Abrahams's recollection of who came up with the Statue ending is different. "That was Rod," he says simply. "That was Rod's ending."

Serling's wife, Carol, believes that that is the more likely scenario. "It was always my belief that that was his idea," she explains. "And it certainly is the kind of twist, O. Henry ending he had in so many episodes of *The Twilight Zone*. What we have come to expect from a Serling piece is *exactly* that type of thing."

Between then and December 22, it was obvious that quite a bit of dialogue had occurred between Jacobs, Serling, and Edwards, with Jacobs issuing a note to Blake Edwards on that date that read, in part, "I absolutely concur with you that the last scene should end with a nightmare quality—no hope—that Thomas should not say: 'This is Earth,' but that we should see it in the last shocking shot. I must say that I feel the last three pages must be kept a total secret, and would like to explore with you some sort of phony final three pages that we could put in the script for the purpose of everyone except those directly concerned, that would not reveal Earth and the Statue of Liberty. I am also keeping under lock and key Don Peters's sketch of the statue."

Interestingly, Jacobs was discussing a type of secrecy campaign that probably wasn't very widely used in Hollywood during that time period, but one which has become the norm in the present, as emphasized by Steven Spielberg, George Lucas, and the *Star Trek* films.

Things continued moving steadily, until Warner Bros. prepared a budget for the film on January 25, 1965, which totaled $7,478,750, and the project was suddenly dead. Just like that, all of their efforts were apparently for nothing. As Mort Abrahams notes, "At that time, [$7 million] was like $40 million today, and they said, 'Pass.'"

So Arthur P. Jacobs was back at ground zero. Blake Edwards threw his hands up in despair and departed the project, undoubtedly due to the fact that their "sure thing" at Warner had fallen apart; and Serling's script had to be pared down, with the writer himself admitting that perhaps he had written himself out on the project—that he had nothing left to offer.

At about that time, Mort Abrahams joined APJAC as associate producer, working with Jacobs for the first time since the 1950s. "I had produced a TV series called *The General Electric Theater,* which was a dramatic anthology hosted by Ronald Reagan," he explains. "Arthur Jacobs had handled press relations for the program and, therefore, came in contact with a lot of the General Electric people. Of course, being the producer, we met. After the show went off the air, we each went on to other things and I didn't see him, except for passing by, for a number of years. Later, I was producing a show at MGM called *The Man from U.N.C.L.E.,* and Arthur was putting together a project for Metro about World War I aviators. It was to be a big, spectacular film. And he was also at the beginning of a project for Fox simultaneously called *Doctor Dolittle.* So we were on the same lot and we accidentally ran into each other at the commissary. Arthur asked me whether I'd give him a hand with the WWI project. That started to fall apart because of its enormous cost. It was very difficult to put together. And Arthur and I started to meet on weekends to discuss projects and how we could further them. This went on for several months. In the winter of 1966, the [*Man from U.N.C.L.E.*] production company asked me to renew for another year as producer. Simultaneously, Arthur asked me if I'd become a partner of his. We didn't have a firm project, but there were several things, as I indicated, that were sort of 'in the works.' The question was, would I take a calculated risk? I said, 'Yes' and notified my people that I wasn't going to renew. So Arthur and I started at Twentieth Century Fox on the first project, *Doctor Dolittle.*"

Simultaneously, *Planet of the Apes* was in development, the script to which Abrahams says he began devoting much of his attention.

"Rod Serling did a screenplay," Abrahams says, "which really cracked the problem of translating the book to the screen. But it wasn't in good enough form for anybody to get excited about it. He'd also had the inherent problem which plagued us for five years of, 'How are you going to do a picture about apes that talk?' It was a terrific script, because it really solved, I'd say, eighty percent of the story problems. But there were serious flaws in it. So while I'm working on the script, Arthur's trying to set it up in other studios and gets turned down every place in town. They're afraid of the picture. It's too much of a risk—the apes will make people laugh. How are you going to do the makeup so that it looks realistic—and on and on and on. They all said the same thing: 'It's going to be a laughable production.'"

Jacobs refused to give up on his vision, and doggedly continued to push the project. He approached Irvin (*The Empire Strikes Back, Never Say Never Again*) Kershner to direct and Peter Ustinov to star at Zaius, but was turned down by both due to prior commitments. In addition, he contacted Pierre Boulle and asked him to take a look at the script to see if it could be improved, to which the author responded on April 29, 1965.

Boulle offered his opinion on various aspects of the script, but emphasized (quite strongly) that he truly did not like the Statue of Liberty ending, feeling that it cheapened the story as a whole, and served as the "temptation from the Devil." In fact, if Boulle was to contribute anything at all to the screenplay he would, in his words, "have to dismiss it entirely from my mind."

Ironically, the Statue of Liberty has become a cinematic icon, and one of the strongest moments in an already strong film.

Not surprisingly, Boulle was not asked to actually take a crack at the script.

APJAC vice president Jack Hirshberg wasn't surprised by the difference of opinion between Boulle and Jacobs, recognizing that the difference in mediums would result in very different takes on the story.

"Frequently," he muses, "books are not transcribed faithfully to the screen. They're two entirely different mediums. They're two different ways of telling the story. In a book you can take pages to describe a person's emotions or their thoughts and unspoken feelings and reactions and motivations and all that sort of stuff. You can't do that on the screen. And a book can be as long as you want it to be, but there are certain time limitations for most commercial movies so that you have a certain number of runs during the course of the day or an evening. And those limitations are very rarely broken. They are broken from time to time for certain spectacles and so forth. The turnover at the theater is very important in generating income. So basically you want a picture to be under two hours. Well, that puts limitations on what you could put in it and therefore it affects the way the story is told on the screen."

The next major step forward for the project was Jacobs approaching Charlton Heston on June 15 for the lead role of astronaut Thomas, soon to be renamed Taylor. Born on October 4, 1924, Heston began his career on the stage, first as a part of the Ashville, N.C., Thomas Wolfe Memorial Theater and such shows as *State of the Union, The Glass Menagerie,* and *Kiss and Tell.* From there he segued over to Broadway as a member of Katharine Cornell's company production of *Antony and Cleopatra,* in which he moved from one role to another. This was followed by *The Leaf and the Bough* and *Design for a Stained-Glass Window.* After several other shows, he moved over to the burgeoning world of television and a production of *Jane Eyre* for the anthology series *Studio One.* He made the leap to movies with 1950's *Dark City,* followed by, among many others, Cecil B. De Mille's *The Greatest Show on Earth* (1952) and *The Ten Commandments* (1956), as well as William Wyler's *Ben-Hur* (1959), Anthony Mann's *El Cid* (1961) and Franklin Schaffner's *The War Lord* (1965). The proof of the importance of Heston's interest in *Planet of the Apes* probably best comes from the salary he ultimately received for the film: 250,000 1967 dollars against 10 percent of the box office gross. A prudent investment of time *Planet of the Apes* was.

"Arthur Jacobs was an *extraordinarily* relentless and resourceful entrepreneur, which is one of the things a producer has to be," Heston reflects. "He went around from studio to studio armed at first with nothing but a set of very well done acrylic renderings of various scenes in the film—then *projected* film—and the book itself, to which he owned the rights. There are really three kinds of producers. There are producers who are marvelous money-raisers. There are producers who are just superb at running a whole film, getting it put together, seeing that nothing goes wrong. And then there are producers who are just very good at ideas and casting and supervising scripts. I didn't know Arthur well, really, except when he was peddling the project, but once we started to shoot, I think he was on set maybe once. Now there are producers who do that. That doesn't make him a bad guy. But he was not a hands-on producer, he was a dealmaker and he did it. Mort Abrahams was a good example of a line producer, making sure that things went right and the film doesn't go over schedule. So you had someone like Arthur, who just would not quit until he got someone to make the goddamned movie.

"What happened," he adds, "was he came to see me, having contacted me—I've forgotten really how he did that, because usually I didn't accept submissions other than those accompanied by firm, fully funded offers—which of course he was not in the position to make at that point, because he had no deal. But I guess I was intrigued by the project—the idea of it. He came and told me the story and gave me the novel and showed me the pictures. I was very intrigued, and wanted to play in it. I empathized to some extent with Taylor's point of view of the world. I think an actor must feel some empathy for any character he plays. I would say, as much as any character I have ever played, Taylor reflects my own views about mankind. I have infinite faith and admiration for the extraordinary individual man—the Gandhi, the Christ, the Caesar, the Michelangelo, the Shakespeare—but very limited expectations for man as a species. And that, of course, was Taylor's view. And the irony of a man so misanthropic that he almost welcomes the chance to escape *entirely* from the world, finding himself then cast in a situation where he is spokesman for his whole species and forced to defend their qualities and abilities—it was a very appealing thing to act.

"It was obvious that Pierre Boulle's novel was just made for the screen. At that time, it was the only science fiction script I'd seen with acting in it. I found it a very complicated plot with considerable social commentary. A researcher's greatest problem lies in keeping up with the wildest flights of their imagination. By the time a science fiction story gets on the screen, it's no longer fiction. Until *Planet of the Apes* came along, it seemed to me that all science fiction, from an acting point of view, seemed to fall into two categories: either a tourist or a fugitive. You were going to the moon or somewhere, and the part consisted of, 'Wow, look at that!' Or you were running away from a bug-eyed monster and the lines were, 'Look out, here it comes again!' That was why I never accepted the occasional offer that would come along—and I was around Paramount at the time they were making *Destination Moon* and *War of the Worlds* and stuff like that. *Planet of the Apes,* of course, offered a very different potential. The thing that I think distinguished it from perhaps *all* of its predecessors was that there was a part to play.

"So, Arthur would call me about every two months and say, 'Listen, I've got it over at MGM again,' and I'd say, 'But MGM turned it down, Arthur,' and he says, 'Yeah, but they've got new people over there.' He remained undauntedly ebullient. Each time he would submit it, he would be *positive* they were gonna go with it. And they didn't. But finally I have to confess that, to me, it was sort of a little private joke. Arthur would call up and say, 'Chuck, we're taking it back to Universal,' and I'd say, 'Gee, that's swell, Arthur . . . great . . . great, they turned it down.' He'd say, 'Yeah, they turned it down, but there are new guys over there and they're changing their whole plan and I think this is the time for it.' And I'd say, 'That's just fine, Arthur.'

"This is an important point to make about the film," Heston emphasizes. "This was the first of the space fantasies and the studios basically all thought it was kind of a bizarre idea. Y'know—spaceships . . . and talking monkeys, and all that stuff. They thought it was *really* very strange and they were *terribly* skeptical. Now in the era of all the tons of space movies that seems a little ridiculous. But at the time they said, 'Come on, this is like Flash Gordon and those Saturday serials RKO used to do. You can't do this.'"

Despite the obvious enthusiasm for Jacobs and *Apes,* on November 3 of 1965, Heston made a notation in his private journals which read, "The *Planet of the Apes* project seems in limbo. Jacobs is now thinking of trying to sweat the budget down to two million, which seems ridiculous. He also wants to go with a mechanical director from television. This seems a mistake. On the other hand, it'd be very good for me if this one came together. It's certainly the different kind of script I'm talking about."

By this time, Jacobs and Heston had interested Edward G. Robinson in playing Dr. Zaius. The actors had worked together previously on *The Ten Commandments* and would again in what would be Robinson's last film, 1973's *Soylent Green*. The duo also approached and intrigued director Franklin J. Schaffner, who had at that time recently collaborated with Heston on *The War Lord*. A World War II veteran, Schaffner's first Hollywood gig was as an assistant director on *The March of Time,* before joining CBS Television where he covered public and sporting events as well as political conventions. He made his dramatic debut on the anthology series *Playhouse 90*. His first feature was *The Stripper* (1963) followed by *The War Lord*. He would follow *Planet of the Apes* with such efforts as *Patton* and *Papillon*.

Of involving Schaffner, Heston explains, "I had just done a film with him, and I mentioned that to Arthur, who obviously thought it was a good idea because Frank was obviously approaching the peak of his career then. Arthur said, 'Could we get a meeting?' We did, and Arthur brought along the paintings and Frank liked the paintings, too. Of course, that's all there was at that time. There was the paintings and the book. Frank liked the idea of the film."

The late Schaffner once explained, "I never dreamed [*Planet of the Apes*] would get made. It seemed to me a fascinating project which would never get made. So when Arthur said, 'Would you do it?', it was easy to say, 'Yes.' Two years later, Arthur called me up and said, 'We have enough money to do a makeup test.'

"This is a satirical comment on our times," he added in explaining his interest in the project. "It isn't science fiction because it has something to say about our society, something about the cynicism of men who choose to exploit others. This is a story about human beings who find themselves prisoners on a planet ruled by intelligent apes. In many ways, these apes 'ape' man. They wear clothes, they use simple tools, permit bureaucrats to govern them, keep animals in cages—but in this case, the 'animals' are human beings. We did not think the apes should have machines and engines. Their leader, Zaius, is a defender of the status quo. He is afraid of what will happen to the apes if they are tempted out of their blissful ignorance. As you can see, the film is not intended as a mockery. It offers a parable, a moral lesson: Knowledge by itself is neither good nor evil. It is what you do with the knowledge that makes it one or the other."

The next progression was Fox's Richard Zanuck agreeing to finance a test which could possibly prove that the film could be pulled off without being laughed out of theaters.

"I think Dick Zanuck made an extraordinary contribution," adds Charlton Heston, "because he asked an interesting question. We were all gung-ho on the project at that time. Dick Zanuck said, 'Look, these paintings look great, but I assume you're going to use actors, right? These aren't going to be monkeys—you're going to use actors.' And we said, 'Yeah, of course, actors . . . makeup.' He says, 'Who's gonna do the makeup? How do you know they're not gonna get laughs? If you get laughs with these monkeys, you're finished, right?' And we said, 'Yeah. Right . . . right. The makeup's gotta be great. Gonna have great makeup.' He said, 'Who's gonna do it?' And we said, 'Well, Christ, let's do the movie, then we'll figure that out.' He said, 'Tell you what . . . we will finance the research up to $5,000 and we will pay for a test of the makeup.' And Frank and I, knowing which side our bread was buttered on—Frank said, 'Well, I'll direct the test,' and I said, 'I'll be in it.' And as you know, Eddie Robinson played Zaius. It was an *extraordinary* executive decision on Dick Zanuck's part. People who make films are constantly bad-mouthing studio heads—but this was *one time* when he had *exactly* the right idea. I think he was being hardheaded and putting his finger on the crucial problem, which was the makeup."

Zanuck explains, "It was a project I had always liked a lot. But when Jacobs first proposed it, it seemed to be just too expensive of an idea. Plus, there was some concern that I had about whether or not the apes themselves would appear comical—whether we could really make them believable to the audience."

Perhaps most interesting is the fact that Fox still had *not* agreed to go forward with the film, whether or not the makeup ultimately worked. Mort Abrahams explains the reasons for this.

"Twentieth didn't say no to the script," he explains, "they said no to the project. They said, 'The screenplay is fine, the project makes us nervous.' But part of our pressure was to keep them alive—they still had a lot of money invested in it and it was our job to convince them to spend another $5,000 to protect the forty or fifty thousand they had already invested. So we said, 'Give us the $5,000 to start working on the makeup and do a test—you can always say no—but what you've done is add $5,000 to your cumulative costs.' It was a matter of salesmanship. We wanted to use every dime to convince them to go ahead with the picture and the makeup was crucial. On the other hand, they wanted to keep our good offices, because we were an active production company. And studios do that—they will allow a producer with whom they have a good relationship and with whom they hope to make pictures in the future. They'll extend themselves a bit to maintain a goodwill relationship. And it was on that basis that they gave us that little money to go forward."

Once the rudimentary makeup was developed (initially by veteran Ben Nye, Sr.), plans were made for the filmed test, which would be shot on the Fox lot for a total budget of $7,455. Fox production manager Stan Hough mentioned to Jacobs in a memo dated January 19, 1966, that there was no budget available for a set or electrical rigging. As a result, they would be forced to use a preexisting set. In essence, this test would be completely no frills.

On February 4, Jacobs responded with a confidential memo of his own to Hough, which read, in part, "In regard to the test for *Planet of the Apes,* it is most urgent that this be done in total secrecy. Charlton Heston and Eddie Robinson have agreed that there will be no publicity whatsoever . . . It is imperative that the pictures be developed in total secrecy and . . . in fact, I would like to hold the negatives in my safe, if possible. It is also most urgent that no one be allowed on the set during rehearsals . . . and that some arrangements be made so that the actors who wear ape makeup are made up on the stage itself and should be given their meals on the stage . . . It is equally imperative that no one be allowed to see the film or the dailies unless approved by me.

"If we proceed, no one will ever be allowed to know what the apes look like until possibly a week before the picture is released . . . If a newspaper or magazine were to get a picture or a frame of film from the test, it would endanger the success of the promotional campaign for the picture."

Later that month, Jacobs forwarded Rod Serling–written pages for the test to

Mort Abrahams, Charlton Heston, Edward G. Robinson, and producer Arthur P. Jacobs.

Heston and Robinson, and rehearsal took place on March 7, as planned. In his journals, Heston noted: "This afternoon I went over to Fox for an hour to rehearse the test for *Planet of the Apes*. I'm a little sorry I agreed to do it, on a film not even approved yet, but I did agree." The next day he added, "Not a very long, or very hard day, doing my part in what, inevitably, is a selling job for *Planet of the Apes*. If the question is whether or not the ape makeup is laughable, the answer is no, it's very plausible."

Today Heston reflects, "Before I took the part, I was worried whether I could act and react with apes—and whether the audience would accept shots of a man talking to an ape. So, for the first time in my career, I made a test. We made the test with Edward G. Robinson in ape makeup and me talking to him, and we showed it around. We found the public would accept it."

Franklin Schaffner concurred. "Was it credible for men to sit down and talk to apes?" he mused rhetorically. "As the story is told through Taylor's eyes, we had to make simian attitudes and personalities appear sensible from the apes' standpoint, while from Taylor's point of view the situation was a madhouse."

The makeup test for *Planet of the Apes* was originally quite different and elaborate, but ultimately proved too expensive to produce. Instead, a series of beautiful production illustrations summed up what would occur in the finished film. Besides Heston and Robinson, the makeup test would costar James Brolin as Cornelius and Linda Harrison (who would eventually be cast as the primitive human, Nova) as Zira. That presentation combined the paintings with voiceover narration by veteran voice-man, Paul Frees.

For the makeup test, Rod Serling wrote a brief script to serve as an example of a human interacting with an intelligent ape. That sequence, rethought and a bit more adversarial in the final film, represents a philosophical discussion between Thomas and Zaius and, as anyone who has seen the documentary *Behind the Planet of the Apes* can attest, is quite effective. Despite the fact that the makeup would be refined later, the test was a success.

Charlton Heston recalls, "My memory of it is that it was the last scene—the confrontation with Zaius. You know—with the doll. And of course they just built a small set, just a tent really. They didn't attempt to get any production values. But they wanted to spend time on the makeup. Obviously the only reason to have me in it since I didn't wear makeup in the picture, was to have something of a full-

Edward G. Robinson portrayed the Zaius character in the 1966 test reel, but declined to continue with the role because of the stress of the makeup.

scale scene. So that you didn't have to have some stock player doing it. We worked, my memory is, most of the day on it. It was the way to do it, because if you do a *scene* with real actors, then you have an idea of what it might look like. If you just have people standing around with the makeup on turning around, why, that doesn't give you anything."

John Chambers, who would actually revolutionize movie makeup with his efforts on *Planet of the Apes,* explains that at that time, Hollywood "was supposed to represent the center of it all with the top skilled artists. What it was, instead, was a cesspool of relatives and friends and they were all buried away, hidden in corners. Of course there was always some exceptional guy that'd come out with something, but that's why you saw so much of this hokey-lookin' monster crap.

"The makeup for the *Apes* test was designed by Ben Nye, Sr.," he continues, "who was a fine artist. And a fine, exceptional person. He was the lab person at the

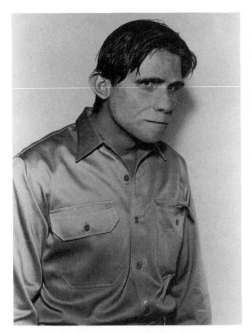

James Brolin was Cornelius in the
1966 makeup test.

Fox contract player and girlfriend of studio head
Richard D. Zanuck, Linda Harrison. She appeared as
Zira in the 1966 makeup test and was later cast as
Nova in the first two *Apes* films.

time, and he sufficed. Ben is a fine sculptor, a fine makeup man; fine beard man. There was the problem with Edward G. Robinson in that he wouldn't take his beard off. He also had restrictions, because he had had a severe heart attack and couldn't breathe well, so he put conditions on how he would look. He had the nose piece, but he put a piece over his own beard, so you could actually see his beard sticking out. And the chimps in that test—they wore slip rubber and had a little slit across the mouth and little round eyes. I mean, holes cut out. The apes were basically wearing rubber masks, and when they talked you'd see the slip kind of buckle. It was just slip rubber like the Halloween masks."

Speaking of the results of the test, Mort Abrahams explains, "The test was completed on 35-millimeter and it was a first-class commercial operation. The scene lasted about five minutes—all dialogue. We all thought it worked. It did reveal certain problems in the makeup, which we felt would be ultimately correctable—and indeed were correctable. Certain lines showed, the makeup cracked and there wasn't enough movement of the lips. It did hold up under the intense light better than we thought. The voice was perfectly clear. It was an arduous task—it took four hours to put the makeup on Eddie. We edited this piece, we put it together, we ran it and Fox said, 'Yeah, we think it will work, but . . . we're gonna pass.' Again. And we went around to all the studios once more with the film, and they all said, 'Very interesting. God, you've come a long way. That's really terrific. But no go.'"

Amazingly, Fox had rejected the project again and Jacobs was off on his own. As incredible as it may seem, though, the producer refused to let go of the idea of bringing *Planet of the Apes* to the screen.

On March 29, 1966, Charlton Heston wrote in his journals, "Arthur Jacobs's office is going on again about Fox's interest in *Apes,* but I can't help but discount it, in view of Arthur's past history on the piece."

An April 11 memo from Jacobs went to Warner Bros., MGM, Pacific Drive-In Theaters and others, explaining that he had brought a writer by the name of Charles Eastman on to the project. "In regard to the rewrites which we are planning on *Planet of the Apes* with Charles Eastman, we have had lengthy discussions with Eastman and Franklin Schaffner. We feel many improvements can be made which will give us a first-rate screenplay and solve many of the elements which can be strengthened in the Serling script. We feel there is much suspense which can be built up and much to be done in the development of the characters. The changes we contemplate are important in getting a tighter screenplay, a more artistic picture and, simultaneously, a less expensive picture.

"We must," he continued, "find a production style which depicts the apes' civilization and culture and yet in no way tips the fact that we are on Earth. In the existing version, Thomas would have to be an

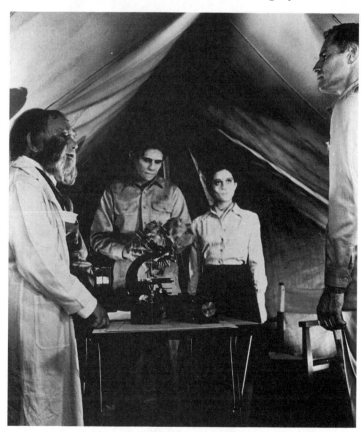

A scene from the 1966 makeup test (directed by Franklin J. Schaffner). Edward G. Robinson, James Brolin, Linda Harrison, and Charlton Heston.

imbecile not to know where he is. We can later justify the strange vegetation, etc., as being a result of the Bomb. While we will use existing streets, buildings, etc. . . . We will have to find a way to dress these exteriors so that again we do not disclose that we are on Earth. A very adroit and skillful art director will be necessary and serious consideration must be given to a perhaps unusual use of color.

"While we are not going to get involved in a nuts-and-bolts script involving scientific jargon, we must still present at least a façade of reality. Therefore, considerable research must be done on probable methods of space travel, etc. Here again, we can refer back to Boulle, who had some interesting ideas . . . Serling's script takes the position that the apes' civilization evolved as a result of atomic holocaust. Pierre Boulle's point of view is that it came about as a result of a natural evolutionary process. We feel that both viewpoints can be combined, so that the impact of our ending is retained and yet have more going for us than the dropping of a bomb . . . We are prepared to discuss very specific changes in scenes and characters based on the above summation."

At the same time, Jacobs had provided Eastman with a copy of the original novel, several of Serling's best drafts, and instructions to punch up the dialogue and breathe some life into the characters. Eastman wrote roughly forty pages and was then discharged, his screenplay almost completely unusable. The obvious problem is that he spent that entire length of time on exposition, detailing who the characters were and their classifications and there was absolutely no sign of intelligent apes anywhere in sight.

On September 23, Heston wrote in his journals, "There seems to be stirring from Fox on *Planet of the Apes,* which I thought had long since disappeared."

Four days later, it became obvious that Edward G. Robinson would have to drop out of playing Dr. Zaius, because the actor found himself getting claustrophobic within the ape makeup. Robinson would be released from his agreement with Jacobs, and ultimately replaced by English actor Maurice Evans.

The next few months were mostly filled with revising the film's budget and tightening the screenplay. To this end, writer Michael Wilson was hired. Wilson was the ideal choice for the film, as he had provided uncredited rewrites on *Bridge Over the River Kwai* and *Lawrence of Arabia,* two of the great cinematic epics of the day. Years earlier, he had won an Academy Award for his screenplay for *A Place in the Sun* (1951) and a Writer's Guild of America Award in 1957 for *Friendly Persuasion.* He had also distinguished himself with the screenplays for *Five Fingers* and the critically well-received *Salt of the Earth.*

Wilson also was a victim of the "Red Scare," being blacklisted by Senator Joseph McCarthy for being sympathetic to Communists and refusing to "name names."

When Wilson read Serling's script, he liked most of what was there, including the scene breakdown, the concept of the piece, and the overall thrust of the action. Like Jacobs, though, he never believed the contemporary feel of the story. Eventually he shortened the story, choosing to restrict the central human figure to long-term captivity and reduced the number of scenes. He displaced the ape culture to one that was both socially and politically in a state of limbo—even though the dialogue was purposely contemporary, the look of the simian world was removed from modern times. Wilson also renamed Thomas as Taylor. Although some additional script rewriting was done by John Kelley, the blueprint for the final version of *Planet of the Apes* was supplied by the combined efforts of Serling and Wilson, through whose imaginations a sci-fi and cinematic classic was born.

In the 1970s, Wilson explained that he had turned Serling's script into a satire. "A satire, really, on the human race," he said. "Because it turned out the apes— these civilized apes—had descended from humans on our Earth and the astronauts had inadvertently returned to our planet only to find out that Earth had been wiped out by a nuclear bomb and, therefore, the dominant species that had evolved was the apes who had descended from and imitated the culture of man, which had preceded it. Which accounts for the satire of the story. That's what I did to it.

"Virtually all of my work was in the final film, with one significant deletion," he added. "In the penultimate drafts, Nova was pregnant with Taylor's child. In this version, Taylor was killed by the bullet of an ape sniper just after he sees the Statue of Liberty. But Nova escapes, vanishing into the Forbidden Zone beyond the Statue of Liberty. The meaning is clear: If her unborn child is a male and grows to manhood, the species will survive. If not, modern man becomes extinct."

Interestingly, it's a theme that would ultimately be resurrected in the third film of the series, *Escape From the Planet of the Apes,* in which Zira gives birth in our time period, implying that should the child grow to adulthood, it will ultimately lead to the downfall of the human race.

At the end of September, 1966—quite abruptly—Fox had a sudden about-face and decided to greenlight *Planet of the Apes,* although interesting the studio was a struggle right until the very end.

"I'll tell you how the picture got made," smiles Mort Abrahams. "We 'conned' Fox. Fox allowed us to do more experimenting on the makeup. They gave us a little more dough. With no intent of follow-through, they said, 'We're doing this as a gesture to you people, because you're on the lot and you're doing other things for us, but don't count on it that we're going to do this picture.' At this point, an interesting thing happened. A picture called *Fantastic Voyage* opened and it was a gimmick picture that opened to *very* big business. Then Arthur did a terrific thing: He got all the box office grosses from that picture all over the country—pulled them out of *Variety*—and we worked to put together a book showing the results of a lot of successful 'gimmick' pictures.

"We went up to see Dick Zanuck," he continues, "and he said, 'If you guys bring up *Planet of the Apes*—I don't want to talk about it. I told you my decision, we're not gonna go. We pass. We're not gonna do the picture.' And every time we went up, we brought it up again. So, finally, Dick called me one day—actually, he was returning my call—and I told him I wanted to see him about something. He said, 'I want you to type an agenda, and if I see *Planet of the Apes* on it, I'm not gonna let you in the office.' So Arthur and I went up to see Dick. Took up a couple of things on other projects, then I said, 'Dick, I'm going to make you a firm, solemn promise.' He said, 'I know what you're gonna say, you're gonna bring up that damn *Apes* picture again!' I said, 'I promise this is the last time we'll ever mention the film in your presence.' He said, 'I trust your word. I give you three minutes and it is the last time, because I'm really bored with it.' He took his watch off and put it on the table. Then he said, 'Go.'

"And Arthur and I went into this sales pitch about how *Fantastic Voyage* was doing this fantastic business, and who the hell was in it and nobody ever heard of it, and it wasn't based on a best-selling book and on and on. If you look at grosses, it shows you a gimmick picture can work, and this is the greatest gimmick picture of them all. And he said, 'Okay, stop—your three minutes are up.' Dick leaned back in his chair and said, 'How much is the picture gonna cost?' We'd already done a budget. We said, 'Five million eight.' He said, 'I'll tell you what—you guys have a point. Let's see if *Fantastic Voyage* has legs. Come back in four weeks. If the picture's still doing well, I'll talk to you about it. Now I'm not promising *anything*. Nothing. I'm just saying I'll talk to you about it again.' We said, 'Okay,' because we'd done our job for the moment, and left.

"We watched. I mean *we watched* those grosses like you couldn't believe and the picture did have legs," laughs Abrahams. "Four weeks later to the day we went up to see him. We said, 'How 'bout it, Dick?' And he said, 'Okay, I'll tell you what. If you can bring the picture in for five million, I'll try to get it through the board.' He had the approval of pictures up to, I think, three million or three and a half million dollars. He could say okay on his own, but anything over that limit, he had to go to the board of directors. So we had to get the budget down about $800,000, and Stan Hough and I worked on that, and we got it down to four million and nine hundred and ninety something dollars—literally. Just under five million. Dick went to New York and stuck his neck out. They fought him bitterly. He said, 'I want to do this picture.' It became his baby. And he convinced them. He came back and said, 'Okay, go.'"

Of course Jacobs and company were then faced with one profound question: Having been given the green light from Zanuck and Fox, how the hell were they going to bring *Planet of the Apes* to life?

PLANET OF THE APES

2

Although the contribution of *Planet of the Apes'* cast to the film's box office success, and status as a classic, cannot be underestimated, neither can the physical representation of this simian world as represented by its architecture, clothing, and, of course, makeup designs.

William Creber served as the film's production designer, bringing a visual style that was integral in achieving the filmmakers' goal of making this seem like an alien planet. Creber began his career as an assistant director on such films as *The Greatest Story Ever Told, The Detective,* and *Justine,* as well as the pilot episodes of Irwin Allen's TV sci-fi efforts, *Lost in Space, Voyage to the Bottom of the Sea,* and *The Time Tunnel,* in addition to the producer's big-screen disaster epics, *The Poseidon Adventure* and *The Towering Inferno.*

Mort Abrahams, Franklin J. Schaffner, Arthur P. Jacobs, and Charlton Heston.

"Our objective," explains Creber about creating Ape City, "was to find something really original and different, in line with and opposed to Pierre Boulle's concept, which took place in a contemporary environment. His story was based on a very involved visual joke where the apes lived in a city much like ours, but altered to fit their physical abilities, i.e. they crossed streets on overhead 'monkey bars,' had autos driven by their feet, etc. It was one of those literary descriptions which is very hard to translate to film. The final concept was to keep any reference to Earth a secret until the tag scene of the picture, the Statue of Liberty shot. It became apparent that we needed to provide a concept that wouldn't give away that they might be on Earth, in order to reinforce the dramatic impact. This led to the alien look we finally designed."

Creber explains that a variety of ideas was explored, including shooting in Brasilia and utilizing modern aspects in the design, but Arthur Jacobs rejected the notion. "We looked at some of the work of Gaudi, and the Turkish city of cave dwellers called Goreme Valley," he says, "and these concepts came through a little."

As Mort Abrahams explains it, as one of the first people hired on the production, Creber definitely had his work cut out for him. "The big problem," Abrahams explains, "was to get a concept for the village where the apes lived. It was a long, arduous research project which started with very futuristic designs. It started with H. G. Wells's *War of the Worlds*-type things. And Bill and I, who worked very closely together, decided this was probably the wrong approach. And after months of looking through all kinds of periodicals, magazines, screening films—the clinical kind of research—we came up at pretty much a dead end. Nothing really looked right, didn't feel right. The texture was wrong. And one day I said to him, 'Let's start all over again; let's take a different approach.' Given that this is a race of primitives which have the ability to speak and a very high intellectual level, if they went about building residences—a small village, a town—what would it look like? Forget the chrome and steel, forget the high-tech stuff (although at that time they didn't use that phrase). I said, 'Let's start much more primitively and see if we could get something exotic rather than try to get a scientific sense to it.'

"So that started us on a whole new program of research," he adds. "And one day I was in the art department with Bill and we were looking through one of probably fifty or sixty books of architecture, and he was thumbing through them and showed me pictures of various things. I suddenly opened a book on Gaudi—the Spanish architect, and I looked at some of his wonderful churches in Spain and thought, 'Jesus, this is very, very interesting.' Because if you look at his architecture, a lot of it resembles trees and I said to Bill, 'If apes were gonna build something, they would have some kind of a primitive, primal instinct to build it toward the kind of habitation that they're familiar with—namely trees. Why can't we look at these Gaudi things?' And he said, 'That's absolutely right,' and he started making drawings of variations of Gaudi's work. And that's basically what the look of the village became. It's really almost primitive. But it comes out of a kind of logic—that if they were to build these kinds of dwellings, they would build them in a sense that made them comfortable. That is, it would resemble the kind of area in which they've lived for millions of years. It would *not* be steel and chrome and glass. It would be wood or at least it would take the form of vaguely resembling trees. That began an evolution which Bill developed into the village as it looked in the film."

Having arrived at that design direction, discussions of actual construction began as sketches started to evolve into a form that could be photographed and which would look interesting. "The first approach, of course, was to make them out of wood," says Abrahams. "That was not practical because it was terribly expensive. So when the form was laid out, we knew that we had to build a fairly big village with a lot of buildings. And then the economics came into play. How do you do it and not spend two million dollars on the thing? So Bill Creber started working with the construction people on new ways, new materials, of fulfilling his designs."

"At the time," Creber picks up the scenario, "the studio had been experimenting with a substance called polyurethane foam, and one day, some fellows had attempted to build something with this foam by spraying it on cardboard, and it had the exact look we were after. So we sculptured the buildings, using [tiny] models, with welded rods covered with cardboard and they'd spray them with foam. Towards the end, we didn't have enough equipment and we weren't making good time, so we had to go into plaster and cement and construction, plus the foam. It worked pretty satisfactorily, though."

Details Abrahams, "It was very light, yet it withstood all the abuse that it had to withstand. They withstood pretty well. Subsequently, after we were finished, they deteriorated badly, but they did have to withstand all of the elements."

Other production challenges to the filmmakers were conveying the idea that this was an alien planet that could, in the end, logically reveal itself to be Earth. "We had to find a place to shoot the picture that looked as unearthly as we could make it look," says Creber. "I had done some work in Utah when I was up there on *The Greatest Story Ever Told,* and I always felt that would be a great place to make a science fiction film. The location problem we had is that we were dealing

with a totally barren and void first twenty minutes with not one living thing until the discovery [by the astronauts] of the small planet which led to the 'green belt' and encountering water, trees, and living creatures. The sequence started with a barren area near Lake Powell, Arizona, and an insert of real living weeds, pulling back to show discovery by the astronauts of more plant life. Then the 'scarecrows,' the sound of water and more trees and a reaction on the actors' faces to what they see, then a quick cut to a waterfall— which we created at the Fox Ranch in Malibu, finally our astronauts are shown bathing in a lush pool. All of this worked so well, that I'm still asked where the waterfall is in Utah."

Another integral design problem was within the sequence in which savage humans are hunted by armed gorillas on horseback, which also included the first revealing of the intelligent simians to astronaut George Taylor (Heston). "We had to grow a field, literally," says Abrahams, "and there was a big question of what the hell were we gonna plant that would grow six feet high in four weeks. That was a monster. I forget what we finally used, but they planted something that was absolutely spectacular in terms of growth in inches per week. In the end, it was one huge mother of a field, which was grown on the Fox Ranch. They had to farm it like a bunch of farmers to get it to grow quickly."

While the look of the planet of the apes was being designed, Morton Haak was designing the costumes that would clothe the simian population. As originally conceived, the apes would have "monkeyed" our society with the populace wearing suits, ties, hats, and dresses, but this approach was ultimately abandoned as being fiscally untenable and inevitably laughed off the screen. In the end, it was decided that each species of ape—chimps, gorillas, orangutan— would in a sense be stylistically segregated from the other. Cornelius, Zira, and the rest of the chimpanzees were adorned in primarily green clothing, while Dr. Zaius and the other orangutans wore a brownish orange, and the gorillas wore black as their primary motif. While the chimps and orangutans merely looked like variations of a theme, the gorillas' garb most definitely brought with it a military presence, suggesting the Gestapo. Humans, of course, wore little more than rags.

"Morton must have submitted fifty to seventy-five drawings," says Abrahams of Haak. "At the beginning, they tended to be overelaborate and there was a question of refining and simplifying. But he had the sense of it almost from the start, 'cause he had a leg up thanks to the fact that Bill had beaten the problem of the designs of the sets. And they worked together on color and texture. Again, the question was, what would they make their clothing out of? We always thought on those terms. How would they do it? In terms of furniture, in terms of props. Always back to the ape origins in the forests. What would it most resemble? What would it look like? A chair wouldn't be the kind of chair we sat in—it would have to fit their anatomy. There was a lot of going back into the psyche of various civilizations to search out these kinds of things. There was an intellectual pursuit."

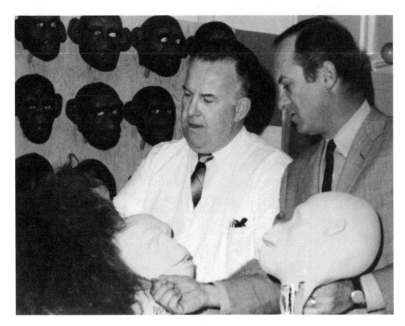

Creber enthuses, "There was a great deal of cooperation on that first one between all the departments. We had fun exchanging ideas and working them out."

While all of this was going on, John Chambers was "working out" the ape makeup, without a doubt the most important component of successfully pulling off the film.

Regarding the makeup, Abrahams emphasizes one particular point, and a rather surprising one at that: "The truth is that the actual groundwork, the labor, the 'hands-on' work, was Dan Streipeke. John Chambers was more of a concept man. Streipeke did the actual experimenting with various materials, including building the casts, etc. A big contributor to this was the sketches made by Bill Creber, although makeup is not his forte—he did do sketches, which turned out to be very helpful, of Cro-Magnon men, etc., etc."

John Chambers *strongly* disagrees with this viewpoint. "Dan is an exceptional makeup artist," he says. "He's one of the rare talented top makeup artists in our union. And he's an executive type, too. He's a very intelligent man. When we were doing the first film, I had my hands full just keeping an organization of people physically working. And then working myself, creatively working, sculpting. All the major principle sculpture was done by myself—for all those principles. No one else touched it. The subordinate sculpture was done by artists that I picked. Copies were made later. But all the original concepts were sculpted by myself. Purposely, so no one twenty or thirty years later would say, 'I created this.' And I've documented it, too—while I'm alive, because several people have got me buried already and are taking credit. But I did it. It's very warped. It's like the Germans who are saying the Holocaust never happened.

"I say this not to be selfish," he continues, "but because I feel once in your lifetime something comes along that you get a chance at the grand slam. And I wasn't gonna let that thing get out of my hand. I had absolute faith in it. I was in my forties at the time and I remember saying, 'Well, I gotta make a go at it.' And I told everyone we were going for it. I said, 'This is a good chance to take home an Oscar.' Everyone knew this, and everyone was striving for it."

John Chambers, the first person ever awarded a special Academy Award for his efforts in makeup, began his career following high school by designing jewelry and working in carpeting before joining the army, where he served as a dental technician. His natural skills led him to develop a new line of adhesives and rubber compounds, which he utilized at the army's Fitzsimmons General Hospital in Denver, Colorado, and eventually in other hospitals, to create prosthetic devices for the wounded. His "creations" included arms, legs, noses, chins, and, for women who had suffered the ravages of cancer, artificial breasts. But then it all got to be too much for him. "I got very involved with my patients," he explains. "It became a very personal thing. After constant dealing with personal tragedy for so long, it became very difficult for me. I took everything too seriously."

Looking for a change, he turned his focus to television in 1953, finding himself underwhelmed by what he saw; makeup designs that were far more primitive than was necessary. Finding himself fairly quickly hired, among Chambers's early television efforts was transforming Paul Newman's boxer character in Hemingway's *The Battler* from "normal" in one sequence to battered in the next—despite the fact that these scenes were only a few seconds apart from each other and being broadcast *live;* transforming Charlton Heston into a Beast in a Shirley Temple production of *Beauty and the Beast;* and such live efforts as *Matinee Theater* and *Lux Video Theater.* His success on the small screen led to work on the feature films *The Ugly American* (1962), *The List of Adrian Messenger* (1963), and *Bedtime Story* (1964), where he truly revolutionized his craft, bringing makeup to levels it had not reached before. From there, he would segue back and forth between the mediums, moving back to television and such shows as *The Outer Limits, Star Trek, The Munsters, Lost in Space, The Invaders,* and Rod Serling's *Night Gallery.*

Chambers was in Madrid working on *I Spy* when he received the phone call from Ben Nye, Sr. and Fox concerning *Planet of the Apes.* At the same time, Stanley Kubrick was shooting *2001: A Space Odyssey* in England, creating revolutionary makeup for the so-called "Dawn of Man" sequence involving primitive apes. Arthur P. Jacobs, looking in all directions to help *Planet of the Apes* along, asked if it would be okay to send Chambers to England for some tips. Initially the late Kubrick was open to the idea, though ultimately the invitation was rescinded when the director realized that there might be a conflict of interest involved. That was fine with Chambers, who had no desire to go to the set of *2001* anyway.

"Some years before," says Chambers, "I had taught a few of the English a lot of laboratory techniques. But I felt I couldn't learn anything more from them. They were working on some gorillas and thought we might absorb some technique, which could help us on the picture. I took the whole idea as a personal affront. I'm an Irishman and I said, 'Anytime any Englishman can teach me anything, it's going to be a cold day.' In fact, I taught what most of the English have learned and what they've passed on to each other. This was on a picture called *List of Adrian Messenger.*"

In detailing the evolution of the makeup for *Apes,* Chambers says, "We had to determine what the makeup concept would be. I read the script and with Franklin Schaffner decided that the apes would not be made to look like hair-faced human beings, they should be animals, apes, with perhaps some minor concessions here and there. In other words, we carried the evolutionary process only very slightly beyond what you might call basic ape."

While experimentation continued, Chambers had one particular memory in mind: the Cowardly Lion from 1939's *The Wizard of Oz.* The makeup for that film, created by Jack Dawn, allowed actor Bert Lahr to be completely covered in makeup and costume, yet the prosthetic placed on his face allowed all of his own expressions to get through, which played no small role in making the character so appealing to audiences across the decades. Unlike Nye's attempts, which were *extremely* primitive, Chambers realized that the makeup for *Planet of the Apes* would have to be as powerful as Dawn's had been thirty years earlier. When Bill Creber brought a variety of stuffed apes into the makeup laboratory, they proved a major influence on the final design. "When I came onto the film," Chambers explains, "they had a concept of a Neanderthal type, where he was fringing more on the human than the animal."

Utilizing his background in creating prosthetics for the wounded, Chambers started developing "life masks."

"To arrive at our final concept," he notes, "we turned to sculpturing. We would take a base human head in plaster and then in clay, model on this head our ape variations. We came up with things looking like the Neanderthal Man and so forth, which we discarded. The concepts were too ambiguous, lacking the strength of the animal face and personality. We needed the pleasantness, yet the strength, of the animal without being too grotesque."

As evidenced in the documentary *Back to the Planet of the Apes,* Chambers's early test subjects were, for some reason, Asian, which thirty more politically correct years later, raised more than a few eyebrows. According to the makeup maestro, this actually had more to do with eyes than brows.

"We didn't just go for Orientals, we also put the call out for Mexicans or Latins because of the brown eyes," he says. "Initially we put the call out for anyone with dark brown eyes."

Eventually, Chambers received criticism from other minorities, most notably blacks, who felt they were being shut out of the casting process. "At the time," he explains, "the head of the NAACP, who also happened to be a stuntman, came to me and said, 'John, every one of us knows who you are and we know how to talk to you. We know you call the cards right, but we want to ask you a question: Why aren't us blacks being hired for jobs?' I explained that the reason I was going after minorities is because of the need for flatter noses and dark eyes. This was about a year and a half after the Watts riots, and I went to Arthur Jacobs and said, 'Arthur, we're worried that we might offend the blacks.' He said, 'What do you mean offend them?' 'Well, they might think you people are recoiling so you're trying to make fools of them by making them look like gorillas and apes.' He said, 'You're kidding.' 'No, I'm not kidding. It's logic.' So I went back to this guy and explained that we were trying not to hurt anyone and he said, 'I tell you personally, if any black makes any intimation that way, we'll make sure we talk to him. We need to work.' And that's how we got blacks into the thing. The truth is, everyone had the best of intentions, but boy, that was a problem."

Chambers details some of the challenges facing him and his team: "We had to worry about voice projection," he says, "so that the actors could properly enunciate their lines and speak them clearly enough for sound recording. The actors' own lips had to synchronize with the outer lips—the ape lips—so that when any word was spoken, the ape lips would properly form this sound visually. And we also knew that heavy rubber makeup can absorb sound, so we had to invent a manner of makeup which allowed the dialogue to sound natural and not as though it was coming from a cavern somewhere inside the ape's body.

"Our final concept," he elaborates, "involved our modifying the simian wrinkles so they did not appear too grotesque. The simian nose was somewhat modified by making it a little pleasanter, softer and longer. By doing this, we were able to change the ape nostrils a little. On apes they look like big slits in the middle of the face. Since our actors would be on screen in this makeup through all the film, we felt they should look a little more attractive. It wasn't that we wanted to beautify it, but also we did not want it so grotesque that it would distract from the story."

In many ways, Chambers's makeup design was shaped like the letter *T,* with

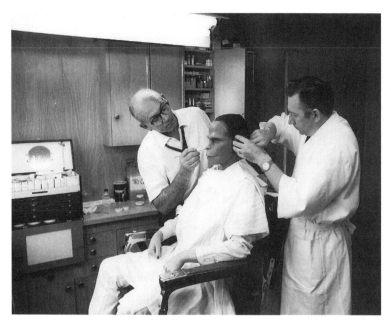

the brow ridges covering the eyebrows of the actor or actress, which brought the forehead out in more of a slope. Makeup was placed over the thespian's nose, upon which a curving surface was built up. This was extended to the base of the upper lip, creating quite a different mouth than the person had started with. Wrinkles were added over the new mouth which ended with a lip that curved downward and ended just a bit beyond where the actor's actual lip was. A small nose was added, the nostrils of which were located approximately halfway up the person's nose bone. An additional piece of makeup altered their chin and lower lip. Then a thin coating of plaster was added, which when dried, transformed the individual pieces into a makeup alliance mold.

"Basically," he says, "we made an individual mold of each component of each actor's face. From this mold we were able to make all of the cheeks, chins, and noses that we needed. We did not use the same makeup twice, because the liquid latex bonds to the foam rubber, and usually tears when we removed the makeup. Our main concern was not the safety of the makeup, but the safety of the actor's skin. So we used gentle chemicals to remove the makeup, threw it away, and used a fresh supply the next day. The appliances tore easily, especially on the edges."

When the mold was ready, actors would come to the makeup area before dawn and sit in a barber chair. The makeup appliances would be placed on their faces and thinned down. The face would be covered in a cream that would serve as protection to the next step, the addition of spirit gum that would effectively glue the appliances to the actors' faces. Once the appliances were dry, the "victims" would slowly move their mouths to see if it would hold (usually it did) and, that by forcing their facial muscles, they could generate genuine emotions.

After that, Chambers applied greasepaint to their face so that the skin and makeup would blend in perfectly. Lips were painted, and the eyes made more deep-set by having circles added under them. The fur, actually made of crepe hair, was threaded into a gauze base a few hairs at a time, eventually turned into sideburns. A skullcap was used to cover the actor's hair, with wigs glued on top of the cap. The final touch was rubber ears and false teeth, with the actor's natural teeth being painted black so that they wouldn't show up on the camera.

In summarizing the makeup, Chambers says, "Our task was to develop a believable chimpanzee, gorilla, and orangutan makeup that could be worn as long as fourteen hours at a time. So we experimented with a foam rubber so meticulously constructed that when worn like a mask, it allows the human skin to breathe naturally under it. Then we came up with a paint—a makeup paint—with which the rubber can be covered without closing the invisible pores. And we also produced a new variation of adhesive which allowed us to fasten the foam rubber appliances— be they full masks or just cheeks, chins, brows, lips, or even ears—to the human skin without irritating it or clogging the pores. We had already used this technique on some of the war-wounded. Now, if a man sustains a horrible scarred cheek in an accident or if his nose or lip is eaten away by cancer, we can in some instances give him a corrective appliance which returns his appearance to normal."

Needless to say, the makeup process was quite a challenge to pull off for one actor on a continuing basis. One can only imagine the nightmare of transforming a large number of actors into a city of apes every single day. "Before production," he explains, "I was training people to do it in six hours, then five hours, down to three to three and a half hours."

One frequent headline-grabbing aspect of the production of *Planet of the Apes* was that one million dollars was spent on the makeup. Associate producer Mort Abrahams smiles sheepishly upon hearing this figure.

"A million dollars sounded like a good piece of PR," he admits. "My memory is that we had a half a million dollar budget."

One thing that was true, however, was that Chambers

led something of a university course to train the technicians necessary to pull off the scope necessary for *Apes*.

"We had to not only bring in makeup technicians, but we had to run a school because they had to be taught how to do this," Abrahams explains, "not only how to make the appliances, but how to put them on. Nobody had ever done this before. As a matter of fact, one of the biggest problems was finding space. They finally put up a couple of trailers on the lot and the guys ran a school for about twenty-five to thirty makeup artists. And they spent hours a day teaching them how to do it. It was a real, from-the-ground-up school."

The lessons, according to Chambers, was an absolute necessity for everything to work. "When I agreed to do the film," he says, "I was not being a prima donna, but I felt there was a time when the pennies were saved and the dollars lost. I felt there were areas where I had to maintain director and camera control. We had to confer if I felt the shot was not good for the makeup. If the acting or shot, no matter how good it was, wasn't done properly for the makeup, it would have to be redone. There were very few faults in the makeup on the first one because I was on the set every day."

The Academy Award he would win for the film would go a long way in proving that Chambers and his approach were absolutely right.

Casting the *Planet of the Apes*

At the time that *Planet of the Apes* was approved for production by Twentieth Century Fox, the only actor already signed was Charlton Heston, with Edward G. Robinson having dropped out for health reasons. Names were immediately bandied about for various parts, among them Julie Harris for the role of Zira and the late Rock Hudson as Cornelius.

"Rock dropped out very early in the day," offers Mort Abrahams. "Rock was a pretty big name and we wanted to let Chuck stand out. I'll tell you a story on Julie Harris, though. I called her in New York, told her what we were up to and asked her if she would be kind enough to come out. I'd sent her a copy of the screenplay. She said, if I recall correctly, 'I'm not sure I understand this picture—how are you going to do all these things with the apes talking?' And I said, 'I will show you a test—it's very crude—that we made a long time ago, but it will give you an idea of what we're into here." She came over to the studio, I ran the Eddie Robinson test and the lights came up in the theater. She sat there quietly and I didn't say anything. I was waiting for her to speak. Finally she said, 'It's absolutely fascinating and I like the screenplay a lot, but I have no idea of how I can inject a human quality into that makeup. I don't know how any emotion is going to come through; anything I would express or contribute to the interpretation of the part is going to be lost in that horrendous makeup.' And I said, 'One of the reasons we want you is because we feel your specific personality will shine through those makeup appliances.' We discussed it for about ten minutes and she finally said, 'I really feel that I can't do it. I just can't do it. I think I'd just be walking around in a lot of makeup and costume and I think you can get anybody to do that.' So I said, 'No, we *can't* get anybody. We need a first-rate actress and I'm sure that you could make it all come through.' She said, 'I really doubt it, let me think about it and I'll call you tomorrow.' She did and she said, 'I've thought about it and I really must pass.' I hesitate to tell the story because I don't know whether Kim Hunter knew that she was not first choice. Kim was so brilliant in it—and she performed the very thing that Julie said she couldn't, which was she made her personality come through.

"Kim was the next name on the list," Abrahams continues. "When she read it, she got so excited about the script that all she did was speak to me on the phone. She'd say, 'How are you going to do this?' and I said, 'You come over and I'll show you a crude makeup test.' And she said, 'No, as long as you assure me that I can do it, I'd like to meet with you and the director and we'll talk it over.' So we met with Frank and we both assured her that there was no problem. We did advise her that there was going to be long makeup and hard work, etc. But it never phased her. She really loved the role."

Kim Hunter was born on November 12, 1922, in Detroit, Michigan. She began her career as an actress in summer stock and ultimately climbed the upper pantheons of show business, carving out a niche for herself in live television and such anthology series as *Climax, G.E. Theater, Playhouse 90, The U.S. Steel Hour,* and *The Hallmark Hall of Fame.* In between she appeared in such films as *The Seventh Victim* and *Stairway to Heaven,* then scored on Broadway opposite Marlon Brando in Tennessee Williams's *A Streetcar Named Desire,* winning an Academy Award for her role in Elia Kazan's motion picture adaptation of the play. And then . . . she was blacklisted; forced to join the ranks of Hollywood actors and filmmakers whose careers Senator Joseph McCarthy's Communist-hunting (read: witch) activities derailed.

"It's hard to think of anybody who wasn't blacklisted," says Hunter. "If you signed a petition protesting somebody being lynched—which was on a pure civil-rights basis—you were immediately popped into that extreme-left camp and were suspect. Once you were blacklisted, other things went on your list. I appeared in a Lillian Hellman play, a revival of *The Children's Hour,* and so obviously I was a Communist and that got added to my list. I worked with a director who'd been named by somebody at the House of Un-American Activities Committee. I was a member of the Actors Studio. What we were doing there that was in any way political I never could figure out, but they decided that we were. It all became insane."

It was *Planet of the Apes* producer Arthur P. Jacobs, who was Hunter's publicity agent at the time, who got the actress' name removed from that list. "Actually," she clarifies, "he was instrumental in making it quite clear that I was being blacklisted, because he was in New York at one point and he said, 'Jesus Christ, you should have a film,' and I said, 'I'm not sure, Arthur, that I'm going to be allowed to have a film. I think I'm being blacklisted.' He said, 'That's ridiculous. I don't believe it. When I go back to California, I'll figure out a way to find out.' And he did. At that time John Huston was his client as well, and Huston was about to do a film. I don't know what the film was, but at any rate he had some little plot put in some column that Huston was thinking of me for a role for this film and so forth. And Arthur—I don't know whether he got a letter or a phone call—was contacted almost immediately by someone who said, 'Huston is your client, isn't he?' And Arthur said, 'Yes.' And he said, 'I presume you care a great deal about him?' Arthur said, 'Yes.' And he said, 'Well would you get to him please and tell him he's jeopardizing his own status in the film industry if he hires Kim Hunter.' And Arthur said, 'What is all this about?' And he said, 'Well, if you want more information, this is a chap you could write to.' Well, he did. He wrote to him and got a letter back saying, 'Oh, yes, indeed, and for two hundred dollars we can tell you exactly why she's blacklisted.' So Arthur called me in New York and said for two hundred dollars we can find out why I was blacklisted. I said, 'Arthur, tell him to go chase himself. I know exactly what I have done. And probably why I am blacklisted is for various petitions I'd signed for something or another. And, no, we're not going to pay two hundred dollars.' So Arthur wrote back and said we had no interest in that. And then he got a letter back, a vicious letter, saying he wouldn't believe me on a stack of bibles or something or another whether I was pro-Communist or a dupe or anything else at this point if we wouldn't pay the two hundred dollars.' I actually found out much later that this chap should never have put it all in writing. That was a great mistake of his. There was the mentor of all these vigilantes in New York who got wind of those letters and told this chap you get her off that blacklist fast; that it was a stupid thing to do. And he did. This man who wrote the letters got me on to a television show, the first I'd done for five years. It was a hysterical period. And any relationship with Arthur was long-lasting and very loving."

Hunter explains that at the time she accepted the role of Zira, she had not read Pierre Boulle's novel. "In a way," she muses, "you know when you're doing an adaptation of something sometimes it's better to stay away from the original, particularly when there's always the possibility that there may be things in the original that you will desperately long for to be in whatever it is you are doing. Sometimes it's better not to know what those things are when you have to deal with what you've got. It was quite a surprise to me to find out how similar it was and how different it was all the way throughout when I did read it. In the end, there was nothing in the book that I really missed. In fact, I think they did a remarkable job in terms of adapting it for an American audience. In a way, I thought our script made an extra comment that Boulle's book didn't. Boulle took the whole thing of the universe being taken over by the apes. But I thought the interesting thing out of the original *Planet of the Apes* was the satire on our respective civilizations and how people are frightened of those creatures that they do not understand. Using the simian civilization to make a point was quite good."

Roddy McDowall was the next person signed for the film, hired to portray Zira's chimpanzee fiancé, archeologist Cornelius. Born Rockerick Andrew McDowall on

September 17, 1928, in London, England, he began acting at age eight, appearing in the English film *Scruffy.* Between 1938 and 1942 he starred in no less than nineteen films. His first major success was in the John Ford classic, *How Green Is My Valley,* which established him as a star of American films. Other films McDowall starred in as a child actor included *Son of Fury, My Friend Flicka, Lassie Come Home,* and *Thunderhead, Son of Flicka.* As McDowall grew to adulthood, he successfully managed to continue his career (no small feat for a child actor), segueing back and forth between film and television. Although he appeared in sixteen films in the 1960s prior to *Planet of the Apes*—among them *The Greatest Story Ever Told, The Third Day, That Darn Cat*—it was undoubtedly *Apes* that would forever change his career.

"Roddy was much like Kim," says Abrahams.

"I sent him the script and he called me and said, 'Oh, this would be so much fun to make. It's so different than anything I've done. It'd be a ball to get dressed up and put on that stuff.' Frank Schaffner and I talked about an ape with an English accent for about thirty seconds and we thought, 'No, he'd be so good and nobody's gonna pay any attention to the accent.' It never really bothered us. And we never did a test with Roddy or any of these people. The point was if we were going to have problems, we were going to have problems with *any* actor. Now the better the actor, in this case Roddy and Kim, the less problems we'd have because they're not temperamental people. They're both very solid, professional actors and they weren't going to be thrown by acting in the makeup and the wardrobe. So we were really not concerned and we didn't do tests from that point of view."

"I'd known Arthur for many, many years," explained the late McDowall. "I forget how we met. We were great friends and had been for many years, and I thought the idea of *Planet of the Apes* was absolutely fascinating. Arthur had flogged the project for, I think, three years. I knew about it because we spoke in an airplane I think a year and a half or two years before it was done. And he confided to me what it was all about and the end and everything else, and he asked me then if I wanted to play Cornelius. This was on an airplane coming back from Europe, I think. I was concerned about the makeup, because I had to face the problem that I *am* claustrophobic. I do have a fear of having my face covered. I can't stand to have a pillow put over my face. But I just had a long talk with myself. You know: What was more important? I really did love the role."

The next most important role to fill for the film was Dr. Zaius, the orangutan leader of the ape community, which had previously been assigned to Edward G. Robinson, who, noted earlier, dropped out. In the end, he would be replaced by Maurice Evans. "We raised the question of Eddie's ability to do such a physical picture with the fact that he'd had a recent heart attack," Abrahams says. "Arthur, who had known Eddie for a long time, and Eddie discussed it on the phone. And Eddie said, 'It sounds pretty grueling to me and maybe it's a good idea if I pass.' And Eddie thanked him profusely and then it went on to, 'Well, who is next?' And we went through a long list of possible alternatives, and again we decided that Chuck was strong enough to carry the picture. We didn't need a bigness, we could get the most competent actor we could find that we did not have to pay exotic amounts of money for. Frank cut down the list to an acceptable few and Evans was such a fine actor and had a kind of innate dignity and strength about him that we thought that would be just terrific. Just a matter of finding the actor who has the requisite qualities for the part. And Maurice wasn't at all concerned about the makeup. I brought him over to the makeup trailer and showed him how they were doing it, and working on it and he was absolutely fascinated. He was totally in awe of the whole operation. He thought it would be a marvelous experience, which it turned out to be."

British-born Maurice Evans began his career on the stage in the 1930s and '40s, appearing in such productions as *Richard III* and *Romeo and Juliet.* In 1941 he became an American citizen, and began to serve in the army the following year. After World War II, he returned to the stage in such plays as *Dial M for Murder, Man and Superman, The Browning Version,* and *The Apple Cart.* His feature film credits included *King Lady,* and Franklin Schaffner's *The War Lord.* On television he had guest starring roles in *Tarzan* and *Batman,* and portrayed Elizabeth Montgomery's warlock father, Maurice, on *Bewitched.* At the time of *Planet*'s release, he explained, "There is no further opportunity for an actor of my type to function as I did in the past, and I do not like to be idle. I took this part [Zaius] for spiritual reasons of keeping busy. Otherwise, you get slack, fat, and lazy."

At the same time, he enthused about the project, "I think they're being very smart here in not going overboard to make this too intellectual or highbrow. It has a nice balance between being a morality play, with a good leavening of science fiction. It has a moral and it's treated with a good sense of drama and to some extent, comedy. The ordinary kind of entertainment on which motion pictures relied for so many years has now been practically taken over by TV. I don't think people, having watched TV at home, want to go out to a theater and see precisely the same thing they've seen at home. So the makers of motion pictures have got to lead public tastes above and beyond what has been the accustomed fare."

The other primary ape role in the film was that of Lucius, Zira's nephew who would ultimately help Taylor and Nova to escape. Essaying the role was Lou Wagner, who had appeared on three television shows prior to getting the gig as a chimp.

"*Planet of the Apes* sounded like an AIP picture, you know, a second-rate B movie," laughs Wagner. "So I went on the interview and I met Franklin Schaffner there. And he asked me some questions and things. In retrospect, I guess he was looking for intelligence that could be seen through the eyes, and manners and things like that. My character was a young, intelligent, radical teenager who was after the truth and honesty. So he wanted to know what I had done, what my credits were, whether or not I was agile. He said the part was very strenuous physically, and wondered if I could take it. Plus there would be extensive makeup and contact lenses. I found out later that day that I had the part."

What few realized at the time was just how important the casting of McDowall, Hunter and, to a lesser degree, Wagner would be in bringing a sense of reality to *Planet of the Apes*. In many ways, they're the ones who established how the simians of this world would be evolved from apes that currently reside on Earth, yet not be quite so evolved that they would walk completely upright like humans.

As McDowall explained it, in the beginning he would put on his green costume and stand in front of a mirror in the wardrobe department. "*Without* the makeup," he emphasized. "Standing in front of a mirror, it just looked like a nice green costume. And I stood there about an hour trying to figure out what the hell could make it really work. And I asked to be left alone. Then I *found* something and went to Kim. I found the physicalization I felt was really valid. And it was really based on Groucho Marx. At first I was walking like an ape and that didn't seem right. And then suddenly I found it. I knew the costume seemed wrong because there was a neck. I asked Frank to come down after speaking to Kim about it. I said to Frank I felt the only way the part could be played—in the physical sense—to be believable was to do a certain thing, but everybody would have to do it. Otherwise it would look foolish. I couldn't be the only one doing it. And that was based on the idea of having locked hips, moving from the *knees,* the knees being your center of the body and the ass being the base of the spine. And I asked that a hump as opposed to a neck shape show. That was complicated by keeping the appliances alive, Kim and I were constantly moving around inside underneath. And doing all that would make the surface just slightly move so the physicalization was just fascinating."

"Everybody was in unknown territory," adds Hunter. "Everybody: the people who were building the sets, the costumes, everything. It was all unknown. We really, with a few knowns, were left to our imaginations as to where it would go, where it would develop if this happened. So it was great fun from that standpoint. Terribly stimulating. Roddy and I had several chats about how we would deal with things from the standpoint of apes who have evolved to this point where they're totally upright, and so forth. We kind of got onto a few ideas of our own, how the body should move and from where, when one pivots where does one pivot from instead of like a human being? We presented all this to Frank Schaffner, who said, 'Looks good to me.'"

The next step was a trip to the zoo, to get an idea of how real apes behaved. "That was interesting," McDowall offered, "but useful only to a certain point. The characters we were playing were much more evolved than the ones you see in the zoo. That's why I hit upon the idea of the sort of crouch and using the knees. It's very, very tiring to stand that way. The whole thing was very tiring."

In Hunter's opinion, the moments of initiative they had were in terms of trying to determine what sort of physical behavior they could achieve beyond what the script offered. "I know I went to the Bronx Zoo, because at that point there were no chimpanzees in the Central Park Zoo," she says. "So we went up to the Bronx Zoo and there was a chimp up there. Jimmy was his name, and he was the only chimp in the house of apes at that particular point. I think he was a very old one, because he was a little testy. I couldn't blame him at all, because I was just watching him like crazy and he got very embarrassed and rather angry at me. I understood that later, when we were out on the set with people staring at us and coming up and poking us. I actually had people come up to my face and poke it, wondering what it felt like. As if we were creatures in a zoo, except that they could touch us. It was wild. Well, I understood Jimmy's problem, absolutely."

Like McDowall and Hunter, Wagner spent time with the monkeys in California. "Once I got the role," he explains, "I had about a month and a half to prepare for it. And so I spent my time practically every day at the new zoo, which had chimpanzees and gorillas. At that time, the gorillas were real babies that looked like chimpanzees. And I just spent my time studying them for minor little moves, quirks, movement of the hands. What they did when they were mad, what they did when they were excited. Just little basic things like that. Then I was thrilled to find later on when I got the role and went to the set, they had a walk they wanted me to do which I had already found on my own, just by studying the stuff at the zoo."

Capturing the essence of apes was one thing, dealing with the makeup, as it turned out, was something quite different. "I don't know if Roddy adapted any better than I did," says Hunter, "but in the makeup chair, Roddy could go to sleep. Absolutely went out cold and that was probably his way of escaping. I actually had to take Valium when I was in the makeup chair. It was the only way, really, I could manage it. I would get so uptight just *sitting* without worrying about anything else. Just *sitting* in a chair for three and a half hours and being immobile that long while someone is working on you is enough to get to anybody."

Added McDowall, "What happened was I came to Los Angeles from New York to do a test in the makeup. I'm slightly claustrophobic, so I didn't like to have the life mask material put on my face. They took the impression. I was in town for about three days. Then I came in and they put the appliances on. I don't think I went ape about it. I don't think I went to pieces. I think I got very quiet and quite concerned. It was very uncomfortable, but I don't think I freaked out. I went back to New York and went to bed for about three days, because I didn't think I could make the film. In the end, I realized that the content of the material was very phenomenal, and the role was just amazing."

Mort Abrahams remembers a more distinct effect of the makeup on the film's performers. "There was a tremendous psychic effect of the makeup," he says. "The actors would come in, they'd sit in the makeup chair and fall asleep. And the reactions were unbelievable, because an actor would come in and he'd start to doze off. The makeup people would work. Fifteen minutes later, he'd sort of jolt awake and look at himself in the mirror and he wasn't himself anymore."

"There should have been a psychiatrist attached to each one of the lead players to observe their behavior and what was going on inside," says Hunter. "I would forget totally what Roddy looked like during the day. Had no concept of what he looked like. He *was* Cornelius. And I would forget what I looked like. Absolutely. Have no idea what I would find when it all came off at the end of the day. And the first thing that hit you was the part of the face, this section of the appliance that already obliterates you which was marvelous in terms of the role as an actor because one look in the mirror and you believed you were a chimpanzee. There was no problem whatsoever. And it was easy to behave that way. But there was an emotional pain in terms of hanging onto yourself. I think everybody involved had rather strange reactions and experiences in relation to the makeup. It was inevitable. There *was* a schizophrenia involved. You were two people, two creatures. You could not lose yourself totally, but you became something else whether you liked it or not. There was no escaping from it for twelve solid hours a day and really longer because from the beginning of the makeup going on you already were losing yourself. Until the final bit is off and that could easily be fifteen hours. Although you lose yourself in a character in the theater, it's not as inescapably as you did in these films. Always I think on stage you are never so totally within a certain character that you don't have control over it. It was an experience that I've never had before and I don't know if there is any other way of having the same kind of experience except with that total physical immersion in a whole other creature, so that there is no way to leave it. *No way.*"

Picking up the scenario, Abrahams reflects on the reaction of McDowall and Hunter to being made up early in the film's production. "Roddy came to the stage first, and he was manic," says the associate producer. "He went crazy. What happened, you see, is that the actor lost his own identity and became truly converted . . . transformed into the animal. I mean, he looked in the mirror and it was impossible for him to realize that that reflection was him. That's how good it was. I went in to see what was going on. Roddy was just finishing. He got up from the chair and he looked at himself in the mirror and manic is the only way I can describe it. Then he started jumping around and acting like a kid who's slightly showing off at a party. He let his arms dangle at his sides and started scratching under his arm pits, and he put his tongue underneath his upper lip and starts making jabbering noises while jumping with two feet. So he went berserk for about fifteen minutes. Everybody stopped what they were doing and watched him jump and leap and chatter and scream and yell all over. Until, finally, he was *exhausted,* and he just calmed down. Then he was fine.

"Let me tell you Kim's reaction," he continues. "First of all, we used the appliances for all the *main* actors. The extras had masks because they were in the background and you couldn't see that much anyway. But if you took, say Kim, and three other speaking lady apes parts and put them in a row, it was very hard to tell one from the other. I'm now on the soundstage. Roddy is finished with his histrionics and I'm waiting for Kim to come on. And in she walks with another small-part actor. The two of them look identical and I don't know which one to greet. I see these two figures coming to me from about fifty feet away, and I think, 'Oh, Jesus, I gotta say hello to Kim and I don't know which one is Kim.' And it's going to be terribly embarrassing. One of the figures starts walking in front of the other, and I still don't know which is which. So now one reaches me before the other and as she comes close, I say very timidly, 'Good morning . . . Kim?' And this actress says, 'No, Mr. Abrahams, I'm Sally' (or whatever). I thought, 'Thank God I got her out of the way.' Now Kim comes over, very slowly. And when she came to me, she started to cry. But she cried for ten minutes. She put her arms around me, put her head on my shoulder and cried and cried. Pretty much ruined the makeup, by the way.

"So complete was her loss of identity," he elaborates, "that she just went absolutely opposite of Roddy's reaction. And kept saying, 'I don't know who I am, I don't know who I am.' It was a very touching moment and profoundly dramatic. Then, of course, she was still uncertain that first day. Uncertain of herself, uncertain of her performance. But she is a tremendous person and a tremendous actress, and of course by the second day she was okay. But she really had a difficult time getting used to it."

Maurice Evans, on the other hand, enjoyed the final results of the transformation. "Once all this makeup is applied, one does, as it were, get into the skin of the part," he said. "You can look at yourself in the mirror and see somebody that resembles yourself not at all. I think it's of great assistance to the actor to depict the character without looking at your own face but rather at this image that has been created for you. It's rather like a puppet master, you are there to pull the strings and make the face work."

In addition to Heston's Taylor, the few other human characters with any screen time of note did not have to worry about the rigors of makeup. Portraying Taylor's fellow astronauts were Jeff Burton (Dodge), Bob Gunner (Landon), and Diane Stanley (Stewart), the lone female crewmember who looks quite lovely before Taylor settles down for cryosleep, but who has mummified in death by the time the ship crashlands on the monkey planet. Then, of course, there was Nova the primi-

tive woman who manages to crack Taylor's cynical heart and fill him with hope for the future of humanity. In the end, the role would go to Richard Zanuck's then-girlfriend, Linda Harrison.

"Dick suggested her, but he did it very nicely," Abrahams says sincerely. "He said, 'I'd like you to consider Linda.' Linda was in the acting school that was on the lot at that point and about four or five times a year the students did little scenes live on a soundstage and the producers and directors on the lot were invited to attend. So I'd seen her act and I said to Dick, 'We will be glad to meet with Linda,' and Frank and I would chat with her and talk about the part but that she would be treated like an actress, not as an affiliation with anybody else. And he said, 'That's the way it has to be.' And we did and we thought she was fine. She was delighted to get it, because she'd only done little tiny bit parts in a couple of pictures before that. I was pleasantly surprised by her. She called me one day and asked if she could bring her sister along with her onto location. I said, 'Sure, of course, no problem.' And I was delighted because she was going out with the head of the studio. She could have been the biggest pain in the ass alive. And I would be in a *terribly* awkward position if she started with the limousines and the special meals and whatever the hell it is—or complaining about whatever. But never a peep out of her. Most pleasant, most charming, very cooperative, very hardworking. She was always there a half hour before her call and she always stayed on for a half hour just in case. Interested in everything that went on, and was a total joy. I couldn't ask for a more cooperative actor."

Truth be told, Harrison was grateful for the job, having come off of a beauty-contest win and looking for a chance to make it in Hollywood. "I think the role fit me well at the time," she says. "I was twenty years old and really hadn't done anything on film yet, so that lent itself to the character because she really didn't know, she wasn't intellectual, aware, or sophisticated. So we just kind of went day-by-day with Franklin and tried to uncover how Nova would react. Of course, Chuck was very helpful. It's something that we were doing spontaneously each day. I think a feature about the film that captivates us now is that we didn't know, as actors and even the director, that it was new territory. So every day we were faced with something new and challenging. It created an excitement in something unusual which I think we sense in the film today. It was just the new territory that no one had walked before."

Of Harrison, Hunter offers, "She was a lovely girl and so pretty, such a lovely figure and consumed with the work. I also remember her in relation to the Valium I used to take to relax because of the makeup. She asked what my strength was. It was five milligrams, or whatever, and she said, 'Oh, my God, that little? I never go to sleep without ten at least.' I do remember that conversation."

With its cast in place, *Planet of the Apes* was ready to swing into production.

Production of the *Planet of the Apes*

There's no denying that *Planet of the Apes* was a difficult film to mount, and that point became even more undeniably true on the first day of physical production, May 21, 1967, when filming was held up because of beards . . . or rather, the lack thereof.

The first sequences to be shot were those taking place on location at the Grand Canyon and Page, Arizona, chronicling the arrival of Taylor and his fellow astronauts on the ape planet. No sooner had shooting begun than the film was behind schedule.

"I've never understood," Charlton Heston mused in his personal journals that day, "why the first day of shooting on a film, no matter how good the crew is nor how well-organized the schedule, never goes well. We were more than half an hour late starting this morning because the beards weren't sent up for the other astronauts, who of course haven't had time to grow their own. They weren't well ap-

plied when they did come . . . The heat is bad here. One of the other two actors playing astronauts [Jeff Burton] passed out from the heat."

Heston was actually one of the few proponents of beards for the astronauts on the film. He viewed the situation logically, pointing out that if the female member of their crew was going to die of old age, then it would be absolutely necessary for there to be some physical change on those astronauts that did survive.

"I said, 'Well, certainly, we all have to have beards, then,'" he explains. "Well, they didn't like that. Astronauts don't have beards. And I said, 'Yeah, but you're in suspended animation for however long it is. People's hair and fingernails grow even after they're dead. If they're alive, *certainly* they'd have beards.' And so they finally allowed, reluctantly, as how this made sense. There are a lot of these film business myths, like, 'No, no, you can't die at the end of the film.' Well, I've died at the end of about half my more successful films. Maybe there's a message there that I'm ignoring, but it was the same thing with the beards. For a long time they said you couldn't have a beard. Well, Christ, I was wearing beards long before they became fashionable—in *The Ten Commandments* and *El Cid* and all kinds of things."

Actor Lou Wagner remembers that first day of shooting distinctly.

"We first landed in Phoenix, Arizona, because Page, Arizona's airport was so small and had such a short landing strip. No jet could fly in there. So we transferred to a prop plane in Phoenix. After we landed in Page and everybody got off, they went to the cargo hold to get the makeup, which consisted of whatever it took to makeup twenty or thirty actors for a week. The most important 'star' of *Planet of the Apes* was the makeup. In other words, nothing could start without that. So when they got to the cargo hold they discovered they had left the makeup back in Phoenix. So they chartered a private plane to bring it in. The plane came in and they all went to the cargo hold to discover they had forgotten the key. So they had to charter *another* plane to get the key to unlock *that*. That's how it started. It was a six million dollar film and at that time we were either going to be the biggest movie of that year or we were going to be the biggest joke of that year."

As far as director Franklin Schaffner was concerned, *Planet of the Apes* could only come to life if an environment on Earth could somehow seem alien, all in a desire to paint a sense of reality to this bizarre world. As director of photography, Leon Shamroy told *American Cinematographer,* "We were looking for a landscape weird and 'unearthly' enough to suggest the possible terrain of another planet. The surface topography had to include formations that appeared tortured, chaotic—yet with a certain heroic, majestic scope. At the same time, we hoped to find a place where the earth was a ghostly gray-green color rather than the characteristic red of Arizona."

Those early sequences were filmed in the wilderness around Lake Powell on the Colorado River in Utah and Arizona. The crash of Taylor's ship, utilizing a combination of point-of-view shots, models, a wooden spacecraft, and blue-screen special effects, was shot at an area of the Colorado River known as the Crossing of the Fathers. This area, as well as nearby Glen Canyon, represented what NASA has called the closest representation to the lunar surface to be found anywhere on Earth. It also represented the first time that the government allowed filmmakers to shoot within so high a security area as the Glen Canyon Dam, through which the waters of the Colorado River traveled to provide electric power to most of the Southwest. As Shamroy noted, it wasn't an easy location to get to. "We could build only one road partway into the area, and from that point on we had to hoof it for several miles," he said. "People were passing out from heat and exhaustion all over the place. It was the roughest film experience I've ever had—but it was worth it to be able to photograph the action in that wonderful terrain. God is a helluva set designer."

As Mort Abrahams explains it, this was a *major* understatement. "We went down on a location scout months prior to the actual commencement of shooting," Abrahams details. "We went down with the production manager [Stan Hough], the cameraman [Leon Shamroy], the art director [William Creber], Frank and I. We got in a van in the morning, we scouted the territory, came back at night exhausted, went out the next morning and picked spots. We lined them all up and everybody was satisfied. Leon would say, 'I think you ought to go this way because the sun in the morning will be shining in this direction.' That sort of thing. We were selecting locations for the desert scenes. Now we go back when we're ready to shoot and it's several months later and *everything* has changed. Not only does the sun not come up 'over there,' it comes up 'over there.' But more importantly, all the colors changed. If you've seen color photos of the Grand Canyon, you know it has wonderful kinds of colors that go almost the full range of the color spectrum. Now Frank wanted a sort of 'flat' look, he didn't want any bright colors. Barren. Moonlike. Well, when we came back, the quality of the light as well as its direction changed and we had to relocate all of the shooting sights. Almost none of the ones we had down worked.

"In connection with that," he elaborates, "I'll tell you a little anecdote that happened during the shooting of that sequence. The trek which begins the picture was scheduled to be shot in three days and we started shooting having now selected new spots. At the end of two days, it was quite apparent that we weren't going to finish shooting in three days. Frank was being very selective about his shots. Very, very careful about them. At the end of the second day we were driving back to the motel and I said, 'Frank, we're gonna go over schedule here.' He said, 'Yes, I need another day.' I said, 'Well, another day is okay, but we have to be really careful because we're gonna start running out of time and money.' He said, 'It's very important—I want to get this absolutely right.'"

So the crew went into a third day, but that still wasn't enough. Shooting extended to a fourth day, at the end of which a troubled Dick Zanuck called Abrahams.

"They had been looking at the dailies and he said, 'You guys are over schedule. When are you going to finish?'" Abrahams relates. "I said, 'I need another day.' He said, 'Listen, you were scheduled for three, you've used four. You're not going into a fifth. I'm getting worried.' I said, 'Please don't get worried, Dick, we're doing the best we can. It's hard work.' Because we'd take a shot and then we'd have to move equipment over rocky terrain. We tried to get jeeps in there, but there were no roads. It was really rough. 'Well,' he said, 'I'm depending on you. I just want you to know I'm a little nervous.' At the end of the fifth day, I got another call from Dick. He said, 'I'm going to go crazy. You're shooting the film like it costs nothing, and I understand that you're not finished yet.' He was getting a little testy. I said, 'Dick, let me call you back in an hour.' So I went to see Frank and I said, 'Frank, I'm getting my ass rolled over hot rocks here. I just got a call from Dick. Let's sit down and figure out exactly where we are. It seems to me we've got enough footage.' And he said, 'Nope. I'm missing four absolutely vital shots.' And I said, 'Well, you better explain them to me.' And he did. He said, 'Listen, Mort, you have to understand—there is nothing more important in this film than setting the mood and the pictorial values of this opening sequence. Unless we make it really nonrelated to Earth, totally alien, the rest of the picture is not going to work.' And he went on to discuss it for another hour and he convinced me that he was absolutely right. He said, 'The whole picture depends on this opening. You've gotta give me another day.' So I called Dick Zanuck back and said, 'Listen, I'm sorry to tell you this, but I need another day.' 'You haven't got another day.' I said, 'Dick, you've got to give it to me.' 'I'm sorry, I'm not going to give it to you. You're three days going into six, and that's enough already with the goddamn rocks and the dust.' I said, 'Dick, you simply have to understand that this is the most important sequence. I will try to make up the time by going faster in unimportant sequences. But this has to work.' I was on the phone with him for about an hour and finally he said, 'I'll give you one more day. But I'm telling you this now, Mort, that whatever

Courtesy Lydia Heston

you have tomorrow is *it,* and you've gotta move on. There is *no way* I'm gonna give you one more hour of work. Not an hour. I trust you, I believe in you, but there's a limit and you've reached the limit.'

"That kind of talk from the head of the studio is perfectly acceptable," he emphasizes. "And he was right. The point is, he was really right. So I met Frank in the morning and I said, 'Frank, this is it. Today is it. I can't give you another hour.' And we *just* made it. We finished up the last shot and Shamroy said, 'I don't know if there's enough light for this shot, but I'll take it anyway.' And it turned out it worked. The basic problem that Frank faced was going from barren to a little piece of green. You remember when the astronauts find one little sprout of green growing? And then gradually increasing the amount of green. It was that progression that Frank was particularly concerned with. And it turned out in the end that he was absolutely right."

The production moved to Page, Arizona, for the sequence in which Taylor and company happen upon a number of savage humans living among the forest; a moment in which Taylor muses wryly, "If this is the best they have to offer, we'll be

Courtesy Lydia Heston

running this planet in six months." These scenes, too, offered challenges, though of a very different nature.

"Page, Arizona, is in the Southern Rim of the Grand Canyon near Lake Powell," says Abrahams. "Page is a very small town—must be a couple of thousand people and twelve churches. It's one of those kind of towns. Now we needed a lot of extras for the sequence where the astronauts first start spotting humans. We needed something in the order of twenty-five or thirty extras. We obviously didn't want to bring them down from Los Angeles. I thought I'd use the townspeople of Page. Well, we were shooting during the day and when I spoke to one of the people in town, there was a problem. As it turned out, while the children were at school it seemed okay, but when they came back from school, the parents wanted to be back in their homes. I suggested to the man who was approximately the mayor of Page that it might be a good idea if I were to meet with some of the parents, the townfolk, and ask them for their cooperation. They were happy to see us there, because, obviously, we brought a lot of money into the town. So we made an arrangement to meet one evening about seven o'clock. The motel where we were staying had a small conference room. And so I met there with about twelve parents-residents of the town."

Abrahams noted that it was a very family-oriented community as everyone introduced themselves. He told the people of Page what they were doing and that the production needed extras. "I described what they would have to do," he says. "I said we would pay them whatever the wages were—$25 or $30 a day—and that we would like to use people from Page rather than bring them in from the outside. They all thought it was a nice idea—all very pleasant, very cordial. Then one woman said, 'I have a problem—when will you need us?' I said, 'We'll need you starting at about eight or nine o'clock in the morning until five or six in the afternoon.' Well, that created a problem because she said, 'I can bring my children to school early, but they'll come back at three o'clock and I have to be at home because there's nobody there.' And several of the other mothers nodded in agreement and verbalized that they, too, had the same problem. So I said, 'Maybe we could work something out—maybe we could get the children into the playground and get some babysitter until five o'clock, then the parents could pick them up or maybe we could just use people that they were used to around the house.' I added, 'I guess some of you folks, if not all of you, have people come in to help you do heavy housecleaning.' 'Yes,' they said they did. Well, 'Couldn't we,' I suggested, 'use those people because the children would know them and they'd be comfortable with them? Couldn't we ask those people to come back and stay from three till five, take care of the children? And I would be glad to have the company pick up the additional expense.'"

A moment of silence followed, with parents looking to each other. Abrahams could sense that *something* was wrong, which was finally voiced by a woman who said, "I'm afraid you don't understand the problem. You see, the people we have to come in and help around the house with chores like housecleaning are Indians."

Says Abrahams, "Now, Page is on the edge of a reservation. And I said, 'Yes, I see, they're Indians.' Long silence. I said, 'Well, you know, that's fine, we'll pay the Indians.' 'No,' she said, 'you don't understand. They're not trustworthy people, you see. We never let them in the house unless we're there. It takes us months to get them to learn how to use a vacuum cleaner. Then once they learn how to use a vacuum cleaner or learn how to dust around and clean up the pots and pans, that's all they're capable of learning. It wouldn't be possible for us to have these people in the house when we're not there doing chores that they haven't been accustomed to doing.' I said, 'Well, maybe we could get a couple of the schoolteachers,' and I kept going. Finally they realized that I didn't understand what they were talking about and one of them finally said, 'You don't understand, Mr. Abrahams, because you've never been around Indians. You just can't trust these people as far as you can throw them. Well, she went into an explanation of Indians and I thought to myself, 'I'm in Mississippi in 1934.' I mean, they treat the Indians exactly the way whites treated the blacks in the worst sense of that term, thirty-five or forty years ago. Their attitude toward the Indians . . . you can't walk around Page without seeing Indians, they live all over the place. It was originally Indian land. But the people of Page had this *terribly* racist attitude."

Given the situation, the irony of *Planet of the Apes'* subject matter didn't escape him. Nonetheless, *something* had to be worked out. "I finally came to an agreement with them," he explains. "First of all, there were a few unmarried people and then there were a few who said they would work as long as they could get back by three o'clock. I mean, there was no way they would allow the kids with the Indians or the Indians in their homes unless they were there—no way. So we'd break at 2:30

and let those few people go home and keep the singles ones; the ones that didn't have parental responsibilities. But it was a terrible thing to watch this attitude unfold before your eyes. Just awful."

Next up for the production was the shooting of the sequences representing the Forbidden Zone, climactic scenes involving Taylor, Nova, Cornelius, Zira, Zaius, Lucius, and a variety of gorillas—actually the first images of the apes captured on film. On May 31, Heston noted in his journals, "We had a fantastic day's work, in consistently good light, catching up what we missed yesterday, finishing off the apes on the location, which is a blessing. The makeup is only just bearable for them, and the more days off they can get the better they'll be. I'm impressed at how well Roddy McDowall and Kim Hunter act in the makeup; you can actually read emotion through those animal faces."

But you couldn't read their *true* emotions, apparently, because the actors in makeup were absolutely miserable. "The first one *was brutal,*" said McDowall. "It was one hundred and thirty degrees. The other features were not made in the height of the summer like *Apes I.* That was really absolutely intolerable. I remember a day with Chuck [Heston] and I was panting. You couldn't remember anything. You simply couldn't remember any lines because the heat was so dreadful. Once they turned the lights on—oh, God! And because we were black, the amount of light that had to be pushed onto you was twice as much than in a normal situation."

Adds Hunter, "It was interesting with Maurice, because he perspires terribly and they had to keep kind of gluing him back on again. They were constantly taking his wig off and putting fans on him and things to relieve the perspiration, because the first film was shot all during the summer. It was terribly hot. I know that we would look darling outside those cages, but believe me, we had umbrellas beforehand, sunglasses, and we were dying of the heat. And then to appear as if it wasn't bothering us at all for the camera . . ."

According to the actress, a true saving grace during that early period was Charlton Heston. "Chuck did one marvelous thing for us when we were shooting," she says, "because we had to all leave from Twentieth, go out there, which took an hour or more in a car, and then at the end of the day another hour or more back to Twentieth to get the makeup off. It made terribly long days. And after the first day of it, Chuck said to Arthur or Mort, 'You really gotta do something for these guys.' And they brought in a helicopter. So we'd meet at Twentieth, but a helicopter would take us out and a helicopter would take us back so that we could do it much quicker, because we had to be made up out there and then taking the makeup off back at the studio, and it shortened our day considerably. Thanks to Chuck, bless his heart. But of course at that time he was also president of the Screen Actor's Guild, right? At first they assumed that our hours in the day were from the time we hit the makeup department until the time we left the makeup department. And then the producers discovered that that wasn't quite in the rule book. That at the end of shooting, you're on your own, so that hour and a half that I had to spend in the makeup department was on my own time, not the studio time. We went to Chuck and said are you sure this is right? He said he would check. The producers were right. And I think that's when the rules started getting changed; because of our film."

Says Heston, "It was a very uncomfortable makeup for her. It was hot and they couldn't eat well or anything. And she was marvelous about it and I thought *fantastic* in the part. I thought she *couldn't* have been better. I thought she gave a very touching, *real* performance. I thought all three of those castings—Kim, Roddy, Maurice—were first-class. They were all fantastic."

Those early days also demonstrated other problems, most notably the fact that the actors playing apes could not eat as they normally would. "That was difficult," says Abrahams, "because the lips of the makeup protruded several inches out from the face. Some of the people managed to use a fork, but most of them just drank their lunch—liquids. They'd take a long straw and drink their lunch. Heston stayed to his old routine which was we'd break for lunch, he'd run a mile, then he'd come back and we'd sit down and eat. He always ran a mile every day before lunch. But the apes—they had very grave problems and we had to adjust our catering accordingly to give them very soft, mushy food and a lot more liquids than we had anticipated."

Lou Wagner has his own Charlton Heston story to share about that particular period in the film's production. "We were shooting before the dam was built along the Colorado River," he says. "They were building the dam and there was a tunnel to get to the beginning of the gorge and then we'd go down for miles to the bottom of the gorge. It was like the Grand Canyon. Well, they had forgotten the straws. It was like 100 degrees and people were fainting all the time on the crew and cast. We needed straws to drink because our mouth was so far behind the appliance we would ruin everything if we tried to drink. Chuck wasn't in a couple of scenes and he hiked about a mile all the way back to base camp and brought us back straws so we could have some water."

On June 7, 1967, *Planet of the Apes* moved to the Fox Ranch. As Heston noted in his journals that day, "The usual problem attendant on moving back on stage from a location. The prop truck isn't back yet, the crew has to shake down. In addition, the makeup is so rough for the apes, their calls so bloody early, that we've decided to start at ten in the morning and finish at seven in the evening. Personally, I'm not delighted with this plan, but it makes sense overall."

The Fox Ranch, essentially the Twentieth Century Fox backlot, served as the home of Ape City, both its exterior and interior sets. During the production's first week there, filming took place in the animal laboratory where the chimpanzees perform experiments on humans captured by the gorilla army, and where Taylor, shot in the throat and unable to speak, is healing. Reflecting on that period, Kim Hunter remembers it as being one of the few times where director Frank Schaffner stepped in with a "telling" direction. "After having seen the dailies from the location work," she says, "he told us, 'You've really got to keep those facial muscles moving, otherwise whenever the camera's on you and you're absolutely immobile, at ease, listening as people do without moving a muscle, it looks like a mask. Whenever the camera is on you, you've got to be conscious of keeping it moving. I don't know what to tell you to do, what motivation for keeping it moving, but you really must, otherwise it doesn't look like a true chimp face.' So that was why we made all those funny faces all the time."

On June 13, Taylor began having regular "dialogue" with the apes, much to their discomfort, culminating in his plaintive cry, "It's a madhouse . . . A madhouse!" Wrote Heston in his journals, "Today was a really horrible day. I'd caught a cold, something I almost never do while working. I felt lousy when I came to work, and worse every time that damn firehose hit me, topped off when I had to scream the last speech of the sequence, dripping and hose-battered. The hoarse rasp I was able to produce is really ideal; this is the first scene where we hear Taylor speak after his throat wound. Frank's staging was very telling. The cage stuff looks good in dailies, the ragged blanket's appropriately ratty and unheroic."

Two days later, shooting in the cage sets, which included sequences in which Taylor and Nova bond somewhat and presumably made love, wrapped, concluding with Taylor's escape. On the fifteenth, Heston noted that he "had a meeting with Dick Zanuck and Frank on whether or not to make a script point of the fact that the apes speak English. To me, it's patently obvious we should ignore this. English is the lingua franca of film, which is reason enough to use it, but it seemed to require a meeting to arrive at this conclusion . . ."

Actor Buck Kartalian, who portrayed human-handler Julius in these scenes, amusingly smokes a cigar during these sequences. Reflects the actor, "One scene opened on me and there's a knock. I get up to let the other ape in. So I said to the director, 'Hey, I have an idea . . .' He wasn't a very talkative director. I said, 'Why don't I smoke a cigar in this scene?' And he just gave me a look. Didn't say a word. So I let it go. We had

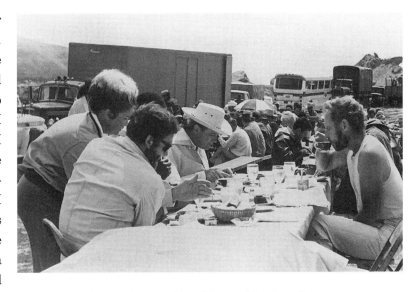

the one rehearsal. And I was standing there afterward and he suddenly yells out, 'Somebody get Buck a cigar,' and that was it—the cigar was in the film."

During the shooting of these sequences, a new problem developed in terms of makeup removal. Roddy McDowall, showing little patience for the notion of having his makeup gingerly removed, literally took matters into his own hands. "At the end of the day," laughs Abrahams, "Roddy would either tear off his makeup— he'd just scratch his fingernails underneath the appliance and rip them off—or, conversely, he took occasionally to driving home or being driven home in a car with the full makeup on, scaring the *shit* out of anybody on the freeway, as you can imagine. I drove with them once and it was absolutely hysterical. They went crazy! And he enjoyed that. Of course after a time the novelty wore off and he started taking his makeup off. But he was able to rip it right off. Kim, on the other hand, had to take one to one and a half hours to take the makeup off. Her skin was too sensitive to just rip it off. Instead they'd lift up a little corner and take a Q-tip, dip it in acetone and do an inch at a time. It was an excruciating process. Here she was dead-tired, exhausted, and then now to go back in makeup for that time to take the stuff off . . ."

In an interview he had conducted for Fox publicity, Maurice Evans agreed about the difficulty of the makeup removal. "The makeup is applied with spirit gum," he said. "It has a great deal of concentrated alcohol as its base and this is very astringent to the skin. It sets very hard and can only be removed with strong alcohol and with acetone. The alcohol removal, I must say, is the best part of the day for me because it takes so long to get it off that one finds oneself inhaling the fumes—it's

180 percent alcohol and you get quite a buzz on."

During this time period, numerous people in the cast and crew began to notice a bizarre segregation of sorts during mealtimes. "It was an instinctive segregation on the set," corroborates Heston. "Not only would the apes eat together, but the chimpanzees ate with the chimpanzees, the gorillas ate with the gorillas, the orangutans ate with the orangutans, and the humans would eat off by themselves. It was quite spooky."

"Roddy could get through it frequently better than I could, because he just had a more playful attitude toward the people," says Hunter. "I don't know what it was like relating human being to human being that he managed any better than I did, but it was easier for most of the human beings to deal with Roddy than it was with many of us, because he would have fun. Oh, he would do terrible things. On the first film I remember he went—I think on all fours—onto another stage where Julie Andrews was doing *Star* and crawled into her dressing room to scare the living daylights out of her."

"I scared the living *shit* out of her," corrected McDowall. "She freaked out. I knocked on her door and crawled into her dressing room, '*Ahhh!*' I developed a way to survive emotionally by actually being very quiet, from the moment they start putting that stuff on, that dreadful anatomical glue."

Beyond this, there was the issue of no one really recognizing the ape actors once they were out of makeup. "One day," Hunter concurs, "I had trouble getting on the set. The reason I went back, really, was because the crew kept asking what I really looked like. So this one day I was through before they would finish shooting, and so I tried to get back on and had one helluva time getting back on the set."

Laughs Heston, "I never saw Kim out of makeup during the whole time we made the picture. She came up to me at one the premieres and she said, 'Chuck how are you?' And I've never worked with her before, you know. I was nonplussed. She said, 'It's Kim. Kim Hunter.' I didn't realize who it was and that was quite extraordinary. I knew Roddy, of course, 'cause I'd known him before and I'd worked with Maurice."

On June 19, filming began on the so-called "trial" sequence in which Taylor attempts to defend himself in front of the orangutan tribunal consisting of the orangutan leaders Zaius, the President of the Assembly (James Whitmore) and Maximus (Woodrow Parfray), plus the "lawyer" representing the simian way of life, Honorious (Jim Daly), with Cornelius and Zira serving as Taylor's representatives. That day Heston wrote, "We began the trial scene today. If this comes off, we'll have something special. I said to Frank, 'I thought from the beginning, we'd have a hit, but we may have a helluva picture, too.' Frank's thought of several telling touches to underline the dehumanization of Taylor."

For Heston, this one of the most important sequences of the film and he gave it his all, even going so far as to suggest that Taylor be stripped during the trial. "It was the only nude scene I've ever done," says Heston. "One of the reasons for that is that I've been persuaded that nudity doesn't have an erotic effect on the screen—it's distracting, and in love scenes it seldom works. But in this case, I saw no way you could more clearly and effectively make the point we were trying to make in the trial sequences—one of the basic points of the whole story—that to the apes, Taylor is an animal. And you couldn't do that any better than by stripping him naked. I mean, the question of whether a dog is dressed or not is something you just don't bother to discuss, because he's an animal. So stripping Taylor naked in that scene worked and it worked better than anything else we could have said or done there."

The sequence also has what is perceived to be a bit of low-brow comedy when the orangutan tribunal, refusing to listen to what Taylor has to say, mimics the "see no evil, hear no evil, speak no evil" image. Indeed, when the film was released—and even to this day—nearly every critic attacked that sequence as representing a bit of low-brow comedy, and incongruous with the rest of the film.

"That seems to be the single point where those who examine the film seriously find fault," says Heston. "Or, if someone has a fault to find, it almost invariably includes that shot. The history of that shot is interesting and reveals something about the way films are achieved. When Frank was shooting that scene—which is, of course, one, the longest scene in the piece; two, in terms of the development of Taylor's character, the most significant; and three, the most important in terms of the comment, the satiric burden of the piece—it is in this scene that the simian world is revealed as a mirror of the human world. And I think it was quite an achievement on Frank's part that he took essentially quite a static and very talky scene—it's about a nine-page scene, and solid dialogue—and kept it interesting. But nonetheless, in the course of shooting the scene, he said, 'You know, I have a terribly funny idea. I don't dare do it; but you know, it would be very easy to do the 'hear no evil, speak no evil, see no evil' thing with those three judges sitting there.

Ah, I can't do that. It's wrong, I know.' And then he said, 'I think I'll do one take, just for fun.' So we did one take and Maurice Evans and Jimmy Whitmore and Woody Parfrey were amused by it and they all did it. They arrived at it plausibly—if not subtly, plausibly—and then he did another version where they didn't do that; and he said, 'I'll just print that up so we can look at it in the dailies; it'll be rather fun.' So we looked at it in the dailies and we all laughed, and then when he was cutting the picture together, he said, 'You know, I think I'm going to put that in the rough cut. I'm sure it's too much, but I'll just put it in.'

"Then," he continues, "the rough cut was refined a little bit and finally refined to the point where you have your first sneak preview, after which you look forward to eliminating a great deal of footage since the preview cut is often fairly loose. But as it happened, the sneak preview was one of the most successful sneaks in the history of Twentieth Century Fox, so everybody said, 'God! Don't touch it! Don't change *anything*.' And Frank said, 'You know, I'm a little worried about that "hear no evil, see no evil" thing.' And Zanuck and Arthur Jacobs said, 'No, Christ! That got a great laugh.' And he said, 'Yeah, but it's a little out of key.' And they said, 'Don't change it, for God's sake. Who knows what we're going to change that's wrong?' So, there you are. Now, of course, there have been criticisms of, for example, in the funeral oration the preacher saying, 'As the dear departed once said to me, "I never met an ape I didn't like."' But an important point to remember is, and the audience does not know at that point, that the society is in fact a monkey imitation of human society, and many, many elements, and sayings and platitudes would be copies of the human foibles. So I think the others are defensible. I must confess, the 'hear no evil, see no evil' you cannot quite defend in those terms; it is, indeed, out of key. I can only say we found ourselves trapped in it by the enjoyment of the preview audience. And you've really got to fight to get something out after that, and he just couldn't get it out. After all, it's not the end of the world—it didn't *ruin* the movie. You just can't justify it. I think he gave in on it. I mean, what the hell, we weren't doing *King Lear* after all."

Hunter explains that she and McDowall truly detested that particular moment. "I remember getting quite upset about it," she admits. "I thought it was taking the film to a different dimension than the rest of it, which was rather faithful, but he just adored it. I can't remember whether Roddy disagreed as much as I did, but I remember that was the only point of contention that I can remember in the whole shooting of the

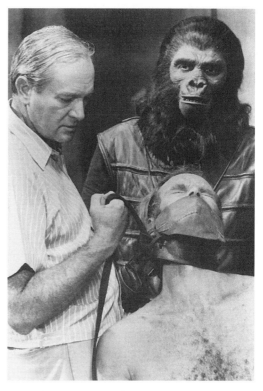

Director Franklin J. Schaffner joins Taylor's list of enemies.

film. I thought it was a bad joke and wrong for the film. I had a sense as he insisted on doing it there that it was a great possibility that he was going to use it, which was why I was fighting it. I was just scared shitless of it because I thought if they all just adore it, it's going to go into the film and that's exactly what happened."

Of this scene, Heston noted in his journals on

Charlton Heston and Robert Gunner: "You cut up his brain, you bloody baboon."

June 20, ". . . The pressure of the scene, the problems of makeup calls for the other actors all combine for a helluva workday for me, too. We have, thank God, some first-class people with us. Jim Whitmore, Jim Daly, and of course Maurice are well worth much more than their salaries. Whitmore, particularly, makes a frightening orangutan (I don't know how complimentary he would consider that observation)." The next day he added, ". . . The trial scene involves, as so many of my parts seem to, another manhandling (or ape-handling, in this case). It hurts after ten takes. They're trying to think of a different way of tying me up from those used in *Ten Commandments, Ben-Hur,* etc., etc., etc."

In true Hollywood tradition, in which films are shot out of order, over the next few days, Franklin Schaffner helmed the sequence in which the still-mute Taylor escapes from his cell in the animal hospital and tries his best to elude the apes who are pursuing him as if he is a wild beast. It's an extremely intense sequence, which culminates in Taylor captured in a net and hoisted into the air, uttering the first words the simians have heard him say: "Take your stinking paws off me, you damn dirty ape!"

It also takes the audience through a rapid-fire tour of Ape City, a sight to behold for both the audience and the cast and crew who were becoming familiar with it for the first time. Back in 1968, *American Cinematographer* magazine noted that this "city" was probably the only one ever to be built by a gun, rather than destroyed by one. As then-head of studio construction Ivan Martin explained to the magazine, "We built the entire set in very quick time out of polyurethane foam. The material is NKC CoroFoam, a combination of resin and a catalyst. When these are fired under pressure from a gun, the mix rises, like bread dough. Then the heat quickly dissipates and within ten minutes it is cold—and solid." Following the designs of William Creber, the construction department built basic outlines of the city's edifices out of pencil-thin iron rods. Basically serving as a "skeleton" for Ape City, they were covered with heavy craft paper that was formed into the necessary shapes. The foam was then hosed onto the paper and, after it hardened, the paper was peeled off. What was left was a city that looked as though it had been carved out of stone.

On June 29, Heston mused, "I spent the entire day pattering barefoot through the undergrowth, picking up more than a touch, I fear, of poison oak; it was luxuriating on every hand. A chase sequence is always easy to act, no matter how complicated it may be to shoot. The fugitive syndrome must lie very near the surface in all of us, ready to burst into the open, panic-stricken." A week later, on July 6, he had changed his tune a bit: "A helluva long day, in the course of which I was finally brought to earth as Taylor. Having evaded clubs, whips, horsemen, crowds, they tripped me ass over teakettle into a thrown net and hoisted me high. It should make a damn good sequence; shooting it took almost all the stamina I was relieved to discover I can still muster. It's surprising the perspective an experience like this gives you. Upside down in a net, a man isn't worth much."

Today Heston muses, "The hunt through the town is a favorite scene of mine. It's extraordinary. I think it's cinema at its best. It's inventive, resourceful, original, well shot, well cut . . . I can boast about it because the acting contribution is almost minimal. I just gotta be scared and running, and hit my marks. But as moviemaking, it's remarkable. I also didn't realize until we got into it that almost throughout the whole picture people were chasing me or throwing things at me or hitting me with sticks or hosing me with water or pushing me around or tying me up. I was constantly mistreated. That, combined with the fact that most of the time my wardrobe consisted of a tattered loincloth, made it really a very uncomfortable film. I had done a lot of pictures on horses, and driven chariots, and parted Red Seas, and a lot of charging around. But you usually get something to ride in. A horse or a chariot and you're an important person. Here, I am being chased by monkeys, for God sakes. Believe me, even rubber rocks hurt."

Heston also remembers that as impressive as Ape City looked, the buildings weren't as sturdy as one was led to believe. "They did a marvelous job," he says, "but a crewman fell through one of the roofs of those buildings. Fortunately he was not terribly hurt, but he could have been."

Reflecting on the chase sequence through Ape City, Franklin Schaffner explains, "Two things are happening. On the melodramatic level, he is seeking to escape, but on an entirely different level we are attempting to show facets of simian society. Showing the latter just by themselves would have been mechanical exposition, which is never really very good. So we do two things at once. Now, as to the crowd's reactions, basically they were rather human. The minute they saw the 'animal' loose, they are frightened, but the moment they saw the 'animal' was about to be captured, or he could be dealt with, they discharged their fright, as human beings do, and started to stone him."

The next sequence to be shot, during the second week of July, 1967, was the hunt through the cornfields, in which savage humans are being shot and rounded up by gorillas on horseback. As such, it is one of the most frighteningly intense moments of the film, and the audience's first image of the apes.

"Frank handled it all beautifully," says Heston of the sequence shot at the Fox Ranch. "He was very resourceful, too, in protecting the initial reaction of the audi-

ence to the apes. The first time you see them is in the hunting scene. You see them in long shots and then the people are running in terror and you think, 'My God, what is this?' And then in closeup you see the gorilla turn toward the camera, and it's quite scary. It just works a ton, and from there on, Frank had 'em. Later, he also bleeds off a little in the chimpanzee scenes. The gorillas are awfully scary; you're not likely to laugh at them. But the chimpanzees you might laugh at, so Frank starts giving you laughs on purpose very early in those scenes. All the stuff with Roddy McDowall has a lot of built-in laughs in it. It kept the whole thing in balance."

On July 18, production moved to the sound-stages and sequences taking place within Taylor's space vessel after it has splashed down. As Taylor, Landon, and Dodge scramble to get out of the ship before it sinks, they discover the mummified body of the female, Stewart. "It was an old lady," says Heston, "and it has to have been the only seventy-year-old woman who ever played an astronaut. The dialogue between the casting director and the agents on this one must have been marvelous."

Filming of the sequence continued on the nineteenth, with Heston writing, "another long day sloshing around inside that space capsule, gargling my lines through torrents of water spraying in from off-camera. It occurs to me that there's hardly been a scene in this bloody film in which I've not been dragged, choked, netted, chased, doused, whipped, poked, shot, gagged, stoned, leaped on, or generally mistreated." Today he adds, "I remember in one of the scenes, Joe Canutt [his stuntman] was having some *terrible* stuff done to him and he said, 'You know, Chuck, I remember when we used to *win* these fights."

Schaffner pointed out that this sequence—in which the astronauts first arrive on the planet of the apes in their spacecraft—was a significant one designed to disorient not only the astronauts, but the audience as well.

"A body of water was chosen for the spaceship to land in, because the craft had been programmed to land on a solid surface," he said. "When the spaceship went out of control, the astronauts had a chance of survival if it crashed into water. Obviously until it got into the lake we didn't want to wake the astronauts up because we didn't want anybody to start reading tapes to find an answer as to how they got to where they were, and so forth. The crash itself, of course, is very definitely the bridge between the men in the rocket going to sleep and waking up in the locale of

Charlton Heston and Arthur P. Jacobs with director Franklin J. Schaffner.

the ape society. One thing the crashdown did do, it seemed to me, was to provide a dramatic coming out from the titles. The prologue for *Planet* was very quiet, and as we came out of the titles we had to get the story going. To get the aerial shots for the crash down, the cameraman was on top of a World War I biplane. We also had a B-25 with a camera in its nose. But when I ran their footage, it simply didn't seem to work, so I said the hell with it, let's shoot the picture and then we'll come back to this thing. When we finished shooting and I sat down to cut the picture, there was one can of film I had never seen and by cutting wide-footage into zoomed-lens stuff, mixing things up, and reversing footage, we put together a sequence which seems to work pretty well for the crash. But it was not planned at all. What was planned didn't get on the screen. What is up there on the screen is what was edited together out of desperation."

Perhaps this is why—on closer examination—the scene has been cut slightly out of sequence, most notably in the first shot in which we see the space capsule in the lake. As the camera pulls back, it's obvious that the ship's escape hatch has already been blown—*prior* to the astronauts blowing it open.

The climax of the film, in which the cave containing Cornelius's archeological

digs are blown up to hide the truth about humanity's history, and in which Taylor collapses before the remains of the Statue of Liberty, was next on the agenda, being shot during the first week of August. Also shot was the cut sequence in which it's revealed that Nova is pregnant with Taylor's child.

Reflects Lou Wagner, "I noticed that Nova was sick and Lucius said to Taylor, 'Your mate is sick.' And then Kim goes over and says, 'I'll take care of her,' and she comes back a few moments later. It was just a darling scene, and Kim's eyes just sparkled when she said, 'Your mate is pregnant.' So in the original one she was pregnant. They didn't want to open a can of peas, so they cut that section out. They never did open that up, but Kim's work was just priceless."

Linda Harrison believes that Charlton Heston is the one who fought the idea of Nova's pregnancy. "I don't think he wanted it; he was weird about it," she says. "Maybe it was too much. When you take the whole picture into consideration, it's just too much if she gets pregnant. There's probably a great deal of footage of it somewhere. I do remember it. Actually it would have been a good turn for the script."

Schaffner pointed out that another aspect of the sequences that many people fought for was the idea of Taylor being killed by the apes and dying before the Statue of Liberty. "That was a debate for a long time," he said. "It seemed to me— as an optimist and one who wants to play fair with the audience—that the man must survive. If he dies in the end, there is no reason to tell this story. But *Planet* went through more discussions in more areas than any picture I have been on—it had to, for there were so many technical and creative problems."

These sequences were shot on a stretch of California seacoast located between Mailbu and Oxnard, with cliffs that towered at 130 feet above the shore. As such, it made access on foot virtually impossible, so cast, crew, film equipment, and even horses had to be lowered in via helicopter.

It was also the only sequence of events, Hunter recalls, for which she wanted a stunt double, most notably during the explosion of the cave.

"All of the horses were lined up, watching the cave blow up," she says. "I noticed that everybody else was astride his horse. I am not a horse woman, and I have to be sidesaddle. Because I am not a horsewoman, I don't know how loud that sound is going to be and what those horses are going to do when they hear it. So I said, 'I really want somebody else to do this because I wouldn't know how to deal with the

horse if it went hysterical.' So they got a guy in my makeup and clothes and he sat on the horse for me. That was the only time I asked for a double on the first one, because I did all the other riding. I had done all of this riding much earlier, so I knew I was insecure riding sidesaddle. Then the explosion wasn't nearly as big as everybody hoped it would be, which was unfortunate."

Also unfortunate was the fact that the fog held up filming on the third, with Heston writing, "The fog didn't creep in on little cat feet; it squatted sullenly on the sand all morning. Not a camera turned till after lunch. Frank still got most of what he planned, though. Mort Abrahams drove out for an inconclusive discussion on what I should say in the final speech, looking at the ruined Statue of Liberty. Fox wants to shoot three versions, giving them all possible choices. I obviously prefer to shoot only the speech I wrote, since this is my only chance to put muscle behind that choice."

In the end, only one version of the ending was shot, with Taylor collapsing to his knees and bemoaning, "They finally, really did it. You maniacs! You blew it up! God damn you! *God damn you all to hell!*" A powerful cinematic moment that nearly didn't make it to the screen.

"The toughest friction on a point of script that I had in the whole piece was my last line, where I say, 'God damn you all to hell.' Well, in those days you weren't supposed to say that. Language was getting more permissive, but still you weren't supposed to say, 'God damn you.' I kept arguing that it wasn't swearing and that Taylor was specifically appealing to God to damn all those people that ended the world. It was literal. There's just no question that that's the only line you can say there. I said, 'What do you want me to say? "Shucks. Darn you!" And with great reluctance they finally allowed it in. I have to point out that I had great respect for Frank. I think he's a marvelous director and an extraordinary professional. Comes to the set as prepared as any director I know. And he is at the same time willing to make extraordinary alterations if it seems like it will improve the scene. Both of us fought very hard for that final line, which was challenged till the time we shot it."

Reflecting on the power of that final moment, Mort Abrahams says, "There is no more representative of symbols, instantly recognizable and instantly associational with the concept of free America. It just symbolizes that. The destruction of that symbol was a powerfully emotional moment." Indeed, two other movies, *Independence Day* and *Armageddon,* followed *Apes'* lead, making a point of decimating Lady Liberty as well.

Adds Heston, "It was so extraordinarily well designed. I don't know exactly how much was built, but certainly there was the back and certainly the breasts, shoulders, and head, with the crown. I think it's the best ending for a movie I've ever seen."

So powerful is the image still, that it is casting a shadow over the new version of *Planet of the Apes.*

"It's going to be very hard to top that visually," offers Richard Zanuck. "That was such a stunning visual image and also it was a shock that we were back on earth and there had been a nuclear holocaust. All of those things were lumped into that one shot. All of those revelations and surprises. I think we can do something just as provocative and just as surprising, but that visual image is something that people carry around with them for a lifetime once you've seen the picture. When you mention *Planet of the Apes* to the average person who'd seen it many years ago, they say, 'Oh God, that ending with the Statue of Liberty . . .' It's the first thing that comes to mind."

Interestingly, these sequences also had Heston shaving off the beard that had

```
                                    October 13
Frank Schaffner                             Mort Abrahams
                    PLANET OF THE APES
```

Herewith is a recap of suggested cuts for your consideration:

1. The first star shot should have the stars passing the
   camera, instead of going left to right.

2. We will have to carefully go over the sequence inside the
   space ship in terms of chronology. When does the alarm
   sound? At what point are the men aware of their danger?
   When does the power go off?   Etc.

   Question: Do we need any more min ature work showing the
   space ship coming up from below the surface and/or the
   angle of the ship righting itself?

3. Look for trims of the sequence showing the men leaving the
   space ship.

4. We must find other actors to dubb Jeff Burton and Buck
   Kartalian.

5. In the scene where Taylor tells Dodge to take the soil test
   and Dodge replies "Yo!", we will correct this in dubbing
   the word "yes" or its equivalent.

6. In the final helicopter shot of the ship prior to the
   sinking, there is either the zoom into the ship or a move
   into the ship which I find misleading, and I suggest that we
   eliminate the move in.

7. In scene No. 39, where Taylor says to Landon, "Still can't
   accept it, huh?" I would like to eliminate Landon's line,
   "You know it." I think Landon's look is sufficient to
   make this point.

8. The Trek footage is long, especially after the finding of the
   planet. The following are suggested trims:
        a) Cut the first shot of the man slipping downhill
           on the rocks. This is before the first lightning shot.

        b) I think we can do some trimming in the ascent up to
           the scarecrow.
        c) I think we can eliminate the rope descent since it is
           really not very exciting.

grown during his cryosleep. "I started with a beard," he says, "and we shot *all* the beard stuff. Then I really shaved my beard during the scene where I was supposed to shave it because we thought that was a good touch. The reaction of the ape to it is interesting and so on. And then after we did the actual shaving scene on camera, we did the end of the movie. The very last scene shot was the beginning, in which I was the only speaking actor, of course."

Mentally, production finally took its toll on Kim Hunter as filming started to wrap. "It was a lunchbreak and we were again waiting for sun," she says. "That was for one of the last scenes when we were shooting out at Point Dune and we had some hours off because they'd heard the weather report that we would get sun later on and they could shoot. But we were standing for the moment for a couple of hours and I went to my trailer and took a nap. The only way to take a nap, really, was to lie flat on your back. The wig could be combed out again, but to lie anywhere near on your face could damage the appliances, which we all avoided like the plague. And I fell asleep. I had taken rests many times during lunch hour before, but I'd never fallen asleep. And this time I fell asleep and had the nightmare of the world for that film, because in my dream I was absolutely convinced that I had become a chimpanzee. And of course you're never unconscious of all this on your face, that was clear and it was there. I couldn't see over it lying this way to see if the rest of me had come back. I woke up, shaking, absolutely shaking, and had to loop immediately out of this dream."

Planet of the Apes wrapped production on August 10, 1967, with Taylor back in his spacecraft, musing about the plight of humanity he left behind, having no clue as to what adventure awaits him. As Heston wrote, "An ideal kind of scene for any actor . . . everybody else lay mute and motionless while I had all the words. More than three minutes of them, for that matter, and they were pretty well worked out, too, after the usual intense effort with a red pencil. We did two different masters on it, then the usual coverage. I think it's good. I think the picture will be, too. It'll certainly be different. If the social comment comes off as well as the wild adventure, we may get some attention."

Over the next few months, *Planet of the Apes* went through the normal stages of postproduction, with special effects (primarily the actual sinking of Taylor's ship), editing and scoring. In terms of the latter, Jerry Goldsmith, who today is considered one of the great composers, was hired and his score was as otherworldly as the bizarre ape planet itself and is itself a classic in a classic motion picture.

In many ways, Goldsmith set the musical tone for all of the *Apes* pictures with his groundbreaking score. His score is crucial in creating a feeling of an alien landscape even before Taylor's ship crashlands early in the film. His serial-based title music, launching from a few foreboding, hand-stopped piano notes, features metallic blasts of air and a devious, well-developed melody for solo flute and clarinet, leavened by echoing percussive effects. Always influenced by Bartok and Stravinsky in his early scores, Goldsmith put the violent, grim sound of both composers to work in the film's action music and added his own characteristic touches, in particular some virtuoso, staccato solo piano performances.

His work is particularly important in creating an alien atmosphere early in the film as Taylor and his follow astronauts explore the desolate expanses of territory of the ostensibly unknown planet. After the violently pulsating and lengthy music for the astronauts' escape from their sinking spaceship, Goldsmith establishes the terra incognito feeling with extensive use of echoplex effects and the even more unusual touch of steel mixing bowls played by legendary percussionist Emil Richards, heard against thrusting orchestral rhythms as the astronauts slide down a rocky hill early in their exploration and later as they run toward a source of life-giving water. Goldsmith employed another signature device, a sliding horn glissando as Taylor and the other astronauts climb a rock face while investigating a line of primitive scarecrows.

The centerpiece of the score (ironically left off all soundtrack releases of the film score until the late eighties) is "The Hunt," a massive and terrifying primitive ballet for full orchestra, including a battery of percussion and the distinctive call of a ram's horn, first heard in the opening moments of the cue as the human explorers see a line of gorilla soldiers mounted on horseback. Goldsmith builds terror and suspense through this sequence with rapidly building figures taken up by larger and larger sections of the orchestra as the humans flee from an organized hunting party of apes until a shrill and overpowering climax is reached as Taylor is shot in the neck and captured by the gorillas. Thereafter the score reclines in grim irony as the ram's horn calls slowly over scenes of the human beings caged and photographed. Goldsmith scored Taylor's scenes in the ape veterinary hospital in a dismal Bartok mode, particularly as the astronaut is paired with Nova, a scene underscored with a dolling, funeral bell and plaintive strings. He provided another frenetic and spectacular piece of chase music as Taylor breaks free of his captors and flees through the streets of Ape City. Wild, virtuoso piano runs over orchestra alternating with satirical passages for scratcher combs and a perverse trumpet solo until Taylor is captured in a bravura section for percussion and frenetic exclamations from the orchestra. Recreations of the sounds of ape hooting in this cue and at several other sections of the score were made by a Brazilian in-

Director Franklin J. Schaffner and Arthur P. Jacobs visit a scoring session with composer Jerry Goldsmith.

strument called cuika, which consists of a drumskin with a rod inserted through its center, which is dragged through the skin at various speeds to create groaning or hooting noises. The cue ends with a staggering dramatic crescendo as Taylor utters his famous line, "Take your stinking paws off me, you damn dirty ape!"

Throughout his *Planet of the Apes* score, Goldsmith provided a musical marker for the oppression of Taylor by the ape civilization with an angry, ascending five-note figure, and primitive sounding pulsations from woodwinds and throaty, growling effects from trombone added to the feeling of this "upside-down civilization" in which Taylor was the mistreated animal. The height of these effects is reached midway through Taylor's hearing scene with the orangutan tribunal, when he is brought to his lobotomized fellow astronaut. The score coils and eventually explodes in righteous fury along with Taylor. The ironic, satirical aspects of the score return as Taylor's "simian sponsors," Zira and Cornelius, help him escape Ape City to the tune of a jaunty march for trumpet and pizzicato strings. Later, the atmospheric effects used early in the film to characterize the Forbidden Zone return as Taylor, Nova, and the chimpanzees return to the region in order to investigate one of Cornelius' diggings. Goldsmith employs his most striking use of the cuika as gorilla soldiers track down the group and invade their encampment on an isolated beach, with the Brazilian instrument providing a bizarre rhythm of apelike grunts over a lurching, Stravinskian counter-rhythm. While he dramatically underscored Taylor's final departure from the apes and the destruction of Cornelius's archeological site, he wisely left the film's final revelation of the Statue of Liberty play out without music, only the pounding crashes of ocean surf for accompaniment.

Following the scoring of the film was the process of looping, in which the actors would come in and attempt to remouth the words that their filmed counterparts had spoken, but which for one reason or another had been muffled or unclear. Amazingly, the makeup *did not* cause enough problems to warrant much in the way of looping. "In the beginning," reflects Kim Hunter, "we spent quite a long time in a sound theater just reading stuff and experimenting to see how we could get through all of this foam rubber and still be understood. We discovered that you really had to place everything far forward into the teeth to get it out so that you didn't sound nasal or muffled. We only had to loop when there were exterior sound problems. Those are the only looping bits that I can recall having to do. Of course when we did loop, we had to wear the appliances. Just the nose and the chin part, but basically the nose so that the timbre of the voice would be the same."

Although Buck Kartalian's voice is heard in the final film as Julius, the actor found himself in the unusual position of having to dub all of his own dialogue. "After the picture was done," he explains, "I got a call from my agent who asked me for my permission to have another actor overdub my voice. We all had already come in for looping. We projected pretty good through the appliances, but they wanted it to sound more uniform. So we watched ourselves on a screen and we did the lines without any makeup on. So I went through that! But apparently someone didn't like my voice and they wanted to dub it in. I was kind of thrown. I said, 'Gee, what does a gorilla sound like when he talks?' Then I said, 'Yeah, go ahead, I don't care.' I found out later from John Chambers that they had five or six different actors they paid to come in and dub the voice for my character. Then I got a call to come down and do my voice again. So I did all my dialogue again—the same way I did it before. So they ended up using my voice anyway."

Heston remembers a lot of looping for the astronauts' desert trek sequence. "The reason for that," he explains, "is primarily that in *my* experience that was the first movie where we used radio mikes. First movie *ever*. And the technology was brand-new and *very* precarious. We had to loop almost all of that stuff. The technology of course was improved beyond *measures* since then. But *that* was, in my experience, the first movie when they were used. Not *throughout,* you understand, just on the desert scenes."

After that, it was on to the film's editing, and, of course, its premiere in April of 1968. As Heston noted in his final journal entry of 1967, "*Planet of the Apes* is still an unknown quantity."

When the film finally was released, it performed spectacularly at the box office, breaking records and ultimately grossing $22 million. It also went on to win a special Academy Award for makeup effects, long before that particular honor became standard practice. Explains Richard Zanuck, "I personally went after the Motion Picture Academy and wrote them numerous letters and had many telephone conversations about having an Academy Award given to John Chambers for the makeup. It's a special award—they don't give one in that category normally, but I felt strongly about that contribution. After all, this picture would not have been successful without the dedication of the makeup people. I thought it just had to be officially recognized by the Academy—and it eventually was."

The critical reaction was mixed, though the majority of the nation's reviewers generally liked the film.

The Denver Post: "*Planet of the Apes* has to be one of the best science fiction films to have been done in a long, long time. Heston's is believable as the cynical astronaut leader who has become so fed up with the world that he thought he could find something better. The film is not a thriller in the popular sense, but it is diverting in theme and so well executed that you are absorbed from beginning to end."

The Courier-Journal: "If *Planet of the Apes* maintained the pace and fantastic mood it establishes in its opening reels, it would be a dandy bit of escape fiction. But there are morals behind its methods, and the movie soon turns into a ponderous allegory that frequently preaches more than it entertains."

The Seattle Times: "A fantastic cosmic joke, a 112-minute gag in which the human race gets a walloping kick in the ribs—which most moviegoers will feel it deserved. This film puts everything in perspective—the perspective of a detached observer watching a bunch of hopelessly stupid ants doing their darndest not to solve the riddle of the ages."

Daily Mirror: "This topsy-turvy evolution theory is a neat idea and makes for a brisk, jolly piece of sci-fi entertainment. But it is not treated with enough satire or original thought to make it the serious sociological study the producer presumably intended."

The Bulletin: "The sociological approach makes it, up to a point, the most interesting of the futuristic films we have had to date. The civilized apes vs. the wild humans is a device which leads itself to pointing up, in the tones of one of Rod Serling's moralistic television dramas, the baser nature of man."

The Guardian: "A promising idea, and yet ultimately too cute: it is a one-to-one allegory, and much of the film is spent exploring this not-very-rewarding vein. It's a film to see, all right, and it does confirm Schaffner's talent. It is only that one can now see more clearly the limits of that talent; limits which are much narrower than I had hoped."

Chicago's American: "If you can live through one of the worst collection of puns assembled in a single movie, you'll find *Planet of the Apes* a thoughtful, exciting examination of what it means to be civilized. What seems a routine space opera to begin with is really something more."

Cleveland Press: "The film is best on the level of pure adventure. It has moments of satiric comedy that are enjoyable though occasionally ranging from clever to overly cute. The movie has the usual escape and chase, but it achieves a twist at the end that makes it important that it be seen from the beginning."

The Independent Film Journal: "Those movie-goers who have yearned for a splendid science-fiction adventure film will happily embrace Twentieth Century Fox's *Planet of the Apes,* a highly entertaining futuristic tale which, along with its breathtaking photography and imaginative direction, offers an effective blend of satire, meaningful comments, and escapist fun."

The New Yorker: "*Planet of the Apes* is a very entertaining movie, and you'd better go see it quickly, before your friends take the edge off it by telling you all about it. They will, because it has the ingenious kind of plotting that people love to talk about. If it were a great picture, it wouldn't need the protection; it's just good enough to be worth the rush."

Whatever was said by reviewers three decades ago, the only barometer that carries

Andy Warhol and Kim Hunter at the premiere.

Credit: Joe Russo

weight is whether or not the final film can stand the test of time. Needless to say, anyone reading this book or who was thrilled with the American Movie Classics documentary *Behind the Planet of the Apes,* will attest to the fact that *Planet of the Apes* has done exactly that.

Kevin Burns, executive producer of that documentary as well as numerous others, points out, "When we started to do this program, and we were asked by Twentieth Century Fox and American Movie Classics to produce something to commemorate the thirtieth anniversary, I had to guard myself from all of my friends in this business who were anxious to participate in this show. I mean, they all asked me if they could be involved. I was able to pick some people that I'm very close to, personally and professionally, who all wanted to participate in this show. In fact the director, David Comtois, who I've known for twenty years, was a film student with me. And I had the best researchers and writers, and associate producers and people who worked with us on this program behind the scenes.

"And all of us are *Apes* fans together," continues Burns. "In fact, I said to Dave, 'Fifteen years ago we were going through trash cans looking for *Apes* posters to glom.' He said, 'Well, we're still going through trash cans, but now we're looking for footage to put into shows like this.' The pay is better now. What was amazing is that when we approached the people who appeared in the show, we got similar enthusiasm. Never in the productions that I've done before have I encountered that. In other words, when you go back thirty years and seek people—actors and creative people who worked on a motion picture, even a motion picture series as popular as *Planet of the Apes*—many of them will say, 'I'm not interested; I don't care anymore; that was thirty years ago; I don't have fond memories of that experience; please don't bother me.' And I have to tell you that in this, it was an incredible exception. Everyone we approached was not only willing to participate but anxious and happy to contribute. And I have never encountered that kind of enthusiasm or support for anything in the years I have been working at Twentieth Century Fox, and the years I've been producing these kinds of programs."

Shortly after *Planet*'s release, Mort Abrahams had an experience that *should* have indicated to him the power of the film. "Arthur and I were in London, at a restaurant," he explains. "We walked in and Sammy Davis, Jr. was there. He was sitting at a table with some friends and he saw Arthur, who he knew. He got up from the table and came over to us, threw his arms around Arthur and he said, 'I've just seen your picture,' and he went into tons of praise—imaginative, fantastic, wonderful, exciting, and on and on. Then he said, 'And [it's] the best statement of the relationships between blacks and whites that I've ever seen on film.' I didn't know what the hell he was talking about. He assumed that we were *conscious* of this as an allegorical treatment of the relationship between blacks and whites. It *never* occurred to any of us that there was *any* of this level. But he read into it. It was an amazing thing to hear. He gave us great marks for this statement about the relationship of the races. At first I was quite taken off guard, because it was so alien to anything I've ever thought of that I didn't have an immediate reaction. Then, later, I started thinking about the picture in those terms and I thought that—unconsciously—I suppose we made the statement. But it was totally on a subconscious level."

Looking back on *Planet of the Apes,* Heston opines, "I was quite delighted with the way it worked. I've never made a film with which I was completely satisfied, of course. I don't think anybody has. It's not a *profound* film, but it's a *good* film. It makes some valuable observations on the human condition. It's kind of a black satire, if you like. And it takes a rather gloomy view of the human condition, but I don't think an inaccurate one. I think it's important to make a strong distinction between the first film and the others. I don't mean that to be pejorative, really, but obviously on each of the succeeding films they spent a little less and made a little less. On balance, they made a great deal of money on the whole series. And it's *understandable* they would spend less, *that's* not the point. But the whole structure of the ape society changed markedly in the other films. In the first film, the ape society is kind of 'monkey-see, monkey-do' imitation of human society, inevitably including the worst traits. It's a little like *Gulliver's Travels,* somewhat Swiftian. But in the subsequent films, the focus shifts to the nature of the ape society and there's a great deal of carrying on about the gorillas being fascists and the chimpanzees are good socialists, and there's a great deal of confrontation on these terms. And there was no hint of that in the first film. Indeed, in the first film, the gorillas were simply the strong guys; the guys that you made into soldiers, but the later films get very political; very 1960s political."

"I thoroughly enjoyed the whole thing," enthused Roddy McDowall. "And one of the major things I enjoyed was Arthur's mind and the joy that he had—and the fact that what he believed in worked. Not just worked, but worked a bonanza, which I don't think the studio ever forgave him for; I don't think they ever actually forgave him for being so dead-on. I know each subsequent film we always started without the green light. The studio was always dragging their feet. But Arthur was an extraordinary man. I wish that the industry had more like him, because he *never* gave up."

And that perseverance took what had started as an intriguing notion some five years earlier, and turned it into what became a cinematic classic. Most amazing of all, however, is that the phenomenal success of the original *Planet of the Apes* was just the beginning.

Planet of the Apes

Planet of the Apes (Released February 8, 1968). 112 Minutes. Produced by Arthur P. Jacobs. Associate Producer Mort Abrahams. Based on the book *Monkey Planet* by Pierre Boulle. Screenplay by Rod Serling and Michael Wilson. Directed by Franklin Schaffner.

CAST

George Taylor: Charlton Heston; Cornelius: Roddy McDowall; Zira: Kim Hunter; Dr. Zaius: Maurice Evans; President of the Assembly: James Whitmore; Honorius: James Daly; Nova: Linda Harrison; Landon: Robert Gunner; Lucius: Lou Wagner; Maximus: Woodrow Parfrey; Dodge: Jeff Burton; Julius: Buck Kartalian; Hunt Leader: Norman Burton; Dr. Galen: Wright King; Minister: Paul Lambert.

PRODUCTION CREW

Music: Jerry Goldsmith; Creative Makeup Design: John Chambers; Director of Photography: Leon Shamroy, A.S.C.; Art Direction: Jack Martin Smith and William Creber; Set Decorations: Walter M. Scott and Norman Rockett; Special Photographic Effects: L. B. Abbott, A.S.C., Art Cruickshank and Emil Kosa, Jr.; Film Editor: Hugh S. Fowler, A.C.E.; Unit Production Manager: William Eckhardt; Assistant Director: William Kissel; Sound: Herman Lewis and David Dockendorf; Costume Design: Morton Haack; Makeup: Ben Nye and Dan Striepeke, S.M.A.; Hairstyling: Edith Lindon; Orchestration: Arthur Morton.

BENEATH THE
PLANET OF THE APES

3

When Charlton Heston collapsed before the shattered remains of the Statue of Liberty and realized that this bizarre planet of apes was actually Earth, audiences were stunned.

So was Hollywood.

After all, *Planet of the Apes* was a science fiction film about talking monkeys, for God's sake. On the surface, it had virtually *everything* stacked against it, and in no way precipitated the success that it would ultimately garner. And as if being a hit science fiction film wasn't enough in Hollywood, it also gave birth to a sequel in relatively short order.

While in 2001 a hit film inspiring a sequel would barely inspire a yawn, thirty years ago it was perceived as a desperate means of wringing the last possible dollar out of a subject (on second thought, perhaps things haven't changed as much as one would have thought). Yet discussions of a follow-up to *Planet of the Apes* began shortly after its release.

Associate producer Mort Abrahams gives much of the credit for the sequel to Fox production executive Stan Hough. APJAC productions was heavily into the development of *The Chairman* and *Goodbye, Mr. Chips* while *Planet of the Apes* was breaking records.

"We were very happy about it and we went up to have a kind of catch-all meeting with Dick Zanuck," says Abrahams, "and Stan was in his office. So we were talking and patting ourselves on the back. Plus we were giving Dick credit for putting his neck on the line and so forth. So Arthur, Stan and I left Dick's office and we walked downstairs and across the lot. Stan then said, 'Why don't you do a sequel?' I said, 'You've got to be kidding—we just blew up the world. How are you going to do a sequel to that picture?' He said, 'You think about it' and I said, 'If we could, we should—it's a natural to follow up. But I don't know how the hell we could do, Stan.' And then he left, went back to his office, and Arthur and I walked back to the APJAC office. I said, 'It's a terrific idea, but how?' Later, I got a kind of a flash of an idea and I went into Arthur's office right next to mine and said, 'Listen, I've got this crazy idea about how to do a sequel,' and I told him—a one-sentence line on what turned out to be the next picture."

Abrahams and Jacobs discussed the concept with Hough, and then brought it to Zanuck, who seemed to like it, telling them that Fox would outlay the money to have a screenplay developed. Going back to *Apes'* roots, Abrahams first contacted Rod Serling to see what he could come up with. The answer came on April 8, 1968.

"When you start from scratch, like we're doing," wrote Serling, "I guess the prefacing word is always 'what if?' So I put this to you—what if Heston and the girl take off to the dark side of the earth—the unexplored part. They're given twenty-four hours of unjeopardized exodus time, but then are told, prior to their departure, that after the twenty-four hours of grace, they'll be subject to extermination. Dr. Zaius retains, as do all the apes, a desperate fear about the rise of Man. This is integral: It's the underlying motive of the entire ape society—the ever present concern for what would happen if Man reachieved his ascendancy.

"So," he continued, "Heston and mate cross rivers and plateaus and totally uninhabited places. But Heston is struck by the fact that things are beginning to look greener, life is beginning to sprout out of the ground, the earth seems to be awakening from a deep sleep, and there are birds and small animals and the like. Then what becomes noticeable is evidence of the other civilization—a wrecked remnant of a building, a place of rusting farm machinery, or even a skeleton. But the impression is that wherever they are, it was once the site of a city—maybe like Buffalo, New York, or something. At least it's a city identifiable as to location by virtue of the geographical surroundings—like Lake Ontario or Niagra Falls, or something of that sort. Maybe there's an earthquake or some trauma of nature that splits open a mountain or knocks the front end off of a cave or removes the top of an excavation. And Heston finds the remnant of a city street, some canned goods and the like. He's haunted by the familiarity of the other time and the recollection of the way it was. Perhaps during this time he's followed by war parties of apes, and this keeps him moving and running. Anyway, then he discovers the remnants of this town—there, maybe he finds a Piper Cub airplane and maybe guns and ammo. Perhaps with this find, he realizes that he is Man's only hope for eventual redemption. And he is also Man's army. It's altogether reasonable that when he first tries to battle the apes, he does so out of a sense of simple survival and the defense of the girl. It might also be a saving grace here if the girl were killed, perhaps at one point, and this adds fury to Heston's hunger for survival.

"My guess," Serling mused, "is that perhaps a half of the picture would be spent in pitched battles with the apes. There might also be a hint of another strange factor hovering around—perhaps lights in the sky at one point or other that are noted but knock the shit out of the apes in a marvelous poetic justice moment when they are about to close in on him—and instead, he strafes them from the air and sends them fleeing. And what if—just at that wondrous moment when he thinks he's won and frightened them sufficiently to leave him alone, the plane is cracked up or the cave closes or his access to arms is denied him and it looks like he's a gone goose. And maybe at this moment from the sky comes another spacecraft. Ship #2, with men on that he knows, including women in the crew. And they land relatively unscathed. They become his allies and they knock off the apes—perhaps in a miserable slaughter that sickens them as they do it. And then Heston has the chance to go back with them—back, perhaps, to his own time or back to a future time or back someplace . . . at least, to a civilization. And it's then that he makes his decision to remain on the planet of the apes and try to bring humanity back to the planet through the offices of Man. And if the crew, indeed, did have women on it, he could pick one. You'd get out of the Tarzan-Jane syndrome if you had an attractive, literate broad who could stand at his side and talk with him in his own language.

"This," he closed, "is all rough-skeined and is really only suggestive of departure points in a general direction. But I think it may be close to what we're looking for in terms of action, a point of view and a philosophy, plus a legitimate extension of the original movie."

At roughly the same time, APJAC apparently received word from Pierre Boulle's agent, Alain Bernheim, that the author had an idea for a sequel. "My memory," says Abrahams, "is we didn't get him to do it. Alain Bernheim suggested that he had an idea that he would like to develop."

On April 9, Jacobs told Bernheim that he had met with producer David Brown, who had started working with Dick Zanuck (prior to their heading to Universal and such hits as *The Sting* and *Jaws*), and the response regarding Boulle's possible involvement was extremely enthusiastic. There were, however, three things that needed to be considered: 1) the ape sets, costumes, and makeup from the first film would be utilized in the sequel; 2) new ideas from Boulle could not make the film prohibitive cost wise; and 3) that Jacobs agrees with Boulle's basic concept. The plan was that Boulle and Abrahams would meet in Paris on either the seventeenth or eighteenth. If the meeting went well, a deal would be struck for $25,000 for an 80–100 page treatment, plus $50,000 upon the start of principle photography.

The following day, Abrahams issued a letter to Serling in response to the writer's initial thoughts concerning the sequel. "I wish I were able to write 'Eureka!', but in all honesty I can't. First of all, I think we are missing the visual shock which is the equivalent of the disclosure of the gorilla hunters. Secondly, I think we are missing the big shock ending equivalent to the Statue of Liberty. Without these two factors, I don't think we would stand much of a chance for a follow-up version. I'm not even sure if we can give Heston and the girl twenty-four hours of grace, because that would mean backing up on the end of the original version of *Apes*. I suppose we could cut back to the scene on the beach after Heston sees the Statue and write a scene in which Zaius changes his mind about letting them go and decides that after twenty-four hours they should be tracked down. I suppose we can do this, but it somehow does not appeal to me. It's too pat. I also have reservations about spending half of the picture or even a good portion of the picture, with the apes tracking down and fighting with Heston . . . Instinct tells me that we must begin with the two points we discussed in the office—the visual equivalent of the apes, and the shock ending—and then build the story around those two items. . . ."

On April 15, Serling pointed out that he wouldn't push for his idea because "I'm not too satisfied with it. I do suggest to you that if, indeed, you're trying to do another picture, responsive to the popularity of *Planet of the Apes*—it's a picture that

I suppose should have to do with the apes. If, on the other hand, you want to do a film in which the original is simply a jumping off place to yet another picture—then the world is our oyster and we can try myriad paths. The idea in my letter to you to continue the conflict between astronaut and ape was based on a surmise that what made the other picture such a corker *was* this very relationship and this very conflict. Now, Mort—*What if* they uncovered another spaceship intact and went forward in time or backward in

time, or what-all, and we began a film and then paused it, using the Statue of Liberty and this planet as we have seen it, as the jumping off place to yet another new and bizarre adventure that in no way related to what we have already seen? Now, is this possible? If it is, my fertile—though aging—brain could come up with a whole raft of possibilities."

Upon receiving Boulle's initial treatment, Abrahams wrote back to Bernheim, providing yet another tantalizing look into the scripting process of *Beneath the Planet of the Apes*.

"The preliminary outline," said Abrahams, "was rather straightforward and simple. I do not mean to understate Pierre's creative work here, but merely to say that his approach to the story of the second film, while interesting and logical, did not seem to present any surprises. It would seem to be an imperative for the sequel that we have two visual surprises for the audience—a surprise hopefully of the intensity and novelty of the two contained in the original [described above] . . . Now, as I understand Pierre's original book, he was saying that the apes (or at least Dr. Zaius) knew the history of mankind and that Man had destroyed the world—in short, he was saying to the audience 'What are we doing to ourselves?' His concept of the new film is more hopeful in tone since it says that the human race can be reeducated along less destructive lines; in short that there is hope for men. Now I do not know what visual presentation this leads to at the end of the film, but whatever it is, it must fulfill the obligation of hope.

"The more vexing problem," he added, "is the visual shock midway in the film, since the reintroduction of the humans will not satisfy us in this respect. Not only have we seen them before, but there is no visual impact in seeing them for the first time, even if now they speak or use tools. I have the feeling that some new element must be introduced to provide that surprise. What it is I do not know, but I might indicate a line of thinking for Pierre which might be useful."

Abrahams went on to note that since neither the apes nor the humans would provide the surprise they were looking for, perhaps Boulle should look in another direction, notably a third species of life living in the Forbidden Zone. "Not," he said, "heaven forbid, a race of giant lizards or human trees, but either something startling that we have never seen before or some aspect of human life that can be treated visually in a startling manner. I will give you a couple of examples that I consider unusable because they have been used before, but will more concretely indicate what I have in mind. Let us assume that Heston's spaceship was not the only one launched from Earth, let us assume further that it was the detonation of the bomb which destroyed Earth's telemetering system which caused Heston's spaceship to go off course and to go into a giant parabola and return. Suppose another spaceship—larger and more populous had been launched shortly after Heston's. That ship, too, would have been misdirected by the same bomb explosion, and therefore the course of the second ship followed the course of the first. It landed some 2,000 years [from now], deep in the Forbidden Zone, the crew consisting of several men and women who survived and began a new civilization. The attitude of this new group of people was that although they were highly technically trained, the new civilization which they would find would not be devoted to technology because of the disastrous history of mankind. Rather, they would devote themselves to a new and beautiful culture based upon the improvement of the human mind and human resources.

"They live a simple, essentially agrarian life in which all of the basic needs are cared for," he added. "But their mental and spiritual resources have been elevated to an incredible level. (If Pierre Boulle is familiar with the world of the Huxley's, he will have some idea of what I am making reference to). They have developed all their senses to new heights, so that, for example, their sight and hearing is such that they would appear to have built-in telescopes and amplifiers. They have no need for speech since they communicate telepathically. As an extension of these attributes (and here I get into an area I am not really sure of) they are able to make themselves appear in any form they desire. This is a technique which they evolved as a matter of protection, for they know that the ape civilization exists, but the apes do not know that they exist. They know that if the apes discover them, they will be destroyed since they have no arms or weapons, nor indeed any inclination to violence even in their own defense. Therefore, after thousands of years they have been able to perfect a method of seeming to appear to an alien visitor variously as trees or rocks or insects or any other living or nonliving form. Now into this civilization walks Heston and Nova (and perhaps their child). Our 'new people' are afraid that Heston will be the means of exposing their existence to the apes, so they must get rid of him. Since violence is not a part of their lives, they try to drive him mad. He is confronted with a succession of situations calculated to throw him mentally off balance. For example, he is walking through a forest and suddenly, as if a cut had been made in the camera, the forest is replaced by the ruins of a city and just as suddenly a minute later he finds himself walking down a long road past a petrol station.

"While I do not actually suggest the use of the above, I am trying to indicate a basic situation in which a new life-form of surprising variety is discovered and which functions at first against Heston so that once more he is fighting alone. He will then ally himself to these 'new people' in a battle against the apes. The battle occurs because Dr. Zaius, in violation of his truce, has sent gorilla hunters into the Forbidden Zone to find and destroy Heston. Heston must then marshal the resources of the 'new people' and utilize their extraordinary gifts in an effort to save themselves."

Ironically, despite his protestations to the contrary, a variation of this scenario is precisely what Abrahams would use as the basis of the final film.

On April twenty-fourth Serling called Jacobs with what he termed an "interesting idea." Serling proposed that a twentieth-century civilization is discovered by Taylor and Nova, as well as parts of a spacecraft. They encounter a couple of hundred humans who are former astronauts. Although he admitted that he hadn't figured out what would happen in the second act, toward the end Taylor tries to get the lethargic humans to build a new civilization. The apes plan an attack while Taylor starts to rebuild the spacecraft. As the attack begins, he and a handful of humans escape in the ship. In a nod to the original Boulle novel, they eventually find a planet with a civilization, only to discover that it, too, is populated by apes.

Over the next few months, Boulle wrote the sequel screenplay, entitled *Planet of the Men,* which picks up immediately where the original left off and follows Taylor and Nova as they reeducate mankind to reclaim the earth, at the same time reducing the apes back to their primitive state. In fact, the script ended in a circus where the monosyllablly articulate Dr. Zaius is little more than a trained ape. In between, Nova gave birth to Taylor's son, who grew up to lead a faction of humans in rebellion against his father. In the end, this material was handed over to Rod

Serling, who offered his notes on how to improve Boulle's take on the material.

In mid-July, Richard Zanuck related to Jacobs that both he and David Brown felt Serling's notes were an improvement on Boulle's treatment, but they nonetheless believed that a more stunning and visual surprise was needed. Zanuck was not in favor of a sequel unless it was equal to the original in creativity.

On July 22, David Brown made his feelings regarding the script known to Zanuck. On the up side, he felt that the film's theme was a valid one one that current youth could identify with. He also liked the conflict between Taylor and his son, Serious, as well as the "dehumanization" of the apes at the script's conclusion. He did, however, feel that the film's visual possibilities were not exploited in the script as successfully as they might have been. Since we've seen the Statue of Liberty, he mused, what about the Empire State Building and other significant aspects of the New York landscape? New elements for a story, he reasoned, could come from beings living within the Forbidden Zone.

Today Mort Abrahams reflects, "When we made arrangements to do the sequel, Allain, who had apparently spoken to Boulle, said Boulle had an idea to make a sequel script and he sat down and wrote it. There was no commitment on our part. We didn't invite him, we didn't have a deal. As I recall, we didn't even pay him anything. He wanted to do it, but it did not seem to work. We read it, and we talked about it at some length. Neither Arthur or I were enchanted with it, but we were flattered by the idea that he sat down and wrote. I don't recall any of the details, but the story itself simply didn't work. There was a lot of, as I recall, conversation. Not an electric story. It was more in narrative form. I think it would have made a relatively good novel. But for visual purposes, and as I explained we went for visual in the sequel, it didn't have the gimmick—it didn't have the visual possibilities. Just didn't have the excitement of the first piece."

On July 30, 1968, a frustrated Jacobs wrote to Zanuck, "Having carefully analyzed Boulle's and Serling's ideas and the comments from both you and David Brown, I've come to the following conclusion about *Planet of the Men:* There is much that is valid and fresh in the Boulle material and Serling's ideas, but they have a basic weakness in their underlying concept since they depend much too strongly on a primitive military engagement between apes and humans. With all the combined thinking, the weaknesses can be strengthened."

On the same day, Abrahams agreed that Boulle's story lacked visual excitement. It was his feeling that the production must look at the sequel as an independent film, separate from the original. In opposition to this approach, Boulle's material would be a fairly straightforward story with little that was original, with the possible exception of the reversion of the apes to primitive status. "I must repeat," he wrote, "that once we have seen the apes get down on all fours, grunt instead of talk, climb up trees, etc., the circus sequences does not provide the visual shock that we want for the end of the film, because the previous antics of the apes have telegraphed this point. I think it is a laugh, not a shock . . . In short, I believe that Boulle's treatment is pedestrian. At the risk of being downbeat, I must say that I do not feel that Rod's treatment offers substantial improvement . . . I think the basic failure of both the Boulle and Serling treatments is in the lack of definition of an underlying statement around which the story must be framed . . . One of the reasons for the success of *Planet of the Apes* was that it made several important points: First, it said Man is destroying himself and gave a picture of what the world would be if his insane self-destructive tendencies were to continue; second, it made the point that Man's scientific advances were being used to destructive ends; third, it parodied contemporary civilization's treatment of minorities and made them appear as pretentious and as ludicrous as indeed they are. Unfortunately, the equivalent issues are not dealt with by either Boulle or Serling, and the result is that their two stories are naïve and uninteresting and that nothing explosive happens in either. In attacking the problem of the sequel, it is imperative that some equivalent sets of values be exploited. I believe that until this fundamental question is settled, we will not be able to come up with a satisfactory story."

Since, he reasoned, as depicted in *Planet,* Man was depicted as destructive, a different tact would have to be taken for the followup. If men were the warlike creatures under Taylor's tutelage as Boulle had suggested, it felt to him as though they would merely be going over familiar territory. "It seemed to me," he pointed out, "that Taylor must have learned a lesson from his experience in picture number one, and particularly at the sight of the Statue of Liberty and his realization that Man destroyed his own world. If Taylor does not understand this, then I'm afraid he is rather a fool and we have failed to make the point of our picture; we are, therefore, *forced,* I believe, to take the position that Taylor assumes leadership of the new society and attempts to build that society along the most peaceful, nonaggressive lines. On the other side we have Zaius, who in picture number one has taken the position that scientific progress must be halted since its end is desolation and that Man must be eradicated since he is the means of such desolation. I think both viewpoints must now be progressed in picture number two. Taylor must be intent upon building a society in which war and violence are unknown; Zaius, on the other hand, believes that Man is intrinsically incapable of such development and therefore continues to pose a threat to simian civilization. As in

Boulle's treatment, Zaius has human society constantly under observation, and becomes increasingly more concerned with the success and progress of that society, but believes that beneath it all, Man's evil propensities cannot be conquered and therefore Taylor and his people must be destroyed. Taylor's problem is now how to protect his society from the threatened onslaught of the apes without resorting to violence, and here, I think, is where Rod should build his story."

The sequel, he felt, should *not* be a story of a battle between apes and man in the conventional sense of the word. Instead, it should be a true battle of survival between a military machine on the one side, and a resourceful, imaginative, nonviolent group on the other. From there, he began pushing for his telepathic humans idea. "I am quite convinced that this is the way we should go," he said.

Shortly thereafter, Serling informed the production that he would be tied up for some time in another project and wouldn't be able to devote his full attention to the script. Deciding that little of Serling or Boulle's material would work appropriately, the producers began looking for a new writer to take over the project and found him in the form of Englishman Paul Dehn.

"He was a film critic and a poet," Abrahams explains of the late writer. "A marvelous poet, by the way. Probably a better poet than a screenplay writer and I don't mean to denigrate his screenplay writing, which was first-rate, but he was a *memorable* poet. He had written a couple of screenplays and had a most fertile imagination. I had read several of his books of poetry and two screenplays of his, one of which had been produced and the other hadn't. I read the scripts because I've never heard of an important poet, which he was, that had ever involved himself in a screenplay. Out of sheer curiosity I read the screenplays and they were quite wonderful. Then when the time came to start thinking about the picture, I thought, 'Gee, I wonder if he would be interested,' because the imagery of his poetry indicated such a fertile imagination. I thought, 'If he's interested, he could give this thing a really interesting kind of approach that was not the standard screenplay writer's approach. When I first called Paul in London and said I'd like to meet with him, he hadn't seen the first picture. He'd heard about it, but hadn't seen it. So I screened it for him. When I met with him I thought, 'He's not gonna want to do this. It's out of his camp.' He had never remotely written science fiction, but he was so attracted to the idea and the challenge that he immediately accepted it."

"I've always wanted to do science fiction," Dehn told journalists Chris Knight and Peter Nicholson, "and that's why I leapt at it. I am one of those writers who likes darting from one type of film to another. When I'd collaborated on *Goldfinger*,

I wanted to do a truthful spy story instead of a fantastic one, whi
The Spy Who Came in From the Cold and *The Deadly Affair.* Then
God, I'm going to be typed as a spy writer,' and then I did *Taming of*
I've always wanted to do a Shakespeare play and that really has been
of my life, that I don't want to get typed and in a way it's kind of a cur
I'm quite good at a lot of things but not very, very good at one particular

Paul Dehn was born on November 5, 1912, in England. He began his ca.
film critic for several newspapers between 1936 and 1963, most notably t̲ ̲Sun-
day Referee, the *Sunday Chronicle,* the *News Chronicle,* and *The Daily Herald.* His
first screenplay, *Seven Days to Noon* (1950) earned him and cowriter James
Bernard an Academy Award. Other screenwriting credits prior to *Beneath the
Planet of the Apes* were *Orders to Kill* (1958), the James Bond thriller *Goldfinger*
(1964), *The Spy Who Came in From the Cold* (1965), *La Bisbetica Domata* (1967),
Night of the Generals (1967), and *The Deadly Affair* (1967). In addition, he had
written several volumes of critically acclaimed poetry.

As Abrahams explains it, once Dehn came on board the decision was made to
stop trying to top the Statue of Liberty. "We abandoned the idea," he says. "I discussed it with Paul and Arthur and none of us could come up with any idea that
approached it. So I said, 'Let's not kid ourselves, let's not do a picture for the final
shot, where we're trying to top the fantastic experience of the first picture. Let's
just do a picture, but we have to make it visually more exciting than the first picture and we're gonna have to involve ourselves in either mechanical or film effects,' and we started with that premise: How we were going to make this picture a
very visual experience? Then I got this idea of going one step beyond apes in terms
of the apes being able to create a reality out of their own mental images—the
earthquakes and rock falls and all that sort of thing, which gave us the opportunity for visual effects on the screen. Then we built the story around the idea of the
visual gimmicks. Once we had the idea of their being able to create these things,
making them happen, we then went on from there and built a story around that—
we went sort of backwards. And the idea of the mutants was a natural evolution of
this ability of these people to create these occurrences."

Dehn added that the plot of the film, ultimately titled *Beneath the Planet of the
Apes,* was suggested by the final shot of the original: the remains of the Statue of
Liberty. "This implied that New York itself lay buried beneath what the apes
called 'The Forbidden Zone,'" he said. "It remained only to people the underground
city with mutants descended from the survivors of a nuclear bomb dropped on
New York 2,000 years earlier, and thus, to motivate a war between expansionist

Bill Creber, the man in charge of special effects.

apes and peaceable but dangerously sophisticated mutants."

In terms of the development of the idea of using the remnants of New York, Abrahams adds, "Again, we were looking for not only the visuals in terms of special mechanical effects, but also in terms of settings that would be at once recognizable to the audience and yet looking in a different form. Now we'd already destroyed New York in the first picture, so we had to decide: Did we want to do shots of New York with the buildings on their side? You know, with the Empire State Building gone? We decided that, no, we'd seen that enough. Maybe we should go underground and keep the whole atmosphere underground in contrast to the first picture, which was all above the ground. I don't know where the specific idea of the subway came in, but we talked about doing sewers under the streets of New York . . . oh, we must have come up with a hundred underground ideas. At one point we thought of going into Mammoth Caverns of Virginia. We gave that one up as not really being too exciting. We thought it would be fun to mess around underneath New York after the destruction. This all came from the impulse, which was to create a very, very visual picture.

"The first film depended upon the unusual story and the unusual characters," Abrahams continues. "Presumably most of the audience for the second picture would have seen the first, therefore you *couldn't* do scenes like the sudden disclosure of the apes on horseback and expect the same reaction as that in the first picture. We knew we couldn't depend on the same gimmicks working twice, so the things we looked for were the unusual visuals, not the repetition of anything we'd seen in picture one."

Dehn's first treatment, developed with Abrahams, was entitled *Planet of the Apes Revisited.* Beginning with the final moments of the original, this time Taylor and Nova ride into the Forbidden Zone, where they encounter a race of telepathic humans living below the remains of Manhattan. In the meantime, the gorilla army from Ape City is marching into the Zone with the sole intent of exterminating all humans and claiming the land as their own. The treatment climaxed with both the ape army and mutants perishing in an underground nuclear explosion, with Taylor and Nova escaping. They meet with their two chimpanzee allies, Cornelius and Zira, and go back to Ape City to establish a new order. There is an optimistic ending, in direct contrast to the pessimism of *Planet,* in which all the captive humans are freed from their cages and a new era of peace dawns between man and ape.

The treatment was fairly well received, and it served as evidence that *Apes Revisited* was finally on the road to production. TV veteran Don Medford was chosen as director, Dehn would definitely be scripting, and hopes were strong that things would get rolling quickly.

Then the bottom fell out of the project again when Charlton Heston, who had played the pivotal role in the original, flatly refused to appear in the sequel.

"We had a big thing with Chuck, because he made so much money out of the first one," says Abrahams. "I made the original approach to him and he said, 'Thank you, no.' He'd done it, he didn't want to do it again. Initially, his agent asked for the same deal he had on the first picture. I think in *Beneath* he was only in for seven or eight days, but his agent wanted the same deal as he had on the first picture: $250,000 against ten percent of the gross. That was obviously not in the cards because we wanted him just for a cameo. I got him to the point of saying he would do it if he got some kind of, what he called, 'reasonable compensation,' but we never discussed that because he always transfers those discussions to his agent. All he was saying was, 'If my agent asks for the same deal, I have to stand behind his requirements'—the typical actor's position. Agents and the actors keep fending one off against the other. The agent says, 'That's what the actor wants—it's not *me,* Mort.' Then the actor says, 'Well, then why do I have an agent if he doesn't make the deals for me? Whatever he says is okay with me.' They play that game all the time. Every actor does it. But finally Dick Zanuck got into the act and asked Chuck to come see him personally and persuaded him to do it for a very nominal amount of money. I think he got $50,000. This was a short call and he wanted it done at his convenience, which it was.

"As I remember it, I scheduled him no more than eight days," he continues. "Actually, he was on the schedule for five days, but I wanted to leave myself a little leeway in the event of weather problems or whatever. His agent kept saying, 'Make the deal five days—that's all you're going to get because of other pressing commitments.' The usual agent talk. I do believe we finally got the eight days. When it came down to it, he was a pro."

In reflecting on that period, Charlton Heston offers his view of events that transpired. "Now it's *understood* that everybody does sequels," he begins, "but in those days it was considered faintly tacky. And certainly creatively, particularly with the story, Dick said, 'Chuck, we've got to do a sequel to this . . . it's been an extraordinary hit,' and he said, 'The ending leaves it open for a sequel—you're still there.' Well, a sequel is a bad idea, really, from an acting point of view, which is the reason why I wasn't attracted to Fox's obvious determination to make several more. I mean, where can you go from the Statue of Liberty? I said, 'Dick, we've *done* the story. There's no other story to do—*that's* the story.' The *extraordinary* ironic dilemma of a man who is so much of a misanthrope that he literally exiles himself from the world on a space mission—and then finds himself in an anthropoid society where he is the sole defender of homo sapians. I said, 'We did that story, and that was a marvelous acting part and I loved having it.'"

Laughs Richard Zanuck, "One of the ways I got Charlton Heston to agree to be in it was that I promised I would kill him. He said, 'Kill me so I don't ever have to have this conversation with you again,' and we did."

Heston elaborates, "While as an actor there was no reason for me to do the part, it was *certainly* a wise move from the studio's point of view. So Dick Zanuck submitted the idea to me, even though they didn't have a script at that point. And I just stated the obvious—I said, 'I don't blame you for wanting to do some more, but all it's going to be is more adventures among the monkeys.' And he said, 'Chuck, we *can't do* the sequel if you're not in it.' And I recognized that was true and I said, 'Look, I'm very grateful to you because you were the only studio head that recognized what the piece could be. I understand you owe your stockholders something. I tell you what. What if I'm in it and you kill me in the first scene?' And he said, 'That's okay. We can work out some kind of plot, but you gotta be in it or we can't get *started* on it,' which obviously, in plot terms, is true. So I said, 'Okay, I'll do it. You pay me whatever you want to pay me and give it to Harvard School'—which was the school my son was then attending and which Dick had attended. I *don't* mean Harvard University, you understand. There's a *prep* school out there named Harvard School."

Heston categorically denies the claim that he was seeking the same deal he'd had for *Planet*. "Oh, no," he says. "God, I wish I had. I'm still getting checks from the first one. They donated $50,000 to Harvard School. Of course Dick would take advantage of that. I told him to. Besides, I figured I'd just be in *one scene*. Obviously I had little input on that picture because I wasn't going to be the center of it. And I had no approvals of anybody, which was okay. I accepted that."

As a result of these negotiations, Dehn proposed the following scenario: Taylor finds another wrecked ship containing a single injured survivor, named Ray. Taylor briefs him about the planet before he is accidentally shot by a hotheaded and overexcited gorilla. Taylor dies in the arms of Nova, who for the first and last time speaks his name. In a house memo, the producers mused, "On the underground battle, there are three basic problems: How do the apes get down? How do the mutants defend themselves? Where is Ray during the battle? Ray should be in the cathedral for the final showdown confronting Mendez. Since the picture is to have no sequel, Ray is destroyed with the rest. So far as a possible TV series is concerned, they are not keeping a single gorilla alive—so why keep Ray? They then dissolve from the explosion to its reverberation in distant Ape City, where Cornelius announces a new order and the humans are let loose."

On October 1 and 2, Richard Zanuck's father, Darryl, who had once again taken a more hands-on approach to the studio, effectively negating much of his son's power, offered his opinion of Dehn's treatment: "I'm basically enthusiastic about it, providing the budget is in the neighborhood of the original. Of Taylor's death, suggest that while Taylor is with Nova he sees another ship spinning out of control. While Nova is protected behind boulders, Heston gets killed as the ship ironically crashes on top of him. This is a magnificent irony. The climax of the treatment let me down. It did not have the kick of the original." His followup added, "Heston should remain partially alive from the crash of the second ship long enough to tell the second astronaut of the planet. He then dies in Nova's arms and it is the new astronaut and Nova who first encounter the mutants."

While the treatment was being expanded into screenplay form, John Chamber's right-hand makeup man, Dan Striepeke, wrote a memo on November 1, 1968 in which he expressed his thoughts about the mutants' appearance and motivation for their behavior. On the surface, he wrote, the mutants look normal and to all intents appear unbelievably beautiful. They are "emotional neuters." Under this façade of beauty and tranquility lies ugliness and genetic destruction. "Our astronaut," he continued, "might become physically attracted to a beautiful young girl and cannot comprehend her lack of response to any emotion. When he gets close physically and emotionally, we begin to detect a slight nervous twitch. A sudden great well of water issues from the corner of her eye and travels alongside the nose and down the face, leaving in its wake *complete destruction*. We are shocked into the realization that this society is one big, ugly sham!" He included several scenarios of how to reveal the truth behind the mutants' appearance. As their leader, Mendez, is deteriorating, his basic human emotions get the better of him and cause the destruction of the last of his generation. "As they controlled their lives, emotions, etc. and were able to hide behind the façade of beauty and placidness, the religion was born. They loved the bomb, because it had given them new life."

On December 20, 1968, Paul Dehn handed in his first-draft screenplay based on the revised treatment, which reduced Taylor to cameo status and brought in a second astronaut, named James Brent. In the scenario, Brent arrives on the planet of apes by following Taylor's trajectory. After he vanishes into the Forbidden Zone, Brent meets up with Nova and goes through the originally conceived adventure which pits the apes in a battle against mutant humans residing in New York's underground, with Brent, Nova, and, to a lesser degree, Taylor, stuck in the middle. The film's ending would go through several permutations, all involving the detonation of the Alpha-Omega bomb. In one scenario, everyone underground was killed, the moment of destruction dissolving to a future in which mutant gorillas burst forth from the ground. The first thing they do is take aim at a white dove, killing it. This conclusion was dropped as being too horrific (the description of the gorillas *was* rather intense). Another, following a new order of peace between apes and humans, resulted in the birth of a human/ape hybrid, though this sequence, for which screen tests were shot, was dropped when producers realized that they could be accused of supporting bestiality(!). Finally, it was decided that the film would end with the destruction of *everything*. The latter supposedly came about because Richard Zanuck was leaving the studio and he wanted to, in a sense, bring the franchise with him. "There is no truth to that," he counters. "I just wasn't a big fan of making an endless amount of *Planet of the Apes*. I thought the second one wasn't as good as the first; it never could be, really. I really thought it would go downhill. We did our best to kind of conclude it all, but, lo and behold, after I left, they continued and made three more."

Shortly thereafter, Don Medford left the project, siting the usual "creative differences." On January 20, Ted Post, who had recently scored with Clint Eastwood's *Hang 'Em High,* was brought in.

"Don Medford is a director," says Post, "who was a friend of Mort Abrahams. He was the original choice for *Beneath the Planet of the Apes*. He went to England and worked many months with Dehn and Abrahams, and then ran *screaming*. He called me up one day after he'd left the picture, screaming like a banshee, literally. Because he was horrified that I had accepted it. I asked him why and he said, 'Because you're dealing with madmen—a chaotic group of people who will absolutely reduce this particular project to rubble.'"

Born on March 31, 1918, Ted Post earned his reputation first on a number of stock company stage shows,

Director Ted Post had high regard for actors James Franciscus and Linda Harrison.

including *The Barretts of Wimpole Street, The Glass Menagerie,* and *Dracula,* and on a variety of television series, among them *Gunsmoke, Wagon Train, The Twilight Zone, Thriller,* and *Peyton Place,* before making his directorial debut on the enormously successful Clint Eastwood "spaghetti Western," *Hang 'Em High* in 1967.

Next to the fifth film in the series, *Battle for the Planet of the Apes, Beneath* is generally considered the weakest link. Surprisingly, Ted Post is well aware of the film's shortcomings and did everything in his power to allow it to match the power of the original, but was seemingly thwarted at every turn.

"I was very unhappy with the script," says Post, "and I thought the script was far from what it should have been. And the input of one particular individual— Mort Abrahams—was so cliché and so hackneyed and so absolutely impossible to change or rectify or even in some way improve because of his power and his highly articulate way of getting his power across, that I think he screwed it."

With no choice, Post determined to be as creatively visual as he could be. "That was the only way I could really salvage whatever it was that I was there to attempt to communicate to the audience," he explains. "I'm an actor's director and I like to know that my stories have to be logical and intelligent at least up to a point, so that you can make your performances come out very rounded and very believable and very human. That's the thing I put all my efforts into, especially when I'm dealing with a dimension-and-a-half picture. So I try to make my actors, at least, come across with heart and with soul and some spirit. And I like to tone my pictures that way, with the spirit or the idea behind what it was they were attempting to do. The *horror* of the change that took place in having apes control the world. The reason I wanted Heston to be in the film so badly is that I didn't want to tell the audience that we were sort of going to give them less. Usually sequels come out worse than the original, and the reason for that is they don't have the original performers in it to give it the quality and integrity. To tell the audience that, at least, we're not going to cheat them; that the original individual who made the picture interesting in the first one was back. I wanted to tell the audience that we were not going to shortchange them by putting in secondary or lesser known or lesser qualitative people. I wanted to have him in there because it would legitimatize the sequel."

There was also the issue of the studio having originally given the film a $5.5 million budget, but then taking thirty-nine percent off for, as Post explains it, "overhead."

"At that time," Post details, "Martin Ritt was complaining about his film *The Great White Hope*. They took about thirty-six or thirty-nine percent off his top. They had not had any hits, so they took it off these budgets and it effected what we could do with a very complicated film. We had some wonderful underwater sequences that had to be taken out of the picture because it was too expensive for the budget, but it wouldn't have been if we had the 5.5 million. We ended up with about three million. We couldn't shoot any excessive material. The need to come in within budget was extremely important. That picture made money, though, much to the surprise of a lot of people who don't believe in sequels making money."

Counters Abrahams, "That's a little unfair. The studio always gets overhead. It was very simple. The theory was, 'Yes, we would like to produce and release a sequel. The first one was very successful, but we cannot anticipate that the second one is going to gross as much because, traditionally, sequels go down, down, down.' That was before James Bond and Superman. But that, historically, is true. Therefore, with reason, they cut the budget."

Throughout production, Post felt challenged by the script. "I spoke to Frank Schaffner about it," says Post, "and Frank told me that when Rod Serling wrote the first one, it wasn't a usable script, so they gave it to Michael Wilson, who rewrote

Planet of the Apes. Michael was a superb writer and Frank gave me his number. I called and he said he would be interested in redoing it as he had redone the original. I told this to Dick Zanuck and he said, 'Go ahead, go with him.' But what happened was that over a very short period of time, I lost Michael Wilson so they said, 'You have to go back with Paul Dehn; we'll bring Paul over to the Beverly Hills Hotel and he will work with you to fix it.' I said, 'If he's already worked six or seven months trying to fix it up now, do you think it's wise to go ahead with him? There's obviously something radically wrong.' Anyway, I went and I tried. When I got to the hotel, he was sick with a 105-degree fever and no one knew what it was. When Mort Abrahams and I got there, it was 105. When Mort Abrahams left, his fever went down. So I got a feeling that the experience of Mort Abrahams was responsible for Dehn's psychological condition, which induced a form of illness. It pumped itself up into a shape of some kind. And he was so amenable to all of Mort's ideas, which were so horribly cliché and so unbelievably *bad* for the show. I never really had a chance to work with Dehn. The guy was sick all the way through. The best *I* could do was to make what was given to me work. And I had to apply all my skills and all my insights and all my experience and whatever technique and principles I ever used—in summer stock, as a director, as a theater director, as a live television director or a tape director or a TV/film director and radio director. I had to apply all those techniques and skills and principles to make this picture work.

"My problem," he drives home the point, "was to make out of a messy script, a wholesome, coherent, unified piece of writing. So I had problems making it emotionally valid. I was so steeped in that, that whenever they came to me with the peripheral problem, I probably gave them the consideration, but not deep consideration. Because to me, if the story didn't hit you with any credibility, then all that would mean nothing. For me, it was a very, very tough situation, because of the script not being up to the level I would have loved it to have been. So my concern was so wrapped up and so singleminded and so tunnel-vision—to get what I had to work with to look as effective and truthful as I could make it. And that was my deep intense concern. Everything around me was incidental—was embroidering. I didn't give it that much thought. If I did, I quickly forgot it and walked into the more important areas of where scenes had to come alive and become dimensional and become more credible through performance and through writing. Always to make the writing credible was the biggest wall-banging experience my head had."

The natural question to ask is why Post would sign on to helm a film whose script he could not respect. As he explains it, he did so because he felt an obligation to Fox. "They had released me to do *Hang 'Em High* while I was on a contract with Fox for directing *Peyton Place.* I told the powers that be that if *Hang 'Em High* was a hit, I would come back and finish *Peyton Place,* which I was obligated to do anyway, and I would do anything they wanted me to do if they were ever in deep trouble with a film—that I would try to help as best I could, and I did exactly that. So I came on to *Beneath* with a moral obligation to take an assignment that I promised I would fulfill."

What has essentially been unknown for the past three decades, is that Ted Post is, in some ways, the unsung hero of *Beneath,* although his efforts unfortunately did not make it to the screen. In looking at his notes regarding the screenplay, it's obvious that he had some *very* strong ideas that would have had a positive impact on the film—*if* he had been allowed to implement them.

Wrote Post, "In the original *Planet,* the whole sociology of a world run by simians is exhaustively laid out. Mutant City is arid of this. We learn from *Planet* that we can be scared of the unfamiliar, and therefore as foolish and as prejudiced as more familiar beings can be. We saw a simple radical reversal, where creatures we are taught to be inferior, are suddenly so superior that they have the power to lock up odd specimens like Heston in a zoo and run a few experiments on him to test the causes of his obvious inadequacy. Dramatically illustrate how the mutants go on with the essentially simple, but in detail very complicated business of living. Show how minerals are used—how converted to energy, clothing, water, food, utensils, pottery, paint, light, etc. Must create for the spectator a climate of acceptance of new wonders and a willingness to think at least one step ahead.

"Since the emphasis of the film will be on survival," he elaborated, "the stress on the characters and their problems, their conflicts, their emotions as determined by the environment in which the mutants live, must be evident. The mutants take us into the field of extrasensory perception—show us the use of 'psi' (psionics) faculties, together with any other unexplored frontiers of the mind, including sympathetic magic—Example: A spaceship driven by mental powers; bomb is set off by mental forces."

Giving the script even more thought, Post wrote shortly thereafter, "1) There should be some payoff of the antagonism [in the script] between chimps and apes. We're led to expect revolution or something. Suggest we see the apes forcing the chimps to bear arms.

"2) Might be better to know of Brent and the spaceship *before* Taylor disappears, i.e. interweave the introductory scenes. Might increase the suspense—rather than having Taylor in a kind of a vacuum at first.

"3) The church scene, the mutation of a Protestant ceremony, seems cheap, silly, and ineffective. Ditto the mutation of 'Ring Around a Rosy.' Both seem like high school stunts, tasteless and pointless.

"4) The sociology, if that's what it is, in Ursus's endless speeches and the arguments between Ursus and Dr. Zaius, seems pompous, overdone, and patently obvious. It would be one thing if the behavior differences between men and animals were explored. But here, the animals have simply been given the attitudes of right-wing, militaristic, rather stupid men. What does it prove? Only what we already know: That stupid rulers rule stupidly. I know it blows the premise of the whole movie out of the water, but the fact of the matter is, only men and ants wage war.

"5) The characters of the humans—Brent and Taylor—are one-dimensional. They are our heroes. There is not conflict over the girl. There is no reason for her to like Taylor any more than Brent. I presume the humans are the same as they were in *Planet,* and cannot be changed radically. Too bad. Think what fascinating trouble you could get into if Taylor were a gnarled old scientist who was actually more in love with Zira, the chimp, than Nova, if Brent were more physical than intellectual—thus paralleling the Zaius–Ursus conflict on the human level."

Not content with simply complaining about what didn't work in the script, Post actually had the "audacity" to offer potential solutions, all in an effort to create the kind of three-dimensional characters and societies that had played so integral a role in the success of *Planet*. "Mutant City," he wrote to Abrahams, "is primarily a story of survival. Perhaps mutants are finding it difficult to cope with the overcrowding (population explosion), the stress, the loss of privacy and independence of action, the shortage of food, etc. They must start to explore—investigate. Their environment is undergoing a major change and they're being forced to make changes. They're seeking to remodel their environment and even behavioral patterns.

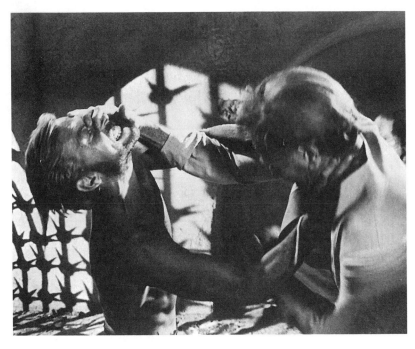

They're finding it difficult to control sudden urges of aggressive and territorial feelings and sexual impulses. They're beginning to realize that their intelligence cannot dominate all their basic biological urges and needs. They will stand a much better chance for survival if they expand, improve and progress.

"The apes," he added, "regard the mutants as prey, symbionts, competitors, parasites, or predators. This will justify (the last scene, if used) an interspecific involvement, unique in the animal world—an integrated animal and human world!

"Justification for the war: Ape scouts and patrols disappear in the same mysterious manner as Taylor. And graineries are ransacked. Land expansion is required

by the mutants. With improper water supply, lack of sunlight and no herbs for medicine, etc., all important elements, to which Taylor opened their eyes, the mutants must resort to external exploration. For centuries they have existed on synthetic foods. Living underground has made them a brittle race of people. Their skin is jellylike, soft, unsupported. Their frames hide undeveloped muscles. They are physically a weak people. Their life expectancy is about thirty-two. Being physically weak has motivated them to strengthen their minds, thereby making them proficient in 'thought transfer' and traumatic hypnosis. (Taylor, kept under house arrest, is living in extremely comfortable quarters—not in a cell, because he is being used by the mutants to expand their way of life, as well as lengthening it.) Brent will, according to them, also be a helpful factor. Like anyone else, the mutants desire to live longer and better. To them, Brent and Taylor mean 'knowledge.' These underground dwellers are not a warring nation. Their entire setup is built entirely around defense. Being physically weak and living underground, they have no need for an army for purpose of offense.

"Suggest that Zira and Cornelius arrange for Brent and Nova to escape, then plan to meet them later. The chimpanzees have decided to visit the Forbidden Zone on a specific mission—to ferret out for themselves who the inhabitants are, what they plan, etc. *It is a fact-finding mission.* Then they can return to Zaius and Ursus, give them a complete report and perhaps a war can be averted. And they will need Brent's help, for all of us fear the unknown.

"Suggested: When Brent and his party, consisting of Nova, Zira, and Cornelius reach the area close to the air vent, which leads to the underground city, the astronaut halts them. He orders them to remain hidden from sight, while he scouts the unknown. If he does not come back within a certain time, they are all to return to Ape City. For then it would be useless to continue if he has failed. This would reveal the inhabitants are not interested in any ties with the outside. It would be suicide for Cornelius, Zira, and Nova to press on with their campaign. (Brent would not endanger the lives of Nova, Zira, and Cornelius by allowing them to follow him blindly into what could be waiting deaths.) When Brent is captured, he is handled roughly by the mutant inquisitors. Their questions and actions stem from a native, paranoid philosophy, based on fear of the outside. After the talk of invasion by the apes, Brent suggests a possible solution for peace. The inquisitors are agreeable. They are not prepared to wage a war against any enemy. But they want proof of Brent's intention. The astronaut informs them there are two emissaries representing the apes nearby. They are eager for a mutual discussion, which can benefit both factions.

"Mendez has Cornelius, Zira, and Nova brought below, but not before receiving guarantee of their safety. Cornelius and Zira explain their mission, aided by Brent. The mutants at first are suspicious, then curious and finally agree to answer questions. The mutants offer information which could assist in stopping certain devastation. When Cornelius motions to Zira to accompany him out of the underground city, Mendez is quick to inform the couple that she will remain behind as a hostage. But Brent will be allowed to go along. And so, while Brent remains in the distant background, Cornelius approaches the mounted army of apes overlooking the underground city. In the vanguard are Zaius and Ursus, who are told about the inhabitants in the Forbidden Zone. The mutants do not seek war. Cornelius describes them, their desires, their hopes, their willingness to exchange scientific experiments and advanced technology. Zaius mulls over the idea, including ideas of a water system, more food, enlargement of boundaries, etc. He is teetering on agreement. It is Ursus who earnestly believes the inhabitants of the Forbidden Zone will desire more and more land as time goes on, eventually absorbing and destroying Ape City. He does not trust anyone, *especially humans.* And they in the Forbidden Zone must be destroyed.

"Cornelius then reveals the mutants own a bomb a thousand times more powerful than anything ever known. If attacked, they will use it and destroy all of Ape City. Ursus does not believe it. If they owned a bomb like this, and it was so powerful, which he doubts, 'They would also destroy themselves, as well.' He gives Cornelius his answer—a gun is pointed and fired at the emissary. Cornelius falls dead, denounced as a traitor to his country by Ursus. Brent, in the distant background, is frustrated and powerless. He returns to the underground city with the tragic news.

"Puzzling: The bomb being worshipped appears to be contradictory. From their history, the mutants seem to be aware that the bomb is responsible for their disfigurement and mode of life. If they want to believe that the bomb is 'an instrument of God,' a means of safeguarding their very existence, in case of enemy attack— *that* would be *logical.* After all, it is their means for survival when all else fails. It can also mean their own destruction and the destruction of *their God. What kind of God is it who can be destroyed?*"

Unfortunately, Post's best efforts were, for lack of a better word, ignored by the powers that were. "I was a young, struggling director trying to make a dent as a motion picture director," he says. "Even though I got great reviews for my first film, *Hang 'Em High,* Arthur Jacobs was not impressed. In other words, I was a low-profile director and he was accustomed to dealing with high-profile people, whether they were stars or directors or producers."

As if Post didn't have enough to worry about in terms of the script, there was a little matter of Heston's agent, Herman Citron. The powers that be decided that they would rewrite the script so that Taylor would disappear at the beginning, but return at the ending. The script was written this way, but Citron demanded that it be *rewritten* so that Taylor would only appear at the beginning. Richard Zanuck was furious, shooting off a memo to Citron on February 11, 1969, in which he expressed his initial frustration over the fact that Heston had flat-out refused to appear in a sequel. Only then did he agree to appear in a cameo. What bothered Zanuck was the fact that while it was true he and the actor had discussed Heston's appearing at the beginning of the film, it didn't make any sense that they would protest the alternate idea of the character of Taylor disappearing at the beginning and reappearing at the end. Heston's shooting schedule would remain exactly the same. At bottom, Zanuck was justifiably annoyed that Heston's demands would "handcuff" the creativity of the sequel. He reminded Citron that Fox took a risk in making a picture where people were "running around in ape suits" and it was entitled to make the sequel the studio wanted.

Two days later, Jacobs informed Zanuck that he had had a lengthy conversation with Heston and was happy to report that Heston will do the picture the way they want, but with some small rewriting for the end sequence. On that same day, Heston wrote in his journals, "Citron is upset with Fox over my appearance in the sequel. The part is longer than I want to do and the latest script is not good. He feels that my relationship with Zanuck is such that I should make some compromise. I'm inclined to agree."

On February 20, publicist Jack Hirshberg wrote a memo to Jacobs in which he suggested a variety of titles for the film, among them *Grotto of the Bomb, Sign of the Bomb, The Inquisitors, The Thought Projectors, Bend of Time, 70 Floors Lower, The Holy Fallout, Blessed Be the Bomb, The Devil's Instrument,* and *Vaguely Kept in Mind.*

Attention was next turned to casting, particularly the role of Brent. Although the producers originally approached then-rising star Burt Reynolds for the role, he eventually turned them down, leading them to their runner-up, James Franciscus. "The curious thing that always astounded me," laughed the late Franciscus, "is that you'd think they'd say, 'Jesus, this guy's gotta walk around in a loincloth—what does his body look like?' And they never inquired. It astounded me. And I recall meeting Dick Zanuck on the street one day and he said, 'Gee, I've seen some dailies—they're great. You just look terrific in that loincloth.' And it occurred to me, 'What if I had a great big fat tummy, and there you have an actor running around in a loincloth that looks like a bit of a tub.' But they never asked me to take my shirt off, ever."

"Franciscus was *my* first choice," says Post. "He was coming up very strong, and working with me, his work has always been a little more . . . *sensitive* (take a look at *Nightkill* to see what I mean). I can see why Jimmy veers away from being sensitive—he thinks it's not being masculine. I just insisted that he play the love scenes sensitively and with a kind of emotional 'pain' that he was trying to hide, that would give it depth. He's a fine actor and a good technician, but somehow he doesn't want his emotions to be seen too visibly for one reason or another. There's kind of a hangup there, though I don't quite know what it is."

James Franciscus was born on January 31, 1934, in Clayton, Missouri. Prior to his death on July 8, 1991, from emphysema, he racked up an incredible number of starring or guest-starring roles on no less than thirty television series [*Studio One, Twilight Zone, Wagon Train, General Electric Theater, Dr. Kildare, The F.B.I.*] and forty-eight TV and feature films [among them, *The Valley of Gwangi* (1969), *Marooned* (1969), *When Time Ran Out* (1980) and *Veliki Transport* (1983)]. He also starred in his own short-lived series, *Longstreet*.

"Burt Reynolds had just turned the script down," recalled Franciscus, "and we had the same agent at that time, Dick Clayton. So Burt turned it down and Dick said, 'Read this, see what you think.' I read it and said, 'The story is fine, but the character is a bit of an ineffectual pussy.' In essence he was lead around by the nose saying, 'Yes' and 'No.' So I talked to Dick and said, 'I can see why Burt turned this down. The story's fine, but the character, the way it's drawn, is no *man.*' Brent is running around in a loincloth, but he's saying, 'What do we do, dear?' to the little gal with him. Anyway, I said, 'Let me think about this.' So I did and I talked to Mort Abrahams, the associate producer and he said, 'We'll fix that—don't worry about that.' Of course, they often say they'll fix it. Fixed after the film is *wrapped.* So I met with Mort and Arthur Jacobs and I told them—based upon the fact that they do some work here and there—yeah, I'd be interested. So the deal was set in terms of *most* of the stuff. I was not yet locked in, but the basic situations had been solved."

Still concerned, he called up Charlton Heston. "I said, 'Chuck, Jesus Christ, have you read this piece of crap?' And he said, 'No, Jim, I'm just in there, this is *your* baby—I do a walk-through. I've already done mine, this is yours.' I said, 'Well, shit, man, you better read this because it's gonna be embarrassing. You've gotta go in there and talk to these people and tell them to do something with this thing, because you're gonna jump out of your loincloth when you read this.' He said, 'Well,

James Franciscus, Charlton Heston, and director Ted Post. The shortcomings of the shooting script were a constant.

look, I can't get involved in this damn thing because I told them I'd do a guest appearance in the sequel and it's not my business to do that.' His ass wasn't on the line because he was in and out. In other words, he wasn't gonna carry the film. Well, the apes were the picture anyway—the concept. So Chuck did have a conversation with Mort and said, 'Jimmy called and said, "Big trouble."' I don't know what occurred after that. I just went ahead and did what I felt I had to."

Picking up the scenario, Abrahams explains, "There was no problem in making the deal with Jim. We'd had a couple of sessions on the script where he wanted certain modifications of dialogue, which were very modest and no problem at all. It didn't affect any other actors, just for his own comfort. So these dialogue changes were made. They were important to him as an actor—to add more dimension. But when the changes were made, he continued to fret. Not in an unpleasant way, but he was really concerned about building the role. I mean, to make it more colorful. Then one day he called me and he said, 'I did some rewriting myself and would you mind taking a look at it?' I said to myself, 'Oh, boy, an actor starts to write—that could be a problem.' So I said, 'If you've done it, I'd be happy to look at it.' He said, 'I'll put it in your mailbox.' We didn't live too far from each other. About a week later when I picked up the mail, I was amazed to find an envelope with a total rewrite of the script. Total."

As Franciscus explained it, over a weekend he took matters into his own hands. "It was outrageous," he conceded, "but I wasn't going to let this be muddled around a line here and a line there. It needs a whole new rework through the whole script. So I called a writer friend of mine, John Ryan, and said, 'What are you doing this weekend?' He said, 'I'm free,' so I told him to come on over and bring his sleeping bag. We spent two days going through the script and rewriting the whole thing. I guess we rewrote about sixty pages or maybe seventy. We concentrated on my part, not screwing up anyone else's part. Had it mimeoed and said to Mort, 'You may want to put me in jail, you don't have to use any of it, but here's my thought.' He looked at the papers and said, 'What have you done?' I said, 'Well, I just went out and had a little exercise—you can throw this in the waste basket if you want. It was done on my time,' etc. So he called me back that afternoon and said, 'Jim, this is a whole rewrite, we can't possibly accept any of this. There's some good ideas, though, which we will certainly incorporate.'"

Abrahams points out that all of this happened about a week before production was set to begin. "I was not happy with the rewrite," he says. "We thought we had a better script in the original with the revisions that we'd made for him. I pointed out why I didn't think it worked and we discussed it for about a half an hour. He said, 'I think this and I think that,' and I said, 'Jim, I really have to take a position. I don't mind line changes if it makes it more comfortable, but we must go with our script. You obliged yourself, you accepted, on that basis and we've got to go on that script. If there are any little adjustments, we'll sit down and talk about it, but I'm not going to change scripts at this point.' He said, 'Well, if you feel that strongly about it—I just think what we have here is better,' and we went into *that* for ten minutes. But that was the end of it. When he lost the battle, he lost it gracefully. Then he went in and he pitched and he worked fine. No grumbling, no nothing."

Franciscus added, "When a revised script came in, there were about fifty-four pages of my sixty pages in it. I do recall that mainly what I did, instead of the man being chased and on the run, asking everyone, 'Oh, please, help me, I don't know what to do, poor little me,' I turned that around to the point where the man was in jeopardy and confused, but still he was a *man*. Asking for help, but if he didn't get it, he was gonna do it on his own, which he did on occasion. As confused as it might be or as wrong at it might be, he was gonna do *something* whether it was right or wrong. He wasn't gonna just sit there. And certain little scenes I recall such as when he went into the subway and saw the phone booth and the festival sign in Manhattan, and he realized, as Chuck did when he saw the Statue of Liberty, and said, 'Damn you!' I felt Brent needed that sort of a scene, too. I recall the lines well because I *did* like them, as he realized what had happened and where he said, 'Oh my God, did we finally do it? All those talks 'round all those tables . . . Did we finally, really do it?' So there were specific dialogue lines and conceptual things, but nothing that really altered the structure of a very nice script. All I did was try and give my character in his loincloth some balls. The things I put in were not monumental changes at all, but they just gave the guy some balls, that's all. It was no great contribution nor did I claim I wanted any writing credit or anything. I was just protecting my ass. That's all I was doing."

Ted Post emphasizes, "James Franciscus helped a lot in the rewriting of it. I spent a lot of time with him trying to get a logical flow. Of course Mort Abrahams and Arthur Jacobs were offended by the fact that he had spent that much time trying to lay out a logical, emotional flow to the story. James is a very concerned, very dedicated, very talented man. And he comes across with a sense of logic that very few producers in town have and understand. He knows something about writing, because he writes! We spent a lot of time together at his home, laying on the floor and laying out the sequences and trying to make the scenes work. And as I said, Mort and Arthur were offended that he went out of his way without consulting them. Mort got angry with me, too, and I said, 'Listen, Mort, actors have to perform this. You're sitting where you are sitting and you don't know a fucking thing about acting—and you don't know a damn thing about whether a scene will work or not. Your ego is writing the fucking scene without knowledge of what an actor can or cannot do.'"

Returning from *Planet of the Apes*—quite surprisingly, in fact, given her aversion to the makeup—was Kim Hunter, who elected to reprise her role of Zira. "The second film I fought like crazy doing," she says earnestly. "Arthur talked me in to it. *I did not want to go back and do that ever again as long as I lived.* But Arthur said, 'Oh, come on, you'll be working ten days, that's all; it's only for continuity, you're not in the script that much and it would be terrible to have someone else doing Zira . . .' 'Uggh! Alright!' But then it was terrible because we had to wait for weather so long. I was out there May or June, and it was that time of the year when in California it tends to be very foggy and not very pleasant, and they needed good weather and we waited and they kept shooting around the stuff I had to do, which was mostly exteriors. And so I was out there with this awful apprehension and anticipation of getting under it for weeks before I finally was in front of the camera."

Maurice Evans, who actually enjoyed the rigors of the original *Planet,* happily returned to the role of Dr. Zaius, ignoring the stigma often associated with the

Kim Hunter reluctantly agreed to return as Dr. Zira after Arthur P. Jacobs promised a less grueling stint in the makeup.

idea of sequels, particularly back then. "I know tradition says that there are great dangers in doing sequels," he said, "but I see absolutely no reason for it. After all, a motion picture lasts, what is it, an hour and a half, two hours maximum with no commercials (thank the Lord). A long play like *Hamlet* or *Who's Afraid of Virginia Woolf?* runs for four hours in the theater, so there is every reason why a story should be expanded if the author has really got anything to say. And I think in the case of the sequel to *Planet of the Apes,* the public will find that the author has a great deal more to say than he had in the first one. In fact, the sequel to my way of thinking is infinitely more profound from a philosophical standpoint. In many ways, more frightening."

Linda Harrison returned in the role of Nova, separated from Taylor and eventually joined by Brent. According to Ted Post, it was a difficult role to do anything with. "Linda was a wonderfully cooperative young lady that needed direction," he notes. "Had no technique and no real acting experience. She was engaged to marry Dick Zanuck. So in *Planet of the Apes* they put her in with Frank Schaffner, then in mine, they underwrote her. They had nothing for her to do in this one, except just be part of the sequel. In other words, she was so badly conceived in the writing, that I had to conceive actions for her to make her belong to the piece. And the big action which I gave her—and I think she came off

beautifully with it—was to try to understand what these people were trying to communicate to her. And struggling to understand and feeling sympathetic vibrations coming from these people. So I gave her something which was *not* in the script to play and she played that, I think, very simpatico, very beautifully."

Enthused Franciscus, "Linda was a joy to work with. I remember we

Maurice Evans returned to reprise his role as Dr. Zaius.

were doing a tracking shot, a camera car on tracks running about one hundred yards down this field. Linda and I were on this horse with no saddle, no reins, just the mane. If anybody fell, that camera truck is there to roll under. It was a very dodgey scene. You're galloping through gopher holes, etc. And they got the mares down at the far end. The stallion getting ready to go is smelling the mares and he's

running like a bat out of hell—and Linda's behind me saying, 'I'm very nervous about this shot.' And I said, 'Join the club. Just hang on and if you feel you can't do it, just don't do it. It's risky. There's no question about it, it's not a safe shot. What a horse is going to do, no one can tell.' But she was courageous, foolhardy or not, maybe me, too. She went ahead and we did it. I recall afterwards Loren James, my stunt man, came up and said, 'You're crazy. I wouldn't have done that. It's too dangerous.' And he's probably right. I thought it was very foolish to have done it. Anyway, Linda was a gutsy little gal and she did it. So she was very pleasant to work with and very nice."

Mort Abrahams, Arthur P. Jacobs, and Linda Harrison.

For her part, Harrison has distinct memories of Ted Post and James Franciscus. "Ted is a marvelous human being," she says. "You could talk to him. He was like a big brother. But Frank Schaffner, because he's quiet it means he's listening to other drums. He didn't say much, but, boy, did he know what he was doing. The leading man kind of disappointed me a little bit. Heston was terrific to work with and so helpful and such a gentleman. I didn't get to know Jim. Jim was a hard man to know. He was very absorbed in himself and the work. I don't know if people handled me differently because I was Richard Zanuck's girlfriend, but he was a strange fellow. He was known for that. You couldn't get close to him. He wasn't 'human.'"

Gone from the mix was Roddy McDowall, who was supposed to appear as Cornelius but asked to be released from the film so that he could make his directorial debut on the feature film *Tam Lin*.

As the actor had not yet become the focal point of the series APJAC agreed. "Although I could have insisted that Roddy stay," says Ted Post, "I never did. A young English actor named David Watson read with a number of people and he was the best. He never imitated Roddy, he just did what he thought was the character. That was his actual voice, though they wanted to give the illusion that Roddy was still part of it."

Offers Hunter, "David and I never really got to know each other very well. We had very little to do in the whole thing, but he was fine and he was dear. But he wasn't Roddy, and I wanted Roddy."

Portraying mutants in the new film was a variety of actors, among them Paul Richards (Mendez, the leader of the underground world), Jeff Corey (Caspay), Arthur Jacobs's wife Natalie Trundy (Albina), Gregory Sierra (*Barney Miller*'s Detective Chano), Victor Buono (Fat Man, perhaps best known to genre fans for his turn as King Tut in the sixties television incarnation of *Batman*) and Don Pedro Colley as the extremely politically incorrect "Negro." "I didn't know about the name until after the movie came out," admits Colley. "I'm looking for my name and there it says, 'The Negro—Don Pedro Colley.' I laughed. I said, 'I'll be damned, look

Roddy McDowall was busy with his first directing assignment—*The Ballad of Tam Lin* starring Ava Gardner. He was replaced by David Watson for the role of Cornelius.

at this . . .' The character's name was Ono Goro. It was Twentieth Century Fox and at the time they were still unable to deal with the reality of the situation and it had to have a label."

"They were mostly first choices," says Post of the film's costars. "These were people we wanted and that's who we got. All of them came and read for their roles, did well, and we gave it to those people we felt could hold their own."

Makeup designer John Chambers vividly recalls the casting of female extras to play mutants in the underground city. "We had to pick out certain women in the age group of twenty-five to thirty-five," says Chambers, "and they would come to the studio in their flats. But then you'd see them come through the gates and they would lean against a wall, put on their high heels and apply lipstick. The truth is, it was like a cattle call; like we were buying cattle. That's how they do it. Anyway, Mort Abrahams and several others were there at like 7:30 in the morning. Now I have to have a certain specific kind that fit the appliance we're gonna make for the overhead masks and stuff, so I'm the one picking them. Now Arthur was always willing to suggest, but it seemed like every one that came along that was bosomly, Arthur would say, 'Look at that one, look at that fourth one.' I'd look at them and say, 'Why? They're too big in the front.' 'Oh, okay.' See, he was always picking the ones with the big breasts."

Next to Brent, probably the most significant role in *Beneath* was that of gorilla leader, General Ursus, who leads a military unit into the Forbidden Zone. APJAC originally approached Orson Welles, who turned them down. Says Post, "Orson said it was 'demoralizing' to have an actor's face covered by a mask throughout the picture. And of course it wasn't demoralizing at all as far as we were concerned,

Paul Richards (Mendez) and Natalie Trundy (Albina).

because if you wanted to go back to where the masks came from, they came out of the Greek theater where in the original Greek plays the actors wore masks."

Their second choice was James Gregory, who in the end made one of the strongest impressions the films have ever offered. The actor was born on December 23, 1911, in the Bronx, New York. Between 1948 and 1983, when a stroke curbed his career, Gregory became one of Hollywood's most in-demand character actors, with a wide range of credits including television (*The Web, Philco Television Playhouse, Alfred Hitchcock Presents, Westinghouse Desilu Playhouse, The Twilight Zone, Wagon Train, Bonanza, The F.B.I., My Three Sons, Mission: Impossible, Barney Miller, Kolchak: The Night Stalker, M*A*S*H, Emergency,* and *All in the Family,* among others) and feature films (*Al Capone, PT 109, The Silencers, The Secret War of Harry Frigg,* and *The Main Event*).

"I was anxious to do it," enthuses Gregory of the film, "because I had seen the first picture and I said, 'Jeez, I could have done that, I could have done that.'" Naturally, like almost everyone else involved with the films, it's the makeup that was a standout for the actor, as well as the time it took to apply it and for him to get into costume.

"They tried to sign me out when we stopped shooting for the day," he reflects, "and I said, 'Wait a minute, it takes me at least an hour to get rid of this makeup.

Now, this is *your* time, not mine.' I finally convinced them of that. And also the wardrobe fittings were quite extensive for the outfit I wore, and they paid me for all that time. One nice thing is that I got to know Maurice Evans pretty well. We'd both meet in the same makeup room, just the two of us at about 3:30 in the morning. We had to get ready for an eight o'clock shooting, so it made quite a long day, but we got to chitchatting with each other. He's a very nice man and I always enjoyed that. Then they'd take a break around 5:30 and send out for scrambled eggs for us. Things like that, something soft that we could eat easily through the mask. Through the 'appliance,' they called it. It had to be augmented with layering on the hair, about eight or ten strands at a time to make it look authentic. I think that paid off because a lot of the other apes just had rubber masks. But you only saw them in the

JAMES GREGORY

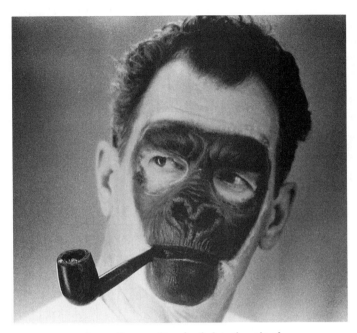

James Gregory fit perfectly into the role of General Ursus.

background, you never had a close focus on them. That's why ours had to be pretty authentic. The costume was pretty heavy. It's a good thing I didn't have claustrophobia, because you felt kinda hemmed in. I was strapped into it, you see, and so I did have the feeling almost of a turtle with his shell on."

On the surface, the makeup for a sequel to *Planet of the Apes* would have seemed to have been a no-brainer. The challenge had been met, and quite successfully so. Yet in many ways, John Chambers and Dan Striepeke, who had developed the apes' look, had to come up with a design for the mutant makeup that was nearly as challenging.

Explains Post, "The final concept for the makeup was mine. When I came in and met Dan and John, I said to both of them, 'I don't like any of these horror things you're making. A neutron bomb or a bomb of that force and impact would skin you alive—you could end up with no epidermis at all, which means you'd see your muscles and your cells and the nerves and blood vessels—that's all in the dermis.' I remember seeing a picture of that when I was a kid studying biology. I saw this in a *Gray's Anatomy* book some years ago—where the epidermis was peeled back and they showed us what the dermis looked like, and I told them what I wanted to have for that mutant look. That got them excited about that and they quickly forgot where that came from. That was totally a hundred percent my idea and I was a little mad because nobody was willing to say that *they* executed it brilliantly, but the concept was mine."

Each of the actors portraying mutants were given full-head appliances made to look like their actual faces, so that in effect they would remove their own faces to reveal the ones discussed above. Each appliance was painted over with a clear silicone coating, the purpose of which was to almost make the skin look transparent. When they worshipped their god—the Alpha-Omega bomb—they would remove their masks to be closer to their maker. It was a complicated and costly effect that only lasts several seconds on screen.

"It actually worked very well," says a justifiably proud Chambers, "and all in just a few seconds. For effect they had all the principles uncover themselves at the same time. I think it should have been like the Rockettes, where the legs go up one after the other, sequentially. You know—one, two, three, four, five, and the camera pans down. Something more effective so you will get more out of it, but they didn't want to overplay it. They wanted the shock impact of the reveal, where you thought you were looking at human flesh, but you discover the faces where the epidermis has been stripped away. For the record, Ted Post is the guy who said, 'Let's take the top skin off.'"

Natalie Trundy, who portrayed the mutant Albina, reflects, "All of that stuff, every little piece, was put on me one by one. I never looked because I knew I was ugly. My makeup man would say 'shut up' when I tried to talk because the minute I moved my face, he'd have to do something over again. I had to drink with big long straws, once that stuff is on you, you can't eat. The first time I actually saw myself as Albina, I looked at the mirror in the makeup room and said, 'Oh, my God, is that me?'"

On April 3, 1969, an in-house memo from APJAC's Joseph Behm addressed some production issues in preparation for the film's start date of April 14. As had become evident, the purse strings were already being tightened. Upon moving the ape army sequence from Los Angeles to Red Rock Canyon, the

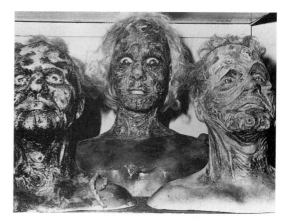

Some original mutant makeup concepts, which were replaced after a suggestion from Ted Post.

army was to be cut from 300 to 150 and, on the master shot, a split screen was to be used which would triple the amount of apes.

The first sequences shot were in Red Rock Canyon, and detailed Taylor and Nova's excursion into the Forbidden Zone where, after experiencing imaginary earthquakes, storms, and fire walls, Taylor disappears. Additionally, shooting would chronicle General Ursus's and Dr. Zaius's military excursion with an army of gorilla soldiers, leading them to the remains of New York City. As happened on *Planet,* the first day didn't exactly go smoothly, with Charlton Heston called to the set and then sitting around, waiting for someone to call "action."

"The one little tangle I had with Chuck, I had on the first day of shooting," says Abrahams. "He was called in for, say, nine in the morning, and we were slow in getting organized on that first day and didn't call him till about forty minutes later. He was waiting on the set. He called me aside and said, 'Ask me to do *anything,* but I ask you for one thing in return—*don't* call me unless you're ready for me.' And he's absolutely right. There's absolutely no reason for ever calling an actor till you're ready for him. It only happened that once."

Concurs Heston, "I try always to be on time and I don't like to wait, because

Natalie Trundy.

other people aren't on time. I hope I did not behave unprofessionally. I don't recall that I did. But that is not unlikely. Usually the first day of shooting, and to the best of my memory I worked that first day—out in the desert somewhere—the first day of shooting is almost always fraught with delays and I remember that was the case."

According to Post, the entire Heston situation was filled with scheduling problems that needed to be addressed. "I remember we had about twelve days scheduled with him," explains the director, "and then it was cut down to ten and then it was cut down to about eight. He was extremely unhappy doing the sequel. They talked him into it against his wishes, because he 'owed' an obligation to Dick Zanuck because Zanuck was the one who sanctioned and said, 'Let's go ahead with *Planet of the Apes.*' Heston was thankful and grateful and Zanuck was collecting his debt from Heston and applied that pressure. And Chuck was resentful of that. So before long he kept on knocking off days, telling me that he had to go to England and that he had to go to Spain, he was going to direct *Julius Caesar* and there was a Charlton Heston 'festival' in the British Film Museum or something and he had to get there. So he gave me only eight days with which to shoot him. I was shortchanged quite a bit."

And not, he emphasizes, just in terms of Heston. "We went to the desert in California," Post explains. "You see, Frank Schaffner went out to Utah and all those lovely areas. Well, they couldn't afford that. We took advantage of whatever we could duplicate here in California. So we were maybe fifty to a hundred miles out, right around the red desert. We just had to use what we had to use and what was available to us about sixty miles from the studio. All of it was shot in California. Frank's picture was shot in the different states, he had a greater budget and was given more leeway. I wasn't. They looked at it as a sequel, which had to be done cheaply. *Very cheaply*. And whatever they could get away with, they would try to get away with. In other words, not really giving it the same kind of care and attention and production qualities that Frank Schaffner was given. I had to work with lesser production values."

James Gregory remembers that desert sequence well. "Red Rock Canyon was up by Mojave," he says. "They used the landscape because it was quite remote and it photographed, I thought, very well for some remote planet or isolated area. And it was extremely hot up there for several days. On one of those days, I remember Maurice Evans fainted and fell off his horse. He had quite an extensive costume,

almost as much as mine. We were lining up a shot there and the sun was beating down. It's the scene where all the apes' corpses were hung up on the crosses. And we had a couple of takes and I remember all of a sudden I heard this thump. I looked around and saw Maurice had fallen off his horse to the ground. Sort of a little faint, from the heat."

The actor also recalls a more humorous instance re-

garding the ape makeup while he and Evans were taking a steambath—in character. "We had a lot of laughs in that scene," Gregory smiles. "The makeup kept falling off from all the perspiration. It took us a longer time to shoot it simply because the makeup had to be fixed up and adjusted after every take."

Franciscus also found himself in a situation quite similar to Charlton Heston when it came to mealtimes, causing the actor to make similar observations as to who ate with whom. "The apes and orangutans all had to eat through straws because they couldn't chew, so their meals were all liquid," he said bemusedly. "The smokers had long cigarette holders so they could get the cigarette in their mouth. During lunch I looked up and realized, 'My God, here is the universe,' because at one table were all the orangutans eating, at another table were the apes, and at another table were the humans. The orangutan characters would not eat or mix with the ape characters, and the humans wouldn't sit down and eat with any one of them. I remember saying, 'Look around—do you realize what's happening here? This is a little isolated microcosm of probably what's bugging the whole world. Call it prejudice or whatever you want to call it. Whatever's different is to be shunned or it's frightening or so forth.' Nobody was intermingling, even though they were all humans underneath the masks. The masks were enough to bring out our own little genetic natures of fear and prejudice. It was startling."

These locations also served as the crash site of Brent's ship, where he sits with his dying skipper, eventually burying the man before encountering Nova. "I was actually on crutches the first two weeks of *Beneath*," said Franciscus, "because I wiped my ankle out on a tennis court. It had swollen up because I'd pulled the ligaments, and this was about four days before we began shooting. When I went in on crutches to get my wardrobe—meaning my loincloth and a pair of sandals—everybody looked at me like, 'What the hell is this?' Especially since it was such a physical part. I explained the first part of the schedule was the crash, and there's not a lot of running around or anything like that. By the time we get to running, I'll be fine. So I spent much of the time between shots with my ankle in and out of hot and ice water, back and forth, trying to get the blood back into circulation and heal it up as quickly as possible. There were just one or two times I recall when I'm running to the spaceship that I'm limping. But that's okay, because in the crash it's conceivable that I could have hurt my foot."

During the first two weeks of production, Heston made several entries in his personal journals regarding his involvement. "I'm still slaving away on my promised chore in the *Apes* sequel," he wrote a few days in. "I'm beginning to regret it.

This is the first film . . . first acting . . . I've ever done in my life for which I have no enthusiasm. I always choose the most expedient solution to a scene and work without watching dailies. I can't adjust to this image of myself. I thought there would be nothing for me but a few simple physical scenes. Instead, I find myself tangled in creative discussions in aid of a project in whose creative validity I have no confidence. At least I've done what I told Dick Zanuck I would do."

During this time, there was also added hostility between Ted Post and Mort Abrahams—as if the script debacle wasn't conflict enough. The two had "issues" over a sequence in which the ape army comes across a group of chimpanzees protesting the war—truly an embarrassing analogy of Vietnam protests that dates the film terribly.

Kim Hunter with makeup man Leo Lotito.

"My son was graduating from Harvard," says Post, "and I told Mort Abrahams what I wanted done. I wanted them to shoot a very innocuous scene. Instead, he shot a scene where they ride into town and deal with the protestors. And he did it so badly. One reviewer attacked me for that scene and I didn't do it."

Reluctantly Mort Abrahams offers his view of events, noting, "I don't want to hurt Ted, but he didn't stage it well at all. I thought it was godawful and I was very upset when I saw it being rehearsed. I took him aside and I said, 'Ted, this is staged very badly.' We discussed it, I made some suggestions, he didn't think that my suggestions were right and I said, 'Okay, look, if you think this is the best you can do with it, we'll leave that. Let me stage a second one and then we'll have both versions to look at. I think we're both professional enough to be objective.' And actually he worked with me on it, although he didn't believe in it, he went along with it. And he said, 'Yes, I think what you've got works. I just think that mine is better.' So I said, 'Okay, fine, let me do it my way and we'll see.' So that's the way it worked, and that's what I think Ted meant when he said I directed a scene."

In an explosion that might rival that of the Alpha-Omega bomb of the film, Post

Ted Post's experience as a director of the first *Apes* sequel was an uphill battle. On more than one occasion he did not see eye to eye with associate producer Mort Abrahams.

retorts, "I never directed a version of it! We never had a chance to do two versions of it—the budget couldn't take *one* version even. And he was not supposed to direct that. He was supposed to direct just horses going by on camera—*that's all!* But not the scene with the protesters. *That* he took it upon himself. I was so disillusioned with him, and with this whole experience of working for that fucking company. You can quote me. It was one of those horrendous, embarrassing and humiliating and demeaning experiences. I *never* discussed that particular scene. He chose that scene himself. When I found out he had done it, I asked him why he had done it, and he used his power of authority as associate producer—and he could do whatever he wanted."

Besides sequences of Ape City itself, also shooting on the Fox lot was the climax of the film, in which the war between ape and man culminates with the dying Taylor—shot by a gorilla and taunted by Zaius—activating the Alpha-Omega bomb, effectively destroying the entire planet. According to Charlton Heston, this was his idea, fulfilling Dick Zanuck's declarative statement that this would be the last film in the series.

"I thought my main contribution was persuading them that the best thing for me to do would be to blow up the world at the end," he laughs. "I thought I'd been very clever, because as we were working on the last scene

I sold the director and the producer on the idea of having Taylor, as he's dying, hit the bomb—like the Alec Guinness character in *Bridge on the River Kwai,* I suppose. And they agreed that that would be very good, so we did that and I thought, 'That finishes the series. You've blown up the world, and that's the end of it.' But of course, they were cleverer than I was, because they managed to keep on going anyway."

Ted Post for one admits that he despises the climax. "I thought it was a very negative ending," he says. "We had other endings, but the order came down from Dick. I guess the reason for that was because his job was being taken away from him as the president of the studio. His father was, at that time, in Paris and Dick had sanctioned a couple of big failures—*Star* and *Dr. Dolittle*—they were big, big failures at the box office and Fox was running low on funds. They were blaming Dick Zanuck and his father Darryl wanted to get rid of him because the board of directors had ordered Darryl to get rid of him. And so that was the picture I was involved with that found Dick Zanuck not in a very happy state of mind. His conclusion about the picture was a reflection either consciously or unconsciously of what he felt."

"I think the ending is awful," concurred James Franciscus. "A picture without hope, especially when it's dealing with mankind . . . It's easy to wake up and say, 'What an awful day it is,' go around and bitch and be mean. It's much more difficult to wake up and say what a lousy day it is and try to make it as good a day as you can. To end the film with absolutely no hope like that, to me, was a copout; an easy way out. A nice big dramatic explosion solving nothing and making no statement. I don't think it was memorable at all. I think Ted and I *pleaded* for someone to survive this mess, be it Chuck's character or the girl or Brent's character—*somebody* far enough away from the explosion for whatever reason so that mankind is still left. Even *one* isolated person, abandoned in the desert and perhaps finding a half-mutant female and starting the human race again. Something like that, but anything except blowing the world up."

During postproduction, the intention was for Jerry Goldsmith to return as composer, but Franklin Schaffner wanted him for *Patton* and he took the assignment. Stepping in to replace him was Leonard Rosenman, another veteran composer who had supplied an outstanding score for Fox's *Fantastic Voyage* in 1966. Like Goldsmith, Rosenman was a modernist with a highly distinctive style, but one that made its own mark on the series while forming a most compatible aesthetic companion piece to Goldsmith's work. Rosenman's score for *Beneath* combined the dissonant, atmospheric passages of *Fantastic Voyage* with two other key ingredients: a mocking and bizarre military march for the gorilla army led by General

Ursus, and a wickedly satirical mass for the atomic bomb worshipped by the movie's underground civilization of mutants.

Rosenman's first job was to return to sequences Goldsmith had scored for *Planet,* as *Beneath* opened with an encapsulization of the final moments of the first film. Sustained, dissonant tones and clanging metallic accents create a more desolate and less rhythmically-defined musical landscape than the one Goldsmith devised, and one that was often marked by a signature Rosenman device: a harmonic brass tone pyramid. Roseman wrote agitated, disturbing music for a Taylor-less Nova's arrival at the wrecked spaceship of Brent, supplying some sophisticated psychological underscoring for the new astronaut character who can't quite believe what he's seeing. In a flashback to Taylor and Nova's exploration of the Forbidden Zone (during which Taylor disappears), Roseman provided striking impressionistic effects for the Forbidden Zone territory and the illusions it generates. Staccato piano and percussion playing and rambunctious chase music (later expanded on in the composer's score for the animated film version of *Lord of the Rings*) mark Brent and Nova's journey to Ape City, where they're pursued by ape hunters: A tone pyramid forms an exclamation for the first full shot of the ape city, along with a hint of Roseman's ape army march as we see General Ursus beginning to make his rabble-rousing speech to the ape council. The first use of heavy percussion in the score occurs later as another group of ape soldiers pursues the human pair, with chattering trumpets and horn glissandos adding a panicky feel to the chase.

Rosenman provides striking music for a sequence of gorilla soldiers training to kill humans, reminiscent of the alarming antibody music from *Fantastic Voyage* but marked by harrowing metallic percussion. The full ape march, a lurching procession marked by mocking accents from woodwinds, emerges in several spectacular sequences of Ursus's gorilla army marching in formation through the Forbidden Zone. Brent's discovery of the underground civilization of mutants and the atomic bomb they worship is greeted by long sustained tones and a dramatic tone pyramid for the first sight of the bomb. His mass for the bomb (with lyrics by the composer) twists a choral mass into a grating, off-key paean to destruction that ultimately becomes a dizzying takeoff of "All Things Bright and Beautiful." Rosenman made sparing, judicious use of electronic effects for some sequences involving the apes attempting to tear down the bomb, and wrote a plaintive, surprisingly tonal elegy for Nova's death at the hands of an ape soldier. But like Goldsmith, Rosenman elected to leave the film's nihilistic conclusion unscored.

In the end, *Beneath the Planet of the Apes* was a much more special effects-heavy followup to the original, concerning itself more with its visuals and spectacle than story and characterization. Additionally, Charlton Heston *was* right:

Richard Zanuck and Arthur P. Jacobs pose with the soundtrack LP for *Beneath,* which featured a rerecorded "rock" version of Leonard Rosenman's score, produced by Jimmy Bowen.

There was no role to play in the followup. The thrust of the story is truly between the apes and the mutants, and the insertion of Taylor and Brent feels more like an intrusion than an organic outgrowth of the story. Considering all this, it's surprising that the film was fairly well received by the critics and was a box office smash. While its grosses sound fairly insignificant by today's standards, one must remember that *Planet* grossed $22 million and was considered a *major* hit. *Beneath* pulled in just under $14 million. Given its lower budget, it made about as much as its predecessor and was deemed a hit.

Of course, the critics had their own points of view on the finished film:

The Christian Science Monitor: "Director Ted Post has made this a more cerebral, satirical film than his predecessor Franklin Schaffner did in the original, and, consequently, I think, a better one."

Castle of Frankenstein: "Its hardly at all as memorable as the original and what bothers me most is that its basic source of inspiration seems to have sprung from a dollar sign rather than an idea."

Evening Standard: "*Beneath* is the more enjoyable film, perhaps because we're able to skip all that tedious exposition about how apes come to be wearing frock coats that wouldn't disgrace Disraeli's wardrobe and behaving in human ways that recall an animal act in a superior kind of circus. Like many a science fiction allegory, it finds space to parody current American dilemmas."

Variety: "The dialogue, acting, and direction are substandard."

Herald-Examiner: "*Beneath* is an amusing, highly enjoyable adventure film. It lacks the moral complexity and the intellectual stimulation of its predecessor, but it is good science fiction, somewhat on the smartly sheened *Flash Gordon Rides Again.* Everyone quite properly takes everything terribly seriously."

The New Yorker: "The film is very strangely conceived. It talks to us as though we were small children, yet there is also something overly sophisticated about it, and children themselves don't like it. The whole movie is often frightening in the wrong way—not by force of satire, but by weight of attitudinizing."

The Times: "Sequels, like remakes, are always a risky business, particularly when the original was a daring undertaking in the first place. Therefore, that *Beneath* combines diversion and allegory in the same effective fashion is no small achievement, especially when you consider that this film cannot have going for it at the outset the sheer novelty of a simian society in which Man is regarded as a beast."

Cinefantastique: "If there is any grievous fault in *Beneath the Planet of the Apes,* it is only that it is a sequel to *Planet of the Apes,* for the two films are of such a self-same nature that they could have come from some science fiction counterpart to *War and Peace* that was chopped in half and released not on alternate weeks, but alternate years. I hold the original film in no high regard, however it and its sequels are, at the very least, excellent entertainment, and perhaps even a mirror for man and a monument to the insanity of our nuclear policy."

Naturally, cast and crew have their own feelings regarding *Beneath the Planet of the Apes.*

Of the finished film, James Franciscus offered, "The reason I wanted to do it was because normally I'm in a coat and a tie and being very intellectual. This was a nice departure for me—and I looked upon it as just a nice big adventure Western. It was something I don't often get offered, so I just had a ball doing it. I enjoyed the picture and loved doing it. And I like the end product."

Ted Post is frank in his admission that he has a difficult time watching the film. "The challenge," he says, "was to really make it exciting, to make it entertaining, to make it interesting. The meaning of it was not too profound and, if anything, it lacked meaning. It lacked human significance. It didn't have a theme or a premise worth anything. If anything, it was cynical and pessimistic because of the finish of it. I don't believe in dampening the human spirit like that. I don't care *how* realistic you want to be—I'm an optimist, basically. That's why I did the picture. I had enough ego in me to say, 'I can make it work,' even with all the opposition. I know I'm a hell of a director. A very important critic in New York said to me, 'One of your big drawbacks, Teddy, is you can make shit look like ice cream.' And that's been my drawback. I've taken some bad material and made it very palatable—but just don't look too close. It worked very well in the theater. Audiences loved it. It made a lot of money. It came very close to almost equaling *Planet of the Apes.* Usually sequels *die!*"

Offers Charlton Heston, "I think most sequels are less good than the originals, I think my point originally to Dick Zanuck was true. We had done the movie—*that* was the story. The rest is sort of adventures among the monkeys. Now you can say you can do those adventures less well or very good, but still that's what they are. You're thinking up different things to have happen on this planet of the apes. Whereas in the first one you had an extraordinary Swiftian idea and I think it makes a difference. I do, however, think that everyone involved in the later films deserves credit for making them as good as they were. Because not only had the central idea been used up, but they were getting smaller budgets to do their work."

Nonetheless, during the post-production process, the studio recognized that they were sitting on a valuable franchise—in the days before studios ever thought a franchise could apply to anything but a fast-food chain (not counting James

Bond, of course). On December 29, 1969, Arthur P. Jacobs wrote to screenwriter Paul Dehn:

"At the moment, Fox is anticipating as big a success, if not bigger, than with the first picture. If it does as well, we hope they would like a sequel."

Needless to say, they did.

Beneath the Planet of the Apes

Beneath the Planet of the Apes (Released May 26, 1970). 95 Minutes. Produced by Arthur P. Jacobs. Associate Producer Mort Abrahams. Story by Paul Dehn and Mort Abrahams. Screenplay by Paul Dehn. Directed by Ted Post.

CAST

Brent: James Franciscus; Zira: Kim Hunter; Zaius: Maurice Evans; Nova: Linda Harrison; Mendez: Paul Richards; Fat Man: Victor Buono; Ursus: James Gregory; Caspay: Jeff Corey; Albina: Natalie Trundy; Minister: Thomas Gomes; Cornelius: David Watson; Negro: Don Pedro Colley; Skipper: Tod Andrews; Verger: Gregory Sierra; Gorilla Sgt.: Eldon Burke; Lucius: Lou Wagner; Astronaut Taylor: Charlton Heston.

PRODUCTION CREW

Music: Leonard Rosenman; Creative Makeup Design: John Chambers; Costume Design: Morton Haack; Director of Photography: Milton Krasner, A.S.C.; Art Direction: Jack Martin Smith, William Creber; Set Decoration: Walter M. Scott, Sven Wickman; Makeup Supervision: Dan Striepeke; Hairstyling: Edith Lindon; Orchestration: Ralph Ferraro; Film Editor: Marion Rothman; Sound: Stephen Bass, David Dockendorf; Special Photographic Effects: L. B. Abbott, A.S.C., Art Cruickshank; Second Unit Director: Chuck Roberson; Unit Production Manager: Joseph C. Behm; Assistant Director: Fred Simpson; Costumes: Head Wardrobe Man: Wally Harton; Wardrobe Man: Normal Salling; Wardrobe Women: Phyllis Garr, Adelle Balkan; Camera Operator: Moe Rosenberg; First Assistant Cameraman: Arthur Gerstle; Second Assistant Cameraman: Mervin Becker; Still Photographer; George Hurrell; Art Illustrator: Fred Harpman: Property Man: Pat O'Connor; Property Master: Bob McLaughlin; Special Effects Man: Jerry Endler; Makeup Artists: Norman Pringle, Jack Barron; Hair Stylists: Madine Reed, Sharleen Walsh; Supervising Music Film Editor: Leonard Engle; Music Film Editor: Kenneth Wannberg; Supervising Sound Effects Editor: Don Hall; Sound Effects Editors: Jack Cornell, John Jolliffe; Sound Mixer: Stephen Bass; Sound Recorder: David Dockendorf; Chief Set Electrician (Gaffer): Fred Hall; First Company Grip: Fred Richter; Script Supervisor: Joan Eremin; First Aid Woman: Helen Jackson; Unit Publicist: Jack Hirshberg.

ESCAPE FROM THE
PLANET OF THE APES

At the moment *Beneath the Planet of the Apes* began to approach the box office success of its predecessor, what had been a sequel was suddenly transformed into a part of a *series,* the idea of a third entry a seeming no-brainer. The real question, of course, was *how.*

It wasn't the "how?" that followed *Planet* as in, "How can they top the Statue of Liberty?" but rather how were they going to work around the fact that they had literally blown up the world and killed *everyone* in the process? As Paul Dehn related it, he was well aware that the studio was painting the *Apes* films into a corner. "The producers wanted it that way to wind up the series," he said, "so I did as I was told. The bomb went off, the screen went white, the earth was dead. No further sequel was intended at this stage, but four months later, I received a

4

telegram that said, 'Apes exist, sequel required.' I was somewhat daunted at being asked to provide a third installment after the commercial success of the second. Obviously we could not go forward in time without moving to another planet, which was out of the question on a reduced budget. It was only the lucky recollection of Charlton Heston's abandoned spaceship that suggested a way whereby three intelligent chimpanzees could travel backwards in time to the year 1973. This was the springboard for a plot in which I tried to combine satirical comedy, an ape love story, adventurous action and a tragic end redeemed by an unexpected 'switch.' The 'switch' was the survival of the baby chimp, whose rise to ape power we follow in the fourth film."

Kim Hunter and Natalie Trundy with associate producer Frank Capra, Jr.

Replacing Mort Abrahams as associate producer on the series was Frank Capra, Jr., whose father, of course, gave us a wonderful life. Capra's first cinematic effort was as the second assistant director on *A Pocketful of Miracles* (1961) and associate producer of *Marooned* (1969) prior to joining APJAC Productions for the proposed *Journey of the Oceanauts,* which was never produced. Instead, he worked on several different APJAC productions, including the last three *Apes* films.

"Before I got there," says Capra, "Mort Abrahams was Arthur's associate producer and worked on a lot of his projects. I got there just after the second *Planet of the Apes* and Mort went on to do something else. Arthur was looking for an associate producer who knew production. I had done quite a bit of that. I had started out as a PA, then second assistant director, then first assistant director. Peter Yates, who was a director friend of Arthur's, suggested me to him in a conversation. So I went to meet Arthur at Fox. I had heard of him, but had never met him before. He had a nice little bungalow at Fox, which was like a little home. That was a far cry from the grungy little offices at some of the other studios. It wasn't that they were very fancy, it was just that they had a nice feel about them. We were right around the corner from Billy Friedkin, and across the street from the *M*A*S*H* people and I'd see Gene Reynolds a lot. There was a lot of talent there at the time and the bungalows just seemed like a nice way to be in production."

Capra explains that at the time Jacobs was one of the most important producers on the lot, and enjoyed a strong position there, helped in no small way that he and Richard Zanuck were close friends. "Arthur left the production pretty much up to me," he explains, "and I gather he left the first two up to Mort. That's what Arthur needed and wanted. Then we became very friendly and close. We socialized a lot and our wives became friends."

As to the development of *Escape,* he offers: "With each film it seemed like it was the end of the series. When Heston blew up the world at the end of *Apes 2,* we were confronted with a real interesting dilemma. *That* looked like the end of the world at the time, so we had to be at a different time period. Then, we were given a very low budget in comparison to the first two, so that really meant less apes. How do we do it? We can't be in the future too much, because that costs money; we can't be too far in the past because *that* costs money. So we were pretty well constrained to do a few apes in the present time, which is why we came up with the concept that we did—sort of a reverse of the original film. Back then, the traditional thinking was that each sequel—and it had been historically true—would only do about two thirds of the original, and if it wasn't a good one it might do less than half. So they made calculations as to what that would be, took the lower number and said, 'That's what your budget has to be for us to make a recovering on it. In the end, I think *Apes 3* was quite successful, because it did better than their preconceived notions."

Prior to Fox okaying *Secret of the Planet of the Apes,* later retitled *Escape,* Arthur P. Jacobs approached Dehn about the possibility of writing a new entry. On June 15, 1970, Dehn offered his initial thoughts.

He offered that it must retrospectively be established early in the picture that in *Apes 2*, Brent's spaceship crashed and is not operable, while in *Apes 1*, Taylor's spaceship landed and while underwater, is still operative.

From this promise, he proposed that viewers would learn that before Earth blew up, Cornelius had obtained Taylor's spaceship and studied it with meticulous care. "Note: Remember here that Leonardo da Vinci 'blueprinted' submarines and flying machines with a technical understanding centuries ahead of his time. Let us turn Cornelius into a young Leonardo—and at some later stage, point out the analogy."

A deleted scene from the film where the apes witness the destruction of the Planet of the Apes from the safety of their spacecraft.

Cornelius and Zira, with friends, Jacobs proposes, will man the spaceship in search of another habitable planet. Thus, the sequel would start with an unidentifiable crew on a spaceship. They witness the destruction of Earth and are then technically guided down to a landing, only to emerge from the spaceship to be confronted by humans.

"We shall trace the adventures (comic, tragic, satirical, and often touching) of these simian strangers in a city which has reached the cultural level of New York or London in the 1970s. What evolves is a story featuring our principles (Zira and Cornelius) who will find themselves in a hostile environment. They and the other two chimpanzees are pitted against the Orionian humans. After the shock, and in some cases panic, of finding apes who are intelligent visitors from another planet, the humans lionise the apes, e.g. they are feted at a banquet (tuxedos, evening gown for Zira, strange food, cutlery, alcohol, speeches). Installed in a Hilton-type hotel with bathroom and mirrored dressing table; and in general the apes are confronted by facets of Orionian culture with which they cannot cope. Zira, perhaps, is the first to realize that they have not come to another planet to let their species die out and she and Cornelius want to escape to some quiet rural spot, breed, and found a colony. The humans up to this point are unaware that the visitors might one day constitute a threat to Orionian society. Here a sympathetic human doctor befriends them, much as Zira befriended Taylor and through circumstances, too early to be specific about, we shall obviously develop a reversal of the *Apes 1* and *2* situation. From being feted, our apes become hunted. Two may violently die. But Zira and Cornelius should survive. We must carefully consider their destiny."

Considering the creative debacle that greeted both *Planet* and *Beneath* in the scripting stage, what's particularly impressive about this proposal was how much of it actually made it into the finished film. Naturally there were some changes, but for the most part all of it was there. The significant alterations were that Cornelius and Zira were joined by Dr. Milo, and although they do utilize Taylor's ship, the shockwave of Earth's destruction sends them backward in time to our world circa 1973. Milo is killed by a modern gorilla while the trio are being held in the LA Zoo. Eventually Zira and Cornelius reveal their ability to speak, and are initially feared and then embraced by the public. *Until* Zira reveals that she's pregnant, and the fear of what could happen to the human race in the future becomes too strong for humanity to ignore. The president's scientific advisor, Dr. Otto Hasslein, takes it upon himself to rid the world of this problem. In the end, Zira and Cornelius are killed, but their newborn child manages to survive, offering tantalizing hints toward the future.

In a very strange sort of way, *Escape From the Planet of the Apes* has a similar structure to Alfred Hitchcock's *Psycho,* in that the film starts off in one way as Janet Leigh's character steals $40,000 from her boss and hits the road, but then shifts gears dramatically once she meets Norman Bates (Anthony Perkins). At that point, the story suddenly becomes about the ultimate mama's boy and his murder spree. "That's true," concurs Capra. "Once they find out she's pregnant, it changes the view. All of a sudden, they're a threat. At first they were pleasant oddities and fun to be around. Now all of a sudden, at least in the mind of some, they become a threat, so it takes a darker turn with the chase for the baby and it becomes pretty strong."

The obstacle, of course, was getting the studio to bankroll the new film. On June 24, Zanuck received comments from three of his executives regarding the project. Generally speaking, they felt that the storyline as presented lacked the action-adventure element that had played a role in the first two films, but by the same token the studio needed to produce family-oriented pictures and this one could easily fit the bill—so long as the budget could be kept under control.

In the end, Fox gave the go-ahead and Dehn set about turning his brief outline/treatment into a full-fledged screenplay. "I gauge that it takes me at most ten weeks to write a first draft," Dehn related, "but in the case of *Apes 3,* the story suddenly took over and I got totally involved and the first draft was finished after three weeks, but that very rarely happens."

On September 28, 1970, production manager Stan Hough wrote to Richard Zanuck, pointing out that if they want to get the film in production somewhere between November and December so that an answer print could be ready by May 7, and 100 prints by May 27. To accomplish this, they only had eight or nine weeks to get the film shot, which also meant that a director needed to be chosen within the week. His suggestions were Gene Kelly, Gordon Douglas, Noel Black, and Paul Wendkos, the latter of whom had recently scored with *The Mephisto Waltz.*

On October 13, Roddy McDowall, who had been directing *Tam Lin* during the shooting of *Beneath,* was signed on to reprise his role of Cornelius. His deal was structured in such a way that he would receive $5,000 a week, for a minimum of eight weeks.

"Cornelius was actually a dull sort of character," McDowall admitted, "though he was stronger in *Escape* because the film had more humor, with Cornelius bouncing off of Zira. Actually with the first film, Cornelius has very little to do in it. He's more or less true blue Sam. Zira's a much more electric character. She's the one with the humor and the sort of teasing. I didn't mind that, because as it evolved, when we were doing *Planet,* the 'total' was the thing that fascinated me. I thought that Frank Schaffner's managing of that film was fantastic. Because, after all, nobody ever tried that before. But to be an actor in the first film was entirely different than being an actor in the third, fourth, and fifth. *Escape* had marvelous comedy, and Kim is an adorable woman to work with. A great deal of the film came from working with somebody as inventive as Kim. And I found the story very moving—the death and all that. It was a very good story. And Cornelius sort of opened

up a bit. But there was *more* of him than there was in the first film. He's very flat, which is fine. It served the purpose very well. Anything more would not have been right. And there's a marvelous balance for Zira."

A deal was struck with Kim Hunter on October 14, with the actress reprising her role of Zira. Her contract called for a payment of $3,500 per week with a guarantee of ten weeks. "The truth is," laughs Hunter on returning as Zira, "it was just too good a part to turn down and the actress took over from the claustrophobic fool. Actually, if you can understand this, going into it every day was easier than going into it one day and having four days off [as on *Beneath*] because then you would have to psyche yourself up to go into it all over again. Whereas if everyday you were going into it, that was easier to adjust to. It really was. Then you'd have no time to think of anything else in life. That was it. That's what you were doing. It was really easier that way."

Kim and Roddy at the wrap party.

Adds Capra, "Between Arthur and I, we had to convince Kim. We felt that she and Roddy were important to maintain the continuity of the project. She took convincing. I don't think she was working a lot then, and she did have fun doing it. It wasn't the stock part again. She had a lot to do. I think that is indeed how she felt: That it was too good a part to pass up."

On the same day, the film's makeup budget was released: $40,748 (down considerably from the previous films thanks to the fact that there would only be three actors transformed into apes rather than a whole society). Then, on October 29, the budget for the entire film came in: $2,213,600, amazingly cheaper than the $5 million-plus allocated to the original.

In mid-November, Don Taylor was brought on to the project as director. Taylor certainly brought to the table a diversified background. He had attended Penn State University, where he studied law, speech, and drama. Following his graduation he moved to California, where he became an MGM contract player. As an actor he appeared in such films as *Naked City, Father of the Bride, Battleground, Stalag 17, Bold and the Brave,* and *I'll Cry Tomorrow.* Eventually he realized that his true calling was directing, a job he felt he could handle—particularly in terms of interacting with actors, whom he obviously understood, so he took the helm of numerous stageplays and feature films.

Notes Frank Capra, "Because we saw the film was going to be more of a performance picture rather than an action picture, we began looking for a performance-minded director who we also thought would be fast and quick, and at the same time be good for the actors. Don Taylor kind of fit that bill. He had been doing some television and some smaller action pictures. He of course had been an actor and related to actors. We talked to him at length and decided he had a good sense of humor, which we knew we were going to need on the project. Those were the kind of discussions Arthur and I had to try and figure out how to do a third *Planet of the Apes.*"

"Film is a director's medium," Taylor recalled before his death in December of 1998. "As an actor, I miss the theater. Every time I go to the theater, I get a lump in my throat or my heart skips a beat. I do miss acting in the theater, but I don't miss acting in films at all. I do love my work as a director. I find it fascinating and very creative. Even more so than being an actor. I think every actor would like to become a director. I think many actors are not well suited or well-structured for that particular thing. It depends upon your ego involvement. As an actor you are selling yourself. As a director you are selling your talents. What helps, too, is that I do understand how other actors feel. As you are rehearsing, when you feel them

falling into a hole or putting the wrong foot forward—I'm using that as a figure of speech—you can anticipate a great many problems on the set by being able to communicate. I have been very fortunate in getting the best out of most actors that I have directed. I think one of the reasons I became a director is that I wasn't being directed. And an actor, if he's a good actor, wants to have a good director."

As to how he became involved with *Escape From the Planet of the Apes,* he recalled, "They were having trouble finding a director. I got a great review in the *New York Times* for a film I had done called *Five Man Army,* which I made in Italy. My agent knew Arthur Jacobs was looking for a director, so he called Arthur and said, 'Read page twenty-three of the *New York Times* today.' He read page twenty-three and they made an offer. Simple as that."

Taylor admitted that he had not been very familiar with the *Apes* series prior to signing on, having not even read the script for *Escape.* "I hadn't even seen the first film," he related with a laugh. "I had seen the second, which I didn't like. I mean, I didn't understand the concept. If you hadn't seen the first one, then you saw the second one, there was no relationship between the two. If you saw the *third* one, it could still be an entity. So Arthur ran the first one for me, *then* I read the script. I didn't read the script until I saw the first one. It was given to me on that basis. Do I want to read the script and then see the film, or do I want to see the film, then read the script?' I said, 'Hell, no, I want to see the film first, 'cause then I know what I'm reading."

When he *did* read the script, Taylor was admittedly blown away by it. "It was delightful," he enthused. "A lot of charm. It's listed as science fiction, but it's so *real* you almost believe that they come from San Diego. I thought at first I would be a little apprehensive about doing the film. I had a certain amount of trepidation about even accepting it, but the script, like I said, was so entirely different from the first two. The values we were exploring were so completely different. It's a very 'human' motion picture. A tremendously fine script, an excellent cast. The real difference is the fact that whereas the first two films had many apes, there are only three in this one, and one of these is on for a very short time. This is really the story of Cornelius and Zira, who were left over from the original two scripts. I mean it is another ape pilot picture, but as I say, there are marvelous social comments and very human qualities involved. I had some experiences with sequels as an actor, so I understand the concerns about them. I started with Spencer Tracy and Elizabeth Taylor in a picture called *Father of the Bride,* which was a most successful picture and because of that we made another picture called *Father's Little Dividend,* and the third picture was definitely in preparation when Mr. Tracy spoke up and said that he didn't want to become what is known as a serial actor. Otherwise that would have gone on and on, covering a lot of the same ground.

"The appeal of *Escape,*" he added, "was the juxtaposition of two apes returned to present-day society and trying to fit themselves into it, and the resistance by some to allow them to. It was a very human value. I mean, it could be interpolated or put into juxtaposition of almost any similar kind of conflict. I feel that we have more social comment, more honest comment, more intellectual comment, in this picture than there was in the first two. As for the entertainment value, it is just pure, simple—you love these two apes and you want to see them fit into our society, which is a very diffi-

Director Don Taylor with associate producer Frank Capra, Jr.

cult, almost impossible feat because of what their existence ultimately means to the future of man. Everything they do in the film makes a comment because of them doing it. It accentuates just a simple little thing, like peeling an orange, or eating a banana—something that we always do, but them doing it makes a contrast immediately, makes both a social and an entertainment—almost comedic—contrast to what we had before."

At the time that Taylor signed on to the film, McDowall and Hunter had already been cast. He turned his attention, along with Jacobs and Capra, to filling the other roles. In the scenario, the President of the United States is sympathetic to the plight of the apes, wondering if perhaps the world they would one day create

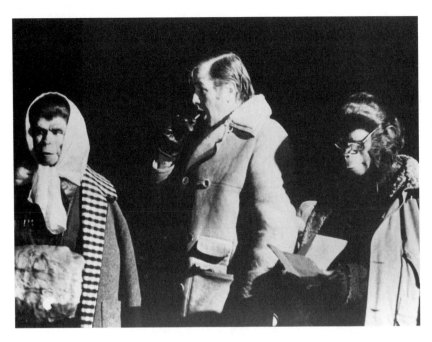

might not be better than the one created by man. At the same time, he is concerned about how history will judge his administration, pondering how future historians will look upon him if the apes are slaughtered. For the role Jacobs wanted to cast veteran actor Henry Fonda, but the director felt that this would be a terrible mistake. His casting choice for the role was William Windom (who *Star Trek* fans will remember as Commodore Decker in the original series episode, "The Doomsday Machine"). Born in 1923 in Manhattan, Windom has an incredible array of character roles behind him on both television and in motion pictures. "I didn't want Henry Fonda," said Taylor. "I thought it was an imbalance. I always wanted William Windom. When I first read the script, I think it was kind of a cameo performance and it seems to me he had done that. I won that argument. When Arthur suggested Henry Fonda, it's not that I was against Henry Fonda—I was opposed to putting a star in the part."

Muses Capra, "Maybe Mr. Fonda didn't want to do it or Fox wouldn't pay the money. I don't think it was very serious or a very lengthy discussion. Don knew Bill Windom as a friend and had used him in other projects, so suggested him. I think Arthur's press agentry was getting the best of him in terms of Henry Fonda, because it wasn't that kind of role: '. . . And Henry Fonda as the President of the United States.' That was *not* what we were looking for."

Next up was Dr. Otto Hasslein, the president's scientific advisor who, in a neat bit of continuity, is mentioned in the beginning of *Planet of the Apes* by Taylor, who discusses Hasslein's theory of time. Hasslein begins the film intrigued by the apes and the future they represent, but grows paranoid and homicidal, electing himself mankind's savior in his determination to kill the talking apes before they can lead the road to ascendency for their kind.

The role went to Eric Braeden, known today largely for his work on the soap opera *The Young and the Restless,* and recognized by genre fans for his portrayal of Dr. Charles Forbin in the computer-taking-over-the-world feature, *Colossus: The Forbin Project.* "We ran *Colossus,*" says Taylor, "and went for Eric right away. He was the *only* choice. We didn't even go any further. That was really Arthur's thinking. He had seen *Colossus*—I hadn't—and he ran it for me and I said, 'Go.'"

Unfortunately, *Colossus* failed at the box office, forcing the actor back to television in a variety of guest roles, usually as a villain. "To be honest," says Braeden, "by the time of *Apes* I was so tired of playing bad guys. They're just so one-dimensional. But I enjoyed working on the *Apes* film. Producer Arthur Jacobs was a gentleman and so was director Don Taylor. The cast was wonderful, so in that sense it *was* wonderful. Plus, I didn't have to put on one of those damn masks."

Emphasizes Capra, "We just thought that Eric was the right sort of guy for this role. He was physical, not just a shrimpy intellectual. He had power and we always knew we wanted to make our heavies have some kind of integrity, power, strength of purpose to make them good heavies. Hasslein was a guy who's not just a crazy guy with weird ideas. He has a serious side. He's trying to save mankind. He really believes in what he's doing. Eric brought with him a strength of purpose, which was important to us. He was not a cardboard heavy by any means."

Arthur Jacobs's wife, Natalie Trundy, who had portrayed the mutant, Albina, in *Beneath,* was cast as Dr. Stephanie Branton, one of three humans who ultimately become friends with Cornelius and Zira, and who does everything in her power to save them when the government's fascination with the apes becomes one of concern and then a quest to destroy them. "Natalie sort of went with the territory," laughed Taylor. "I could have turned her down, but I'd just directed her in some silly little TV show, so she was fine."

For her part, Trundy enjoyed the role. "It was wonderful," she says, "because I happened to be trained as a medic. Therefore, when we had that particular film coming on, I knew exactly what to do as far as animals were concerned. We had the tigers and lions and everything else."

Bradford Dillman portrayed animal psychiatrist Dr. Lewis Dixon, who worked with Dr. Branton at the San Diego Zoo and is just as concerned for the apes as his partner is. "Getting Brad was excellent," enthused Taylor. "I didn't think he'd do it and I was happy when he said yes. I'd directed him before, too." Like Windom, Dillman has spent his career as a highly sought-after character actor who has brought a large variety of roles to life on the big screen and the small.

Dillman admits that he's not exactly sure how he got the part. "I had not seen

the earlier *Apes* pictures," he says, "and, indeed, to this day *Escape* is the only one I've seen. My recollection of it was having particular admiration for Kim and Roddy and their patience in getting in those appliances every single day. Of course, they couldn't remove them until the end of the day, and they took lunch through a straw. If you have any degree of claustrophobia, as I have, I wouldn't have been able to deal with that at all."

Of the casting, Capra adds, "We wanted a clean-cut young guy, who looked semi-medical and pleasant and could work with Natalie Trundy, because Arthur had already promised her a part. I don't remember any outstanding rationale about using Brad, but it just seemed that he was the right choice for us. He was a successful working actor. He seemed to fit the part perfectly."

One of the most pleasant surprises in the film was Ricardo Montalban, best known as Mr. Roarke on *Fantasy Island* and as genetic superman Khan Noonian Singh on *Star Trek,* who portrayed circus owner Armando. It is through the efforts of Armando that Zira and Cornelius's child manages to survive the efforts of Dr. Hasslein, eventually leading to the birth of the planet of the apes. Taylor explained, "The casting of Ricardo Montalban was done by Arthur, who was excellent at casting. He had good concepts. He was able to detach himself. But I certainly didn't disagree. Ricardo and I went back. We were on contract at Metro, and he was very good in the role, too."

The most intriguing casting was Sal Mineo as the third intelligent chimpanzee, Dr. Milo, who is killed by a modern-day gorilla while they're being held in the zoo. Born on January 10, 1939, the former juvenile delinquent made the shift to acting. He made his debut in the Broadway production of *The Rose Tattoo* and, in 1952, portrayed Yul Brynner's son in *The King and I.* He would eventually be nominated for Academy Awards for best supporting actor for *Rebel Without a Cause* (1955) and *Exodus* (1960). His life ended tragically in 1976 when he was stabbed to death.

"You know," mused Taylor, "I'm not sure where Sal came from. Arthur had cast him. The truth is, I never saw him out of makeup. I'd talk to him and never knew who I was talking to. He never came to the party or anything. I'll tell you something interesting, though. I never thought of Kim and Roddy as Kim and Roddy. They were *apes,* absolutely. You couldn't see their faces and the way they talked to you, they were characters. Kim had a little smile, a kind of whispering thing, and Roddy has his thing. They were entities on their

Natalie Trundy, Bradford Dillman, Roddy McDowall, and Eric Braeden.

own. It's the same thing with Sal Mineo. Like I said, I never saw him. I know what his face looks like because I've seen pictures of him, but he and I never met when he wasn't in makeup.

Reflects Capra, "One of the things about the ape makeup that is so unusual is you can act through it. Actors had to get used to doing that; it wasn't simple. But one of the things that we thought would work was that actors who were trained on the stage, because they were more used to broader facial movements so they can be seen by the audience. When you're working through that makeup, you had to create broad movements and when it was translated and seen by the camera, it would seem like a small movement of the face. But you had to think broadly. I think that was one of the things we thought Sal could do. He just seemed to fit the part."

Principal photography on *Escape From the Planet of the Apes* commenced on November 30, 1970, with Don Taylor shooting exterior sequences at the San Diego Zoo that featured Bradford Dillman and Natalie Trundy engaged in a brief discussion regarding the apes. Also captured on celluloid that day was an exterior sequence involving the arrival of Zira and Dr. Hasslein at the Museum of Natural History-USC. Sticking with the history of the *Apes* films, the first day did not go well. "We shot the whole film in thirty-five days," said a still-awed Taylor. "And one of those days we had to shoot twice. The first day's work went in the hopper. A so-

Roddy McDowall with Sal Mineo. *Escape* was Mineo's last film—he was murdered in 1976.

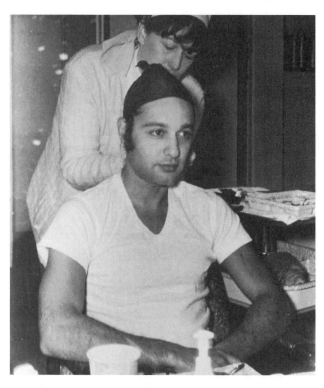

lenoid wasn't tied to the crystal in the camera or something and the picture was not in sync with the sound. All the zoo exteriors and the interior of the Museum of Natural History where they had the bones of the animals and so forth was absolutely no good and had to be shot again. It was a half day at the museum and a half day at the zoo."

The following day, December 1, featured a cute bit in which Cornelius warily accepts oranges from Dr. Dixon for himself and his companions, which they proceed to eat. "That's Roddy," smiled Taylor. "He was marvelous in that scene. Just look at that scene, and watch as the apes try to use silverware for the first time. They had a ball." Following the fruit sequence, the company shot footage of a colonel getting a report about the apes and the chimps being escorted to their quarters by guards.

Between December 2 and 3, Taylor captured the opening sequence of the film in which Taylor's spacecraft is floating on the water's surface, and towed to shore by the army. There was also the moment when the "astronauts" are helped out of the capsule, the officers around them believing this to be Colonel Taylor and his crew. Their mouths drop open collectively as these astronauts remove their helmets, exposing the fact that they're apes. "When they removed their helmets, the audience broke into applause in the theater," Taylor explained. "We premiered it in Phoenix and the cards were, according to the Fox people, as good if not better than the first one."

This being said, it should nonetheless be pointed out that the sequence involving a helicopter and the spacecraft did not go smoothly. "The team had brought out all the equipment that they had left over from, I think it was, the first one," said Taylor. "The only real thing we had that was tough was they had anchored the spacecraft about sixty or seventy yards out in the water. It broke its anchor

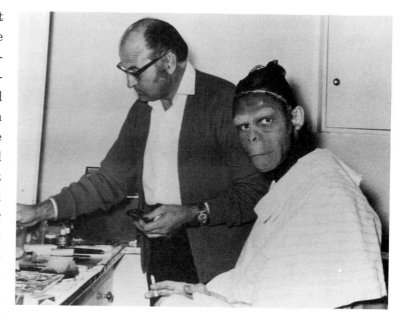

and there were two guys in there, and it was headed for the rocks. We were screaming at them to jump and they jumped out before it hit the rocks. But it damaged the hell out of it. We had to redo the whole nose. I was angry. They came down and said, 'Why the hell . . . ?' and I said, 'Wait a minute, when you anchor it out there, you *anchor* it. It broke its anchor—it was a bad job of rigging.'"

"Let's face it," laughs Capra, "that thing was not built in such a way as to be tremendously seaworthy."

In those first couple of days, another problem reared its head: Sal Mineo was rapidly discovering that he was terribly claustrophobic. "A lot of people had psychological trauma with the makeup," said Roddy McDowall, "because their ego was in danger somewhere. I've always loved makeup, absolutely fascinated by it, so that didn't worry me. Sal had trouble. Sal freaked out. I knew that was happening, so I went and watched him being made-up. I knew him very well and had known him for a long time. I sat and watched about the last forty minutes of his makeup and I could see his eyes full of terror. I went to Don Taylor and said, 'I think you're going to have to wait with Sal.' A lot of people simply couldn't wear it. It was suffocating—claustrophobic—and they panicked. I had to face the problem that I *am* claustrophobic."

"There was a lot of hand-holding with Sal," concurs Kim Hunter. "But I think he enjoyed the work. I think we all enjoyed the work as actors when we were working. It was just dealing with the physical end of it that was always difficult—I

The spacecraft was damaged when it broke free from its cables and crashed into the rocks.

think for almost everybody. I remember one chap in the first one after we got back to California and we were working at the studio, one of the gorillas had a problem. Arthur had brought in these great long makeup tables for lunch hour. You'd order what you wanted and you would have to look in the mirror to eat to make sure you don't muck up the makeup, because it's going to be another hour or two to get it fixed up again if you do. I got very bored with that and ended up drinking a can of Seago with a straw. But I remember while I was drinking my little can of Seago one day, one of the gorillas came by my dressing room and said he had a question. The usual, 'How are you holding up? How are you coping with this?' And I said I was managing, how are you? And he said, 'I don't know. I've been on it for two or three weeks and I've been married a couple of years, but my wife says since I've been on this film, I'm talking in my sleep every night.' And he said that he was starting to get frightened at bedtime. I think everybody involved had rather strange reactions and experiences in relation to it. And that included Sal."

Points out Frank Capra, Jr., "The truth is, nobody realizes just how claustrophobic they are until they put that makeup on. One of the problems is that it takes a long time. If you could just pull a mask over your head, you can get through it. But there are all of the applications that could take two to three hours. So you were in there early in the morning and

Kim Hunter, Sal Mineo, and Roddy McDowall.

you're sitting there all that time. If you're going to be claustrophobic, what a great way to find out. In truth, Sal had a tough time with it.

"I remember talking to him, trying to calm him down," he adds. "I had gotten a phone call telling me that Sal was a little bit freaked with the makeup and that I should get down to the set. We always knew that was a chance, because unless people had done this kind of thing before as an actor, they wouldn't really know what their reaction would be. Even if you tell them what it entails, they said, 'No problem.' It's like actors who used to be asked, 'Can you ride a horse?' and they'd say, 'Oh, sure. Grew up on a horse.' Then you get them out there and you find out that they're scared out of their minds. It was tough for him, but actors like challenges. And the character of Milo, even though he's on screen a short time, was a good one."

December 4 was a special-effects day, with the company shooting the space capsule in orbit around earth. Within the space capsule, the astronauts see the disintegration of earth—essentially the climax of *Beneath* from a different perspective—they exchange some dialogue and then their ship is buffeted by shockwaves before the vessel starts plummeting back into the atmosphere. The shooting con-

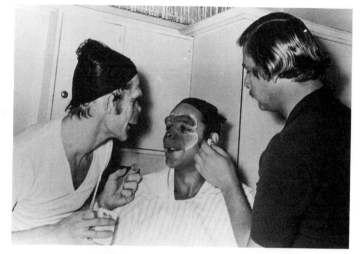

cluded within the capsule as the apes/astronauts hear the voice of frogmen giving them orders. "There's a lot of film somewhere," mused Don Taylor. "That's a whole day's worth of electronics and special effects. Smoke and gadgets blowing up. I don't know why we cut it. I guess we just didn't need it. In other words, it was the same old jazz."

Amazingly, no one can recall exactly why the sequence was cut, but one can assume that it had almost entirely to do with postproduction special effects. In other words, cut the sequence and save quite a bit of cash. Paul Dehn's script for this sequence includes the following descriptions: "Earth's rim whitens to incandescence and a soundless explosion sends a column of fire and cloud mushrooming towards us. Apalled silence. Through the ship's windows the astronauts are watching (and we with them) the nuclear disintegration of earth. The incandescence almost burns through their space helmets . . . Earth burns . . . The spaceship begins to shudder . . . The shock wave of the huge, megatonic explosion hits the spaceship from below. Chaos and pandemonium inside. We multiply normal air turbulence a thousandfold and are bashed, buffeted, whirled, twirled, lifted a hundred miles and dropped fifty, before slowly flattening out to some semblance of equilibrium on (presumably) a new orbit . . . The spacecraft is seared with flames and smoke as it plummets through space. The windows fog and blacken . . ."

In the days before CGI, this bit of F/X magic would have been enormously expensive, so it would seem that it was determined it would be cheaper to cut the bit and lose a day's worth of shooting rather than spend what it would cost to bring the sequence to life.

Capra has his own theories as to what happened to the scene. "As I recall," he says, "it just didn't seem to fit. This was not a science fiction piece as much as the others. We decided to use the spaceship only to get them into the water and started right away on the beach. It just seemed like it was more about people and personality than a science fiction piece. By beginning it in space, people might have been expecting a different kind of film."

While a few other little bits would be shot on the same day, the next major sequence to be filmed—on December 7 and 8—was one in which Zira and Cornelius address the Presidential Commission, answering questions posed to them and pleading for their freedom.

"Roddy and I had a very strange experience shooting that scene," says Hunter. "When we went before the President's commission, in the morning all of the camera shots were on us because they wanted to get rid of the extras behind us— all the press that were up there in the bleachers behind us. So they did all of the kind of general shots that showed the press behind us and then they finally came into all of our closeups. So we were the first ones being shot. That was the direction of the camera during all of the morning until after lunch. When they had finished the camera shooting from that angle and were turning around to shoot the President's commission, and going in on closeups and group shots of them, we had to be there for off-camera lines. But we were not going to be on camera for the rest of the day, so we asked if we could start getting out of the makeup, since that always took time. And we had permission to do this and they were doing it on the set. Well, the wig came off first and then the ears, and gradually they started working on the rest of the stuff. Well, we'd come back to do our of-camera lines, the chin appliance comes off reasonably easily. But then, gradually, as everything started coming off, we both had the same problem. There was a certain kind of speech thing as well as performance level that we always had to be on when we were in the makeup in order to get through it. It was a little larger than life in order to look just like ordinary life. It had to be because of the restrictions of the makeup. But once you take the makeup away, it no longer had the reality that it had with the makeup on for us. And it was terrible because we desperately wanted to give these people the same thing to work with that they would have if we had had just an enormous master shot of the whole scene. We didn't want to hurt their reactions because they were on camera, the President's Commission, to what they should be getting from us. And yet as each section of the makeup came off, we felt like absolute fools doing it the same way as if the makeup was on. It was the most horrendous afternoon that I went through, I think in all three films, just from an acting point of view. To be able to give them what they should get to react to when it was phoney as hell without the makeup to do it that way. Very, very strange. And both Roddy and I felt it, so strongly it was painful. Painful personally, not physically. As we kept losing bit and pieces and we'd come back to do our off-camera lines, we were losing the characters. We really were. Without the makeup, it was not the same. We only went through that that one day, thank God. I think we both decided then and there that if we ever hit another situation like that, we would

not ask for the makeup to be taken off. We'd have to leave it on. It was so much a part of the entire character that without it you couldn't do the same things."

December 10 had the crew capturing scenes in which the commissioner reads the recommendations regarding the disposition of Cornelius, Zira, and their unborn child; Dr. Dixon briefing the apes about the proceedings they're about to un-

dergo (actually filmed the day before in standard moviemaking style); and Zira confessing, while under the influence of sodium pentathol, that she did indeed know Taylor. The eleventh dealt with sequences toward the film's climax in which the government is in hot pursuit of the apes. Dr. Hasslein has found Zira's travel bag, and sees *something* moving on a derelict ocean vessel in the distance. Using binoculars, Hasslein sees Cornelius and has his targets in sight. Also shot that day was the moment when Cornelius, too, sees the shipyard (located in San Pedro, California) for the first time.

From December 14 through 18, the company stayed on the so-called "decrepit ship" shooting scenes involving Cornelius, Zira, and their baby (played by a real chimpanzee baby) trying to make a home for themselves until the hunt for them cools off and they can escape via Armando's circus. Hasslein finds them, though, and executes Zira and the baby, before being shot to death by Cornelius, who in turn, is killed by a shot fired from a national guardsman. (All pretty depressing, until it's revealed that Zira had switched her baby with a present day chimp's, so her and Cornelius's progeny lives on.)

Of the locale, Taylor explained, "Arthur and Paul Dehn had already scouted this and written this whole section to what they found. They went down and found this old ship. Then I went down with Paul and came back and told Arthur the compromises I had to make in order to make it work. But Paul and Arthur had done all their homework, and it was in the script just as we shot it. This derelict ship was actually an oiler from World War II that they were cutting in half and selling in parts to Japan for steel. I think maybe we stopped them from doing the final cut. The whole front had been cut off, so we were just using the back end. They were about ready to do another slice and we stopped them."

Says Capra, "We found the locale after the script was written. I knew San Pedro pretty well and kept my boat down there just off Twenty-second Street, so I was pretty familiar with the area. Today, that area doesn't exist in the same form. There's no ships there anymore—it's a live shipping area. At the time, though, the

ships were kind of mothballed and that was a boat that was not in commission, so we were able to use it very fully. It was sitting right near the road, so it was very accessible, which made it very nice for a company that brings in all its trucks and everything. Nice parking lot, near the highway. You think of logistics when you look for locations. I know we looked at several other places and this was the best all around location."

Kim Hunter remembers these sequences well, particularly those between her and the baby chimpanzee. "We had a terrible disaster," she says candidly, "with the brother or what have you—the mate of our little chimpanzee that came across at the age of six months from Europe. The two were brought over at the same time. The other one came down with and died of hepatitis. And so the entire company had to get the hepatitus shots, because there was no telling whether through our chimpanzee everyone wasn't exposed to something. That was a little painful there for a while, because a lot of people had a hard time sitting down. Those are lousy shots."

"Then," added Taylor, "we had a squirrel that bit the prop man and we all had to have shots again. The trainer almost died from hepatitis. A very young guy. He was in the hospital in very serious condition."

In elaborating on working with the baby chimp, Hunter notes, "Originally when we started working together, they got another woman—I don't know who it was—in costume like mine, and makeup like mine, to work with the chimp to get it used to what it would eventually have to deal with when it would be on film. They found out right away that it took a while for the chimp to get accustomed to this girl. But the first thing they became aware of is that they've got good teeth, and it bit her in the chest. So they made up a thing to go under the costume for her and immediately made one for me as well so that we would be protected. I remember the first day that I was to work with the babe, there was a woman, a handler named Jerry Campanella, who had the chimp in her arms. I was there talking and Jerry was kind of half instructing me as to what was safe and what wasn't safe in terms of dealing with the chimp, and then there were several attempts to pass the chimp over to me, which looked like it was still too soon. It took a while before the chimp was ready to be handed over to me. Maybe an hour or so. But it was very carefully done so we could get to know each other, and to pet a little and talking and so forth and so on. Gradually it came to a point the chimp would go into my arms as opposed to hers. Then she stayed close by for a long time until the chimp felt comfortable in my arms with her talking to him from the side. Then it came time to shoot the scene. And of course—all great luck—the first scene was the one I tripped on with the chimp. It didn't bite me, but it screamed and bared its teeth.

"This was an old derelict ship we were working on in San Pedro Harbor, and the camera was up on a one-flight up kind of thing," she elaborates. "I had to run out—know how ships are, because they have a ledge that you step over. That's the first thing I had done, but when I got over there, there were a bunch of lighting cables and stuff. And after getting over them with the chimp, the damn thumbs of the feet got caught up in them and I went headlong and held the chimp up as I went down. I actually hurt myself a lot. I had a lot of bruises for days afterwards on that one, and Jerry was there immediately, wanting to take the chimp from me and I wouldn't let her. I didn't know much about what I was doing, but I thought if I passed her over to Jerry right away, the chimp is going to have a hard time coming back to me. So I just hung on and made cooing motherly type sounds and reassuring sounds to the chimp, until the teeth sort of retreated, and the chimp stopped yelling. *Then* I passed her over to Jerry so that I could pull myself together because I was shaking like a leaf. And it took me a while to pull myself together because they got the cables out of the way and we did it again. It went on just fine from there."

She admits that she was impressed by the baby chimp's "acting" abilities in a key scene. "I'll never forget when we were on this ship and we were lying down," Hunter says. "Roddy had gone off someplace and I laid the chimp down on the blanket and was down beside it when we shot the scene. Well, somebody, once the camera was rolling, made the noise of our hearing sounds overhead or wherever. Something wakes us and somebody kindly made the sound so that we would be alert to it. Nobody directed that chimp. It was incredible how it responded to everything once the camera was rolling. Between shots I would try to get his attention. You know, it was all over the place like any kid. Funniest little thing I've ever seen in my life. Behaved like a child all the way with its boredom, and being terribly interested in something it shouldn't get involved with, and you'd have to watch it like a hawk. All of this, but once the camera was rolling, the thing was in it. Absolutely responded to everything immediately. It was instinctive. Just miraculous, that kid."

Roddy McDowall remembered Cornelius's death scene, particularly after he is shot and his prosthetic cheeks puff up as he wheezes through the makeup. Quite an effective moment, easily accomplished (surprisingly). "That was done by blowing air; by turning off the nostril, taking a deep breath and blowing out the nose inside the mask," he said. "That would pulse it."

As originally conceived, Paul Dehn had come up with a much darker close. Instead of being "simply" shot, Zira tried to save her baby by literally throwing herself to the police dogs, that chewed her alive. "Sometimes both Paul and Arthur could think a little darkly and we would have to deal with that," says Capra. "Sometimes we had to say, 'Arthur, you really *can't* do that.' In time, things got worked out. One of the nice things I remember about working with Arthur is that he was very amenable to working creative problems out. If we had problems, which every project does, he would listen and talk about it. If I had a problem about money issues, like something was costing too much, he was very good about that. He was very responsible to the studio and he knew how much money we had and he was good about working things out. We tried to work with directors who would be that way, too."

Even as shot, the climactic scenes were extremely violent. These moments, combined with the violence of *Beneath*'s conclusion (Brent is virtually blown apart by gunfire, Taylor's chest is bleeding profusely, and his bloody hand sets off the Alpha-Omega bomb as he calls Dr. Zaius a "bloody bastard"), makes one wonder how in hell these films could possibly be G-rated, the same code governing Bambi and all his wilderness friends. "It's funny," muses Capra, "that the ratings system has changed so much. In a funny way, being apes it wasn't the same kind of violence as if it was happening to people or if you had seen Hasslein shoot a mother and her baby. We tried very hard to keep it a G rating because of the others and we thought it was a picture that would be seen by families. It's kind of interesting that the violence wasn't looked upon as strongly as it is today. One thing we didn't have is a lot of school violence. You didn't have people blaming movies for their doing crazy things. The connection had not been made that much, I guess, and there are a lot of pictures from the time that are pretty violent that got away with benign things."

On December 21, Taylor shot some exterior sequences involving vehicles in motion, as well as characters arriving to and leaving from a military guardhouse. The following day, locations shifted to the zoo infirmary, where Zira slaps a zookeeper who she feels has insulted her (prior to speaking for the first time) plus a few bits involving a man in a really terrible-looking gorilla suit. So hokey-looking was this costume, one has to wonder if it bothered the director. "Did it bother me?" repeated Taylor. "Hell yes. Take a look at the film and see how far back we stayed from it."

"It was a monetary issue," adds Capra, "driving home the difference between putting on a mask and doing the full deal. It was very hard to convince the studio that you needed extras who needed the full deal."

December 22 and 23 saw the shooting of Milo's death, as well as the battery of IQ tests the chimps were put through upon arrival at the infirmary. The tests were actually an audience favorite as Zira proceeded to make a chump—in a good-natured way—out of Doctors Dixon and Branton. "Although the tests were in the script," said Taylor, "we designed how it would function. It looks like the kind of scene that would require a lot of takes, but it didn't. She just did it. We did it all on the set, making it up as we went along. We didn't know what we were going to do. I suppose it worked, because when I saw the film that scene got a lot of applause." The next day consisted of a sequence in which Zira and Cornelius introduce themselves to Dr. Dixon, with a dumbfounded Dixon responding, "Well, I'm a psychiatrist . . . too." Taylor thought this was a pure Paul Dehn moment. "Paul was a very brilliant guy," he enthused. "Some of his writing was just exquisite. I don't know how he wrote it. It's almost impossible to say. It's inverted—it goes back and forth. There's a scene in the film with the President and Bill Windom wanted to straighten out the dialogue. I said, 'Absolutely not! Don't straighten it out, because you won't get this kind of writing again.' Anybody could write it straight. He agreed, but it took him four or five takes before he got it."

Following a Christmas break, filming recommenced on December 28 and continued until the thirty-first, with one of the most intense sequences in the film, as Hasslein's people interrogate Zira and learn about the future history of the world (which, in many ways, paves the way for the next film in the series); the fate of

Colonel Taylor and the ultimate destruction of earth. It is at this moment that the tide changes against the apes. Also shot on this day was Cornelius accidentally killing an orderly he felt was insulting Zira.

Sequences filmed on January 4 basically chronicle Hasslein's increasingly desperate attempts to capture the apes before they lose them forever, deciding to have every zoo, menagerie, and circus searched until they find *something*. The following day, the location switched to Rancho Park and a circus area. The final tag of the scene—in which the slightly older baby chimpanzee, who Armando identifies as Baby Milo—looks at the camera and repeats the word, "Mama" several times. Interestingly, a prosthetic was used on this real chimp to make it look as though it could actually be the offspring of Zira and Cornelius. On the sixth, they caught on film the very pregnant Zira trying to talk to Armando's chimps, an adult ape named Heloise (another phony-looking person in an ape costume) and the real chimp baby. Zira's giving birth was the final sequence shot.

January seventh's footage included the apes saying goodbye to Armando, who can't bring them to the Florida Everglades and freedom as he had hoped because of the intensity of the manhunt. Plus Zira says goodbye to Heloise and her baby in the chimps' cage, unbeknownst to anyone else exchanging babies. Through clever editing this scene gives the impression that there were two chimps in that cage, when in actuality it was only one. "It was the same chimp," says Hunter. "The big fake chimpanzee was played by a person, but Milo—that's what they named the baby—was used for that one, too. Of course it was edited as if it was two chimps as we sat in the cage together at opposite ends. I think the camera was on me and the camera was on her, and it was Milo both ways."

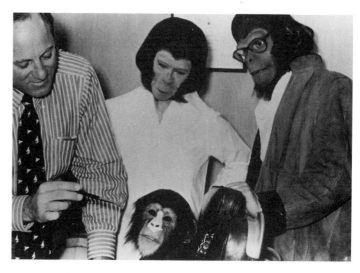

Kim and Roddy with makeup man Dan Striepeke.

The actress recalls another difficulty during these scenes. "There was one problem we had with the baby chimp," she notes. "It was scared to death of elephants. And in the scene with Ricardo Montalban and his circus bit, they had a very small baby elephant that Don Taylor wanted in the scene. But every time Milo saw him, he'd throw the blanket and just grab me and hug and scream. Just scared to death every time he saw that elephant. So Don was unhappy about it, but he was stuck with it and he had to keep the elephant out of sight of poor Milo."

Things lightened up considerably for the production on January 8, when the crew shot scenes involving a TV interview with Hasslein, who explains his theory of time travel to a thoroughly confused reporter. "Listen to that dialogue," said Taylor. "That's Paul Dehn, pure and simple. Eric's got everyone twisted around in a knot—'What the hell did he say? What did he say?' Eric was very good, because he said it like, 'You asshole, don't you understand what I'm saying?' When I read that scene I said to Paul, 'What the hell does this mean?' He said, 'Whatever you want, dear boy.'"

Then there was the bit at Carroll & Company on January 11, where Cornelius is fitted for a suit, and Giorgio's, so Zira can get an outfit as well. All very light and very comical. Also occurring on this day was the apes' being checked in to the Beverly Wilshire Hotel as guests of America.

"Funny story," proclaimed Taylor. "They still had business as usual at the hotel while we were shooting. The parking boy got into a brand-new Mercedes and when he saw the apes getting out of the limo, he backed the Mercedes right into another car. Just smashed the shit out of it. He wasn't paying any attention and he put it in reverse instead of drive."

The shooting on January 12 and 13 dealt with exterior moments of the apes on the run. For the fourteenth and fifteenth, production moved to the Fox stage where scenes in the Oval Office were shot in which the President orders a full security clampdown on the apes as well as the formation of a commission of inquiry, then a further interrogation of the apes and he reads the third recommendation of the commission. The eighteenth saw some light material, mostly comedic bits involving Zira and Cornelius being given a tour of Los Angeles. Things were a little more serious when Dr. Hasslein gets Zira drunk and then secretly records their conversation, gathering incriminating evidence against the apes.

"The champagne scene with Braeden was terrible," says Kim Hunter. "They built me a champagne glass with a lip on it so that I could somehow control the liquid going into my mouth and not screwing up the appliances. But it still did, so they had to constantly come back and reglue me because it would break away. The scene went on and on and on in terms of shooting. It may not have been that long on film, but it took a long time in the shooting because of the various shots they were doing. And I ended up with great sores because of the constant having to reglue. We were having one helluva time with that for a few days afterwards. They had me on antibiotics, creams, and everything else. They had to cut away some of the appliance and shoot around it for a few days after that because I just broke out because of the constant reglueing. It just kept loosening around the mouth, and there was no way to avoid it because you have no control. That was what was so funny when Roddy and I had to kiss each other in the first one and the discovery that when we kissed, everything kind of went together. It all squished in and disappeared and we had to learn how to kiss and not press as we kissed."

January 19, 1971, was the final day of production, and it included a scene that would ultimately be cut in which General Brody is told that there is a report of a spaceship entering earth's atmosphere—despite the fact that there are no ships "up" at the moment.

Although there would be a few pickup shots here and there, production was essentially over with the usual postproduction efforts to follow. Excitingly, Jerry Goldsmith was brought back in as composer, which allowed him to expand on some of the pop stylings he'd brought to movies like *Our Man Flint* while slyly referencing some of the riffs from his original *Planet of the Apes* score. Goldsmith's rocking title music erupts after the astronauts are revealed to be apes. It begins with some striking percussive accents and revs up in a bracing mixture of exciting action music and seventies rock and roll, with heavy rock percussion, bass electric guitar and even some passages for sitar, all accented by steel drum riffs. As Zira and Cornelius enter human society, Goldsmith's score takes on a much lighter, transparent pop quality for several sequences, with only hints of the old ape planet vibe to remind us of the perils to

Director Don Taylor and Kim Hunter.

come. The original *Apes* score is quoted most graphically in a sequence in which Zira is made drunk and interrogated by Dr. Hasslein. The score begins to take a much darker turn, as does the film itself, as it's revealed that Zira is pregnant. A disturbing, impressionistic figure for flute returns again and again with each hint of Zira's pregnancy, making her condition into an unsettling source of tension. Late in the film, Goldsmith begins the progressions of a fast-paced chase ostinato that explodes forth in epic style as the two chimps escape their captors and attempt to flee Los Angeles. The exciting chase music (eventually involving a reprise of the title music) alternates with the grim musical reminders of Zira's pregnancy as the chimpanzees find refuge in an abandoned freighter in San Pedro, but the dogged return of the ostinato motif returns as Hasslein continues his personal pursuit of the pair, leading to a brutal and tragic conclusion. Unlike the first two films, *Escape*'s denouement is scored, and quite dramatically, too, with a grim and regretful piece of end title music following the explosive scoring of Zira and Cornelius's death at the hands of Hasslein.

In the end, *Escape* was shot with relatively few production headaches. "Things went smooth as silk," stated Don Taylor. "First of all, Paul Dehn had written a good script. And, secondly, the two actors knew their parts better than I did. It was just fun and games to see how they were gonna behave, and they were both inventive and we had a tremendous amount of fun. Everybody had a good time, and that's important. It doesn't happen very often. Actually, it's more rare than common. It was a joy making *Escape*. The first problem of doing a film is to get the script right, and we had it right way before I started. So I was able to do many more things that you don't get time to do, because you're usually worrying or working over the script even while you're shooting. I never had to worry about the script. You knew that the scene would play, and didn't have to rewrite it on the set. Every scene just worked beautifully."

Incredibly, not one person speaks negatively of the experience of making *Escape From the Planet of the Apes.* As proof, on March 10, director Don Taylor wrote to Paul Dehn, "All these weeks I've wanted to write to you and tell you what a joyous experience we all had making *Apes 3.* This includes everyone, from Arthur down and/or up to the standby painter. It was such a marvelous experience for us all, that even Roddy was heard to say, 'If it was all like this, I'd even do a series.' I'm not positive that he really meant that he would spend the rest of his life in the makeup room, but it does tell you the level of high humor in which we all worked. Which brings us and/or down to you. Never have I directed a film in which the script worked so beautifully. More often than not, I spend a great deal of time reworking and patching a script while on the set. I don't believe we changed two words and happily I don't believe more than two words have been eliminated in the final cut. So there you are, a fan letter from your director . . ."

On the nineteenth, Dehn replied, ". . . Arthur is bubbling with delight at the picture's reception by the Fox salesmen and, if the public follows suit, insists (as though I needed persuading) that I come to Hollywood to write *Apes 4* in July. Meanwhile, accept my grateful idolatry for so infecting us all with your own enthusiasm that what could have been hard labor became a universal pleasure; *and* for a new friendship, which I truly value . . ."

The audience seemed to value the film as well, allowing it to gross upward of $10 million domestically, which, again by today's standards, doesn't sound like much, but considering the film cost about $2 million to make, it was extremely profitable. Clearly a better film than *Beneath,* its failure to equal that film's box office was nonetheless perplexing to many. "I've tried to analyze why," said Arthur Jacobs, "and I think there are three reasons. First, there were some who were disappointed in the second picture. Second, it's really not so much science fiction as the others were, and I think that was a letdown for some kids, even though it received better reviews and was I think a better film. It was an intimate picture, not a spectacle. Third, I think Fox took the attitude it was presold, therefore not spending too much money in selling it."

If there was any bit of controversy surrounding *Escape,* it is probably from Jacobs's contention that Fox pretty much dumped the film on the marketplace, leaving it to fend for itself. Perhaps it was because they felt it was inevitable that the grosses would continue to go down, or that it was a political move born in the aftermath of Richard Zanuck leaving the studio. Whichever it might have been, on June 28, 1971, APJAC attorney Jack Schwartzman (who would eventually become a producer himself, among his credits the James Bond film *Never Say Never Again*) wrote a letter on the subject to Fox's Dennis Stanfill.

In essence, Schwartzman had penned a several page diatribe against what he and Arthur Jacobs felt was poor marketing on the part of Fox. It was their belief—and they turned to the lack of advertising running in the *Los Angeles Times* and *New York Times* as proof—that in an effort to save money, the studio was banking on the name *Planet of the Apes* to sell the film for them. He concluded the letter by stating, "We respectfully request that an immediate investigation be undertaken to ascertain why this has occurred and what steps can immediately be taken to rectify the situation."

In the end, no steps at all were taken. *Escape* was never given the proper promotional push, and while profitable, it never achieved the financial heights it should have given the film's quality and the critical response. As for the latter point, Don Taylor has his own theories: "Somebody had already created it and got the glory of the moment. We got tremendous press and reaction, it just didn't knock everybody down. Possibly because of its placement. If it had been the *second* one, it might have done something. With the second one, everybody went with a great anticipation and they were let down. I don't want to knock Ted Post or anything, but it just didn't work and I think that hurt us. It lost all the momentum."

"Arthur was very cognizant and knowledgeable about the marketing and advertising part of the distribution game," says Capra. "He would always support his films and he complained about all of them each time, but he had the knowledge to back up his complaints. I agree with Jack Schwartzman's letter. It was a time of change at Fox and there was always a little insecurity about the *Apes* films. The second picture had not done as well as they had hoped. It was an uphill battle to get the third one made, anyway. I guess they were nervous about who the audience for it was going to be, anyway. Since it wasn't a big action picture, there was some question as to how to sell it. Is it a *Planet of the Apes* movie in which you're expecting hordes of apes and battles, or is it a kind of ninety-degree turn, which it was? Which we were kind of constrained to do because we didn't have the money to do much else. We had to find a creative, inventive way of doing it to make a decent picture. I think we were more successful than Fox thought we were going to be. Sometimes those marketing campaigns are laid out in advance and they don't get a chance to change them much. That letter is interesting. I remember that we were upset that they hadn't really gotten behind the picture more. We made money on it. They were pleased, but I think Arthur's view was more that this was a much better picture than they expected and once they realized that, they should have gotten behind it."

Critically, the film—like its predecessors—had its share of detractors and supporters.

Variety: "*Escape* is an excellent film. Far better than last year's follow-up and almost as good as the original *Planet of the Apes*. Arthur Jacobs's production is marked by an outstanding, award-caliber Paul Dehn script, excellent direction by Don Taylor and superior performances from a cast headed by encoring Roddy McDowall and Kim Hunter."

Morning Telegraph: "Surprisingly, *Escape From the Planet of the Apes* is quite good. Better, in fact, than the first two films in the series. All the obvious ironies and turnabouts are handled with good humor and the film moves swiftly to its inexorable conclusion."

The Observer: "The third in the series and as inventive as ever. The science is nonsense, but the slaughter of the two intelligent simians because they come from an ape-dominated future, offers a neat parable for neo-Fascism. The satirical sequences are sharp, too."

New York Post: "As with most sequels, the quality has deteriorated with each repeat. This one goes in for cute comedy and obvious satire in a story which inverts the original subject. Miss Hunter tries gamely to keep her dignity, but playing mother to a baby chimp is too much even for her to handle. McDowall sounds more and more pompous as the outraged husband."

Boston Herald: "Given the incredible premise, it is amazing how organic *Escape* is. Inevitably, it ends tragically, though in the movie's final images is the groundwork for the fourth *Apes* film. The major asset is Paul Dehn's script, which never slips while manipulating material which less sure hands would have mangled. Director Don Taylor has placed Dehn's conceptions on the screen in a straightforward, uncampy way that develops almost every nuance."

The New York Times: "Nobody is going to believe it, but I must say anway that Don Taylor's *Escape From the Planet of the Apes* is one of the better new movies in town and better in a genre—science fiction—that at the crucial middle level where the history of movies is made, if not written, has recently been not so much bad as inevitable. As movie premises go, I think this is quite beautiful and its development in *Escape* does it considerable justice."

The Village Voice: "The problem with *Escape* is that it's loaded with too many good ideas, twenty-four a second, flickering to life for a moment, then dying out instantly: concepts of time-space continuum, racist society, bourgeois society, animal-human parallels, the potential fascism of science, etc. This is the many-cooks school of filmmaking. The results are entertaining, but rarely more."

The Saturday Review: "To prove that sequels need not necessarily lead to disaster, there is *Escape from the Planet of the Apes.* What if these intelligent creatures should come to dominate Earth? The action slows down a bit as all sides ponder the possibilities, but soon the pursuit pattern established in earlier episodes returns—and with it, a final shot to suggest that we have not yet seen the last of these profitable anthropoids."

Frank Capra, Jr. obviously believes strongly in the film and agrees with many of the above-noted critics. "There are people who think it's the best of all of them," he enthuses. "Obviously the first is truly the best and was the most unique. It also had the problems of dealing with the makeup, which was very difficult and important to the project. Once that was done, making sequels was not as hard. But it was a different kind of picture. In the end, we did something that a lot of people said we couldn't do: another successful sequel."

"*Escape* I liked best," said Roddy McDowall, "strictly on content in relation to the characters. Paul Dehn's scripts, I thought, were tremendously brilliant. I thought that the first film was absolutely magnificent. It had a huge tapestry, it was tremendously difficult and I have enormous adoration for Franklin Schaffner. I loved working with Schaffner, a fine man and a great gentleman. The second, of course, I know nothing about. The third was just a wonderful story, deeply, deeply moving. And I loved working with Don Taylor. It was great fun and it was larkey."

Says Kim Hunter, "I wouldn't have missed the experience for the world, but I wouldn't want to go through it again. And I'm delighted that people ask me how I like being identified with this cult of apes. I don't mind a bit, because I really think they were, generally speaking, very worthy efforts."

There are a couple of generations of *Apes* fans who would have to agree with her.

Escape from the Planet of the Apes

Escape from the Planet of the Apes (Released May 26, 1971). 97 Minutes. Produced by Arthur P. Jacobs. Associate Producer Frank Capra, Jr. Screenplay by Paul Dehn. Directed by Don Taylor.

CAST

Cornelius: Roddy McDowall; Zira: Kim Hunter; Dr. Lewis Dixon: Bradford Dillman; Dr. Stephanie Branton: Natalie Trundy; Dr. Otto Hasslein: Eric Braeden; The President: William Windom; Milo: Sal Mineo; Armando: Ricardo Montalban; E-1: Albert Salmi; E-2: Jason Evers; Chairman: John Randolph; General Brody: Steve Roberts; General Winthrop: Harry Lauter; Aide: M. Emmet Walsh; Lawyer: Roy E. Glenn, Sr.; Cardinal: Peter Forster; Army Officer: Norman Burton; Naval Officer: William Woodson; Orderly: Tom Lowell; Marine Captain: Gene Whittington; Curator: Donald Elson; TV Newscaster: Bill Bonds; Referee: Army Archerd; Hercules: Ed Holliday; Brunhilde: Raylene Holliday; General Faulkner: James Bacon.

PRODUCTION CREW

Music: Jerry Goldsmith; Director of Photography: Joseph Biroc, A.S.C.; Film Editor: Marion Rothman; Creative Makeup Design: John Chambers; Unit Production Manager: Franciso Day; Assistant Director: Pepi Lenzi; Art Illustrator: Billy Sully; Sound: Dean Vernon, Theodore Soderberg; Special Photographic Effects: Howard A. Anderson Co.; Art Directors: Jack Martin Smith, William Creber; Set Decorators: Walter M. Scott, Stuart A. Reiss; Makeup Supervision: Dan Streipeke; Makeup Artist: Jack Barron; Hair Stylist: Mary Babcock; Orchestration: Arthur Morton; Unit Publicist: Jack Hirshberg; Animals Furnished by: Roy Kalbat.

Arthur P. Jacobs and Kim Hunter.

CONQUEST OF THE PLANET OF THE APES

5

As the *Planet of the Apes* series continued, it no longer seemed to be a question of whether or not there would be another sequel, but how quickly it would be mounted.

Even before the release of *Escape,* talk had turned to a fourth entry, to be called *Conquest of the Planet of the Apes.* At the time of the fourth film's release, screenwriter Paul Dehn explained, "Within a month of the release of a film, the computer tells us whether it's going to be a success, and we go through a regular procedure from there. We open in the States, pretty well on the day the kids come out of school. If we get the kids we make two million dollars more than we would otherwise. So 'round May the film opens, a month later the computer calculates the figures, and then if it's okay and I have to go out to Hollywood, I leave around the beginning of August and stay about three months working on the next script. If I'm in luck, I even have a director to work with, if not, usually a lot has to be rewritten."

In detailing the genesis of his scenario for the fourth film, Dehn told *Cinefantastique,* "It is about the intermediate stage. If you remember, there was a plague of cats and dogs which was discussed in *Apes 3,* when all the cats and all the dogs on earth had died. So the human race was without pets, which was intolerable and they started looking around for something else and began to get monkeys, which was all mentioned in *Apes 3.* The monkeys were, at first, pets like dogs, and like dogs it was found that they could be taught to do simple things, menial tasks like fetching a newspaper, bringing in master's slippers and, being apes, they were far more intelligent than dogs, so very soon they began to do very much more difficult things like bed-making, cooking, sweeping, and cleaning, and they became the servants of mankind. Having begun as pets, they end, as our film opens, as slaves."

Dehn had handed in his treatment for *Conquest* at the end of March, 1971. On April 9, Arthur Jacobs wrote him, "All the executives at Fox have read *Conquest of the Planet of the Apes* and the reception has been uniformly wonderful. They all agree that it is a perfect followup and, hopefully, can be done within the proper budget range. However, as I suspected, whilst they feel quite certain that *Escape From the Planet of the Apes* will be a big hit, they want to give it two or three weeks to be sure it is holding up before deciding to go forward with *Conquest.* This means that sometime between the tenth and fifteenth of June, we should get a definite okay on the project, which, of course, means we must do an instant screenplay so we can shoot the picture in November as we did the last one . . ." There was also an interesting contingency plan that Jacobs had developed, which he let Dehn in on: ". . . Just in case Fox collapses before June, I'm going to give this very quietly to Dick Zanuck at Warner Bros., so that, if for any reason Fox can't go ahead, we can move it over to Dick . . ." This, of course, was due to the fact that Zanuck had left Fox and teamed up with producer David Brown on what would become a phenomenal string of successes highlighted by *The Sting* and the original *Jaws.*

Haggling between APJAC and Fox ensued, with both sides fretting over budget. Over the next few months, Jacobs remained convinced that a fourth *Apes* film could work. Indeed, in his argument he offered to put APJAC's production fee back into the film. "I strongly feel that the fourth *Apes* has a very strong chance as it has much action and violence and will benefit from the good reviews and reactions to the third *Apes,*" Jacobs wrote to Fox's Elmo Williams on July 22. "I also feel strongly that having the fourth feature, thus completing the entire story, has many benefits in the area of rereleases and, additionally, has a further benefit many years to come when our main television syndication is played out whereby the four pictures can be made into one and then made into thirteen half-hour episodes aimed at Saturday morning children shows, giving us still another source of revenue . . . In these rather risky days, it would seem to me this is a certain bread-and-butter winner."

At about the same time, Twentieth Century Fox began tightening its fiscal reigns, electing to drop its option on a 1966 "first look" contract with APJAC, which had essentially meant that the producer was required to bring the studio any project it was trying to mount before offering it to any other studio. In exchange, Jacobs was given offices on the lot and was paid a fee to cover expenses. Jacobs, through lawyer Jack Schwartzman, attempted to change the studio's mind, but was unsuccessful in their bid to do so. Instead, Fox opted for a picture-by-picture contract rather than an overall deal, meaning that they were no longer obligated to pay APJAC's flat weekly overhead fee, essentially making Jacobs a free agent. Nonetheless, a deal was eventually struck for *Conquest*. The budget would be $1,700,000—an astoundingly low fee for what would turn out to be quite an ambitious undertaking.

To helm the film, Arthur Jacobs turned back to J. Lee Thompson, who was supposed to direct the original *Planet of the Apes* until delays in getting the project set up forced Thompson to depart the project. As associate producer Frank Capra, Jr. explains it, when the fourth film came about, a lot of time was devoted to determining what director would best suit the production.

"The director was going to be an important piece of business," he says. "We needed a director who we thought could handle size and scope and do it cheaply, which doesn't always run together. Of course Arthur had known J. Lee before because he had done *What a Way to Go!* One of the things with Lee is that he had an alcohol problem. So he went back to England and was in England for some years. Just about the time we were looking for a director for this, someone, it may have been Paul Dehn, said, 'J. Lee has done a very nice film here in England for a moderate or low budget; and acting piece, not a big action piece, but the reports are that everything is wonderful with him. He's totally stopped drinking, he's on top of his game again' and all that. We thought, 'Maybe that's an idea.' I mean, God, he had done *Guns of Naverone*—big pictures, and we knew he could handle the action, and here he just finished a smaller project in England that was very sensitive, very well done and done for a low budget. So we seriously began thinking of Lee and we picked him. It's what sold us on Lee. Roddy had known him, of course, and was very much in favor of him. Arthur was, too, because he had really liked

him. But Lee turned out to be a wonderful choice. As it turned out, the film does have a great look and he gave us 125 percent. He was recreating his career again, too. I spent a lot of time with Lee and his wife, Penny, and we had a lot of wonderful moments together.

"He had this wonderful energy," Capra continues, "but he also had this weird habit. He has a lot of nervous energy directing and he would sit there and take pieces of paper, tear them into strips and roll them up into balls and fool with them in his hand all the time. The energy was just going to his hand. It was actually a way that he kind of calmed himself; a self system of his own that worked very well. And he was wonderful to work for. A lot of the time he was confronted with situations that were difficult."

Thompson himself has often said that he "rued" the day that he pulled out of the first film in the series. "The film that I did at that time [*Mackenna's Gold*] was not nearly as good as *Planet of the Apes*," he says. "So I regretted that I didn't stay with it, also from a financial point of view and from a point of view that I loved it. I loved the story and loved the whole idea, which was entirely discovered by Arthur. He offered me the second *Apes* and he offered me the third one. The second one, I tell you, I could have done, but, to be honest, I didn't like the script when I read it. I thought that Franklin Schaffner did a marvelous job on the original. It was a wonderful film. I loved it. I'm creaking with envy and jealousy that I hadn't done it myself, but I did like it. But, as I said, I didn't like the second one. I also thought it would be compared very unfavorably with the first one. The third one I didn't like because it was only two or three apes, if I remember, and to me it wasn't an *Apes* film."

John (J.) Lee Thompson was born in 1914 in the English city of Bristol. He first made his mark in the motion picture world as a screenwriter, having handled scripting chores for *The Strangler* (1940) and *No Place For Jennifer* (1950). He would also serve as writer/director on *The Yellow Balloon* and *The Weak and the Wicked* (both 1953), and *For Better, For Worse* (1954). In 1955 he segued over to the director's chair full-time, helming such films as *An Alligator Named Daisy* and *As Long as They're Happy, Yield to the Night* (1956), *Woman in the Dressing Gown* and *The Good Companions* (1957), *No Trees in the Street* and *Ice-Cold in Alex* (1958), *Werner von Braun, Northwest Frontier,* and *Tiger Bay* (1959), *The Guns of Naverone* (1961), the original *Cape Fear* (1962), APJAC's *What a Way to Go!* (1964), *Mackenna's Gold* (1969), and, of course, *Conquest of the Planet of the Apes.*

Conquest of the Planet of the Apes was a project that immediately intrigued the director. "Going years back when I made films in England, I won a great many awards because the films I was doing were mostly political," he says. "They were not a commercial success. They did not do badly, but they were always the small, social film. And I loved those. Then, if you like, I sold out to Hollywood and the kind of films that I make here bear no relation to how I really began my career. *Conquest* I saw as being that beautiful in between in that you could get a commercial success as well as a good political statement. And quite a few of the critics realized that as well."

Unlike the previous entries in the series, the intention—at least from Dehn and Thompson—was to make a strong political statement, drawing an analogy between black feelings of oppression and the plight of the apes. Jacobs, on the other hand, was more concerned with getting back to basics.

"Arthur wanted to go back to a kind of scale-and-scope-size film," says Capra. "He didn't want to try to recreate something along the lines of *Escape.* He wanted to go back to a more traditional *Planet of the Apes* theme. Arthur's feeling was that each time we had to do something new so the audience would come again and say, 'Gosh, that's something we hadn't thought of. That's a new twist; a new piece of action or a new character.' Because it's pretty hard to keep telling the same story. Although we were within the larger sense of telling this arc of a story of how the apes rose. We had that as an overall umbrella, and we had to figure out how to do it within the timeframe."

Paul Dehn explained his position to the press shortly before his death: "I saw *Planet of the Apes* as a paying member of the public and I thought then that it was the sort of thing I

Roddy McDowall and Arthur P. Jacobs.

would have liked to have written, though I had no idea I would become involved. When Arthur Jacobs suggested that I script a second *Apes* film, I immediately said yes. But you have to think very carefully indeed about sequels, because very few writers and directors will undertake this sort of work as they usually become progressively worse with each film. However, I was intrigued by the apes and I'd always wanted to do a science fiction screenplay. Now, the whole thing is quite fantastic—a splendid experience for me—and really quite bewildering. The *Apes* are a cult, especially among young people and students. In truth, we wanted that film to be very angry; to be the counterpart of the riots in Chicago and Watts. The director, J. Lee Thompson, said we should end the picture on an ape's eyes glinting . . . not evilly, but glinting anyway, in the dark, and we could take it from there next time and have them cool down."

Adds Capra, "So much has been read into it, such as racial issues, revolution, and all this other stuff. I don't think anyone was conscious of it. Paul Dehn may have been socially to the left, but that doesn't mean he was trying to create some kind of allegory about social revolution. J. Lee *was* trying to. The imagery of the Watts riots had been played on television night after night after night. Television covered it enormously, day and night, so these images were just in everybody's mind, especially in the LA area and probably most of the country. They were certainly in J. Lee's mind. Here we were talking about some sort of uprising at night in the city, and he saw there was an immediate connection. Even though he wasn't saying, 'These are black people rising against white people,' the imagery of the riot created in his mind the kind of look that he wanted to create in the riot scenes and did. One of the reasons it was successful is that people who went to see the movie were harkened back to those images from about a year before."

Capra also admits that Dehn and Thompson were proven somewhat correct when *Conquest* was released. "It opened in Detroit and it opened very well," he says. "And to enthusiastic audiences that were probably ninety percent black. I think the marketing guys at Fox began to get the message and so began to play it in more and more black theaters. They realized that—whether we intended it or not—that there was a connection being made, and that it was becoming popular. I was at a theater in Long Beach, which was predominantly African-American, and it was a very enthusiastic audience complete with people yelling at the screen, encouraging Caesar and all the rest. It was pretty interesting, I must say. A more enthusiastic audience I had not seen. It was pretty impressive and obviously the connection was indeed being made."

Dehn's first draft for *Conquest* began with a much different feel than the final film. In pages dated October, 1971, the fourth *Apes* film originally began with clips from the last scene of *Escape*, which serve as a means of reintroducing the audience to circus owner Armando and the talking baby chimpanzee son of Cornelius and Zira. Early sections of the film depict young Caesar's life in the circus, where Armando is passing the ape off as a badly deformed human. Eight years after the events of *Escape* (setting *Conquest* in 1981), Caesar is now the equivalent of a human seventeen-year-old (Dehn's reasoning here being that chimps mature twice as fast). Caesar's cover is blown when he rescues a trapeze artist midact in a manner that would be difficult for a human. A press report of the incident reaches the two CIA operatives from *Escape* (designated E1 and E2, played by Albert Salmi and Jason Evers in the earlier film), who suspect that perhaps the infant ape killed eight years earlier was not the one they'd been hunting after all.

Caesar is even more humanlike thanks largely to the fact that he has associated solely with human beings. Surprisingly, it is Armando who assures Caesar that he wants his adopted son to "fulfill the destiny for which I believe God intended you; to found an ape civilization which will manage this torn old world of ours better than we corrupt and wretched humans."

In an effort to discern the truth, E1 and E2 dispatch operative Arthur Kolp (played in *Conquest* and *Battle* by Severn Darden) and his partner, Hoskins, to investigate the circus. Kolp poses as a circus fan, engaging Caesar in conversation. Caesar identifies himself as Hernandez. At the same time, Hoskins interrogates Armando, who attempts to explain Caesar by noting, ". . . I found him in a hovel in the wilds behind Teotehuacan . . . His father had rotted to death on rum. His mother lived exclusively on marijuana. The result was Caesar."

While Kolp and Hoskins compare notes, Caesar and Armando both conclude that the young ape is in danger. Caesar says farewell to Armando, expressing regret that, as an ape, he cannot shed tears (an ability he decidedly possesses in the final film), and heads for the wilds of Arizona.

While Caesar is living a hermetic life in a cave, astronauts returning from Mars have brought back a plague that spreads like wildfire, wiping out all dogs and cats (as Cornelius foretold in *Escape*). The script contains some suggested scenes dramatizing the epidemic—it's not too hard to imagine why these were jettisoned, as audiences were unlikely to flock to a film full of images of dying pets. Additionally, as Capra notes, "We budgeted the film down and that looked like it was going to be a little bit too much for us. And we also recognized that it's not a story about dogs and cats; it's about apes. That could be covered in dialogue and we could spend our money on the apes and the battle."

More entertaining is a two and a half-page "march of time" montage depicting the integration of first monkeys, then apes, into daily human life. They start as pets, move on to fetching the paper and tending babies, and finally achieve slave status.

When the story continues, nearly a decade has passed since Caesar fled the circus. Still isolated in the Arizona wilderness, he is captured by a pair of human rustlers who don't realize that he can speak, but *do* know that a smart chimpanzee is worth about $1,000. As a result, Caesar is sold to an auction house and brought to a metropolis that is described in Dehn's script: "The location suggested is Century City, where the buildings are futuristic and the shopping center (reserved exclusively for pedestrians) solves the potentially expensive problems of building late twentieth-century cars."

Of the location—which would ultimately be used, despite many alterations in the final screenplay—Capra notes, "Our big question was where in the world were we going to get a city of the future? We looked around and decided to use Century City, as Paul suggested, which was just being built. Some of the buildings weren't even finished. It was adjacent to Fox and it worked out perfectly for us. With interesting lighting and using interesting camera angles, which Lee was very good at, we got a look that I thought was pretty spectacular. Here we had Century City right next to us. The prices were right. We could work and do it for the money we had."

Upon arriving in Century City, Caesar is led by handlers through the bustling area in a sequence that is almost identical to the one in the opening of *Conquest*'s filmed version, save that he is accompanied by unsympathetic handlers rather than Armando. Caesar is stunned to see the ape slave labor force and attracted to the comely chimp Lisa. He does not, however, erupt into speech yet and all other apes he encounters are mute. Caesar is then taken to "ape conditioning," which (again) closely resembles the final film in its psychedelic nightmare of loud sound, strobe lighting, and hoses that shoot flame instead of water.

Breck still purchases Caesar at auction, but he is not the governor in this version, merely "Harvey Breck III," recent widower—his wife was mauled by an ape—and dedicated alcoholic. Unlike the antagonist in the final film, *this* Breck has no suspicions about Caesar's ancestry—he simply brutalizes apes on general principle. Mr. MacDonald is his human overseer, who in the first draft of the script carries a whip.

Caesar is brought to Breck's home and made a household servant. Most of the apes Caesar meets here are Breck's servants: one, Amanda, is a female orangutan. Aldo, a gorilla laborer, is showing signs of rebellious behavior and apparently influencing his fellow apes to do the same. Breck reacts to Aldo's recalcitrance by flogging him. MacDonald flees, unable to stand the sight of Breck's brutality just as he is unable to prevent it. Expressing his disgust in private, MacDonald is thunderstruck when Caesar agrees with him—out loud. Caesar, however, is quick to assure MacDonald that he's really a human freak who simply resembles a chimpanzee and can't stand being stared at. MacDonald buys it, but the conversation reveals that Caesar is becoming impatient with the status quo.

In the first draft, it doesn't take anything as dramatic as Armando's death (in the film he plunges out a window in an attempt to save Caesar from Governor Breck) to spur Caesar into fomenting rebellion; indeed, in this version, we never see Armando again once Caesar leaves the circus. Caesar urges his comrades to ever-increasing acts of defiance. His cover is blown when Kolp discovers that there is an incredibly well-trained ape called Caesar at Breck's residence (in the final film, Caesar is found out because he has the bad luck to smuggle himself into a shipment of orangutans, who hail from Borneo, a land without chimpanzees). As in the final film, Caesar is tortured to make him reveal that he can speak; in the first draft, only now does MacDonald learn that Caesar is simian rather than human.

The riot by the apes under Caesar's command is somewhat more graphic and brutal than what is seen in the final film—which, by 1972 standards for "children's" fare, was pretty intense in any case. In the first draft, Caesar spends much of the conflict on horseback. Aldo utters the word "no" in response to one of Breck's commands; the vicious slave-owner is flogged to death by his victims while Caesar prophesies the future. The final shot is of a statue of Caesar—"Born 1973, Died 2008"—shedding a tear of rain that the living ape could not. This denouement, unused in *Conquest*, would finally end the *Apes* series in *Battle*.

Upon reading Dehn's first draft script, Fox was for the most part unimpressed, feeling that it lacked a certain excitement they were looking for, and that it basically took too long to reach the point where Caesar would lead his fellow apes into revolt. Undaunted, Arthur Jacobs, Paul Dehn, and J. Lee Thompson worked at reshaping the scenario. On December 22, Jacobs shot off a memo to the studio that said, in part, "As you will see from the new attached script, we have made considerable revisions, not only to the beginning but all the way through the script. We believe that these revisions have vastly improved the script . . . and that the production value has been likewise hugely increased. Inevitably these revisions have necessitated a new schedule . . . and we have revised the schedule upwards from twenty-five days to thirty days. . . . We expect that the cost of the picture will now be $1,830,000 approximately, including 25 percent overhead. Although we all feel that the additional money is well spent, the budget can be reduced by approximately $130,000 by deleting the Irvine sequence and the contingent story points so that the budget would come down to approximately $1,700,000."

Of these gorilla film tactics (pun definitely intended), Jacobs added, "We have had exhaustive discussions with Lee Thompson about the schedule and we are all quite convinced that it is adequate to complete the picture, without losing any of the inherent production value referred to above. . . . It is our feeling that the additional money and time are well spent for the good of the picture's 'look' and entertainment value, which will eventually be reflected at the box office."

Fox accepted Dehn's screenplay, and gave the green light for production at a budget of $1,700,000, with a start date of January 31, 1972. The studio's first step was to secure Century City for production. On January 19, the film's location manager, Bill Venegas, wrote to the merchants about the soon to be shooting film.

He provided notice on the start of production of this "family-type-entertainment" and asked for cooperation from all the businesses at the Century City shipping Center Association. The production would shoot for a period of six consecutive weekdays between the hours of 7:00 A.M. and 7:00 P.M. after which there would be seven nights of photography between the hours of 7:00 P.M. and 7:00 A.M. He continued to explain that cooperation was of vital importance to the successful outcome of the film and that inconveniences would be held to a minimum. He finished by emphasizing that the photography would indeed identify many of the store fronts and that publicity campaigns could be coordinated to maximize exposure through television, newspapers, and magazines.

With production twelve days away, the production had to quickly cast the rest of the roles, with Roddy McDowall already cast as Caesar, the grown son of Zira and Cornelius. "When I played Caesar," said McDowall, "it was more enjoyable than playing Cornelius, because Caesar I based, really, on a combination of Zira and Cornelius, taking both qualities, and actually having much more fun because the part had more humor than Cornelius. Cornelius was actually a dull sort of character."

One person completely mesmerized by McDowall's performance was director J. Lee Thompson. "Roddy was marvelous," he enthuses. "He would approach these roles as if he were doing Shakespeare. And each one individually, as if it was the first film. You would think, seeing him in *Conquest,* that he was playing the role for the first time. His enthusiasm and the way he would talk was simply amazing. Some actors have a way of getting rather egotistical—'I've done these pictures before, don't interfere with my character,' etc. None of that with Roddy. He would approach it as if it was the first time there was an *Apes* picture, and discuss the character and discuss each scene as if we were doing Shakespeare—which was marvelous. That was the success of it, because that character became like a real person. It's a wonderful piece of acting, actually. Very underrated."

Concurs Capra, "It was a very dramatic role and it gave Roddy the opportunity to rise as a leader. He certainly did treat it like Shakespeare and J. Lee certainly helped him. He had a real ability to work through that makeup and create real characters. You've got to hand it to Roddy. For so many movies to put that makeup on and take it off . . . Roddy was a serious actor. As he always said, you have to work twice as hard or three times as hard to make the performance work through the makeup. So everything has to be exaggerated. You're thinking, 'My God, he's going way over the top,' but by the time you look at it in the film, you realize that it's not."

Series veteran Natalie Trundy returned, this time portraying the chimpanzee Lisa, who would go on to become Caesar's wife. Jacobs had originally wanted Kim Hunter back, but the actress absolutely refused to put the ape makeup on again. Ricardo Montalban was also back as Armando, the circus owner and Caesar's adopted father.

Then there was Lou Wagner, who had portrayed Zira's nephew, Lucius, in the original. In *Conquest* he is a chimpanzee seen briefly stealing knives and setting fire to the restaurant he works at. As originally conceived, however, his part was supposed to be more significant.

"I had a five-week guarantee," says Wagner, "but the first day there was a funny

feeling on the set and people were gone in meetings all the time. At the end of that day they said that they had had a meeting and that they were writing my character out. My character was to be Roddy's henchman all the way through. That was on my first day, when they filmed me stealing the knives and setting the fire. We had just shot that and there were plenty more things to do. All through the battle I was at his side, fighting all these other people off to protect him. It would have been wonderful. But then they rewrote the script and cut out a lot of different people. Subsequently, they paid me off and I didn't fight, but one of the negotiations that I held out for was my co-star credit. If you notice on that one, I'm co-starring. I have the biggest billing that I've ever had to date. They called me up to ask me if I would please—since I didn't do all the work I was scheduled to—relinquish that billing, but I told them no. I said, 'It's very important to my career; I'm still new to this business and it means very much to me. Nobody's going to know what I did, let alone how much I did.' That was because the only ape in that film that talked was Roddy."

Another returnee from the original *Planet of the Apes* was actor Buck Kartalian, who had portrayed Julius and appeared in *Conquest* as a gorilla named Frank. "They heard I was in the first one," says Kartalian. "My agent got me down there and they gave me this part, which turned out to be very insignificant. The strange part of it is that you'd hardly even know I'm in it, but, oddly, I made more money for *Conquest* because they paid me a five-week guarantee on it. I got paid for five weeks and worked only one day."

New to the series was Don Murray, who was signed for the role of Breck, now governor/dictator of California who presides over ape management and the ape slave trade. Don Murray was born on July 31, 1929, in Hollywood, California. He made his acting debut on the classic anthology television series *Studio One* in 1948. He followed with performances on other anthologies from the Golden Age of television, including *Philco Television Playhouse* and *The United States Steel Hour,* before jumping to the big screen and such films as *Bus Stop* (1956), *Bachelor*

Party (1957), *A Hatful of Rain* (1957), *From Hell to Texas* (1958), *These Thousand Hills* (1959), and numerous others. He has also served as writer/producer of *Hoodlum Priest* (1961) and *Childish Things* (1969), before taking on the quadruple duties of star, writer, director, and producer on *The Cross and the Switchblade* (1972).

"Let's face it," says Capra, "we were looking for a good heavy for that part, but also a guy who we thought could be a little crazy. Or at least a little on the edge in terms of paranoia. We talked about that a lot. The truth is, if you create a heavy who's all villainous, it's kind of a cardboard heavy in a way. You have to give him a little something. Now Don Murray wasn't really well known at the time, but we thought he would be right for the role. Don liked to chew the scenery a lot, and J. Lee had to hold him down at times, but I think he made a pretty credible kind of heavy."

As Murray himself recalls, "It was the first time I ever played a 'heavy' in movies. It was an interesting concept that Arthur went totally against type with me for casting. I usually play the nice guy. Of course it's the actor's job to find out what the purpose of his character is. And then you see how you can most fully serve that purpose. I believe that you really have to give yourself to it totally. Breck is meant to be an antagonist to the hero—the hero is Caesar, the ape. The head of the humans—in this case the dictator of the humans—has got to be the enemy of the audience's emotions. The emotions of the audience have to be worked *against* him, against the character I play.

"I didn't look for any moment for a sympathetic angle," he continues. "In fact, it was just the opposite. As a matter of fact, one of the ways that I prepared myself for the role was that I conceived the man as being a dictator. Dictators are bullies. And what are bullies? Bullies are basically cowards—basically fearful people. Somebody might have physical courage and yet be a coward about losing their *position*—whatever it is. And I figured that was the motivating force behind this man. His fear was losing his position of authority. Even though he did have physical courage and that's why he was so severe on the apes. What I did was say to myself that the ultimate dictator as we can conceive it is Hitler. Hitler of course spoke

German. I went through the entire script and I took my speeches and I worked on them in German. I speak pretty fluent German. I don't even have to translate. I just think in German when I'm speaking it. So I would take my lines and speak them in German during my private rehearsals and so on, to get that kind of a feeling of that absolute, unrelenting kind of harshness. So that was my concept and that's the way I worked on it."

Just as important to the film was the casting of the role of McDonald, the governor's assistant who initially befriends Caesar prior to finding out just what he is, and then saves his life which inadvertently paves the way for the ape revolution. The production locked on Hari Rhodes. Born on April 10, 1932, Rhodes was an actor who segued back and forth between television and film, with credits that include *The Fugitive* (1963, TV), *Shock Corridor* (1963), *I Spy* (1965, TV), *Taffy and the Jungle Hunter* (1965), *Mission Impossible* (1966, TV), *Trouble Comes to Town* (1972), and *The Streets of San Francisco*. He passed away on January 14, 1992.

"We were looking for an African-American actor for the role," says Capra. "We saw a number of people, but Harry was the one we wanted. We liked his look and his demeanor and to be kind of an opposite to Don Murray, even though he was working for him."

Rounding out the new cast members was Severn Darden, who played Kolp, one of Breck's assistants. Hailing from New Orleans, Louisiana, Severn Darden was born on November 9, 1929. Like Hari Rhodes, he was an actor just as comfortable on television as he was on the big screen. His credits include *Goldstein* (1965), *Double-Barrelled Detective Story* (1965), *Honey West* (1965, TV), *The Monkees* (1966, TV), *The President's Analyst* (1967), *Night Gallery* (1970, TV), and *Vanishing Point* (1971). Darden died of a heart attack on May 27, 1995.

Says Capra, "Severn was another one of those kinds of characters that we wanted to be just on the edge, so it would seem the people in command at the time were on the edge, about to go over. He and Don Murray kind of complemented each other."

Production officially began on January 31, and everyone knew it was going to be a tough shoot. Unfortunately, the first day of shooting literally got off on the wrong foot. "In all the films," said McDowall, "the worst thing happened when I sprained my ankle on the first day of *Conquest* while coming out of the goddamn dressing room. We had those iron steps with the holes in them, which I knew would be wrong for the feet on the apes costume. I said, 'You mustn't have dressing rooms with the iron steps. We can't stop now, but get this thing out of here by tomorrow.' Sure enough, the toe caught in it and it was terrible."

Filming was delayed for forty-five minutes while the actor sought medical treatment for the injury which plagued him through most of production. Later, shooting began on an early sequence involving Armando and Caesar's arrival in the transformed Century City, and their movement among "commuters." The next day in the same location covered Caesar's observation of the cruel manner in which the apes are treated by their human masters. Over the next few days, sequences were shot which continued to have the duo moving through the crowds, Caesar observing the cruel manner in which human masters treat their ape slaves, and then a pivotal moment in which Caesar calls a couple of Gestapo-like cops "lousy human bastards" for torturing an ape named Aldo. Armando sneaks him away, but says that he'll have to turn himself in to avert suspicion that Caesar actually understood all that was being said and done.

On February 4, McDowall—in scenes that actually take place later in the movie—acted in sequences in which Caesar inspires a series of minor revolts, such as apes screwing up book filing, shoe polishing, and food preparation.

February 7 and 8 saw production of the integral scene in which Armando has turned himself in for interrogation, where he defends himself to Breck and Kolp, claiming that his ape is incapable of speech. In just a matter of moments, they uncover the truth despite the circus owner's objections. They attempt to force the fact from him using the "authenticator," but Armando rebels—accidentally plummeting out a window to his death. Frank Capra, Jr. admits that there was some concern about killing off such a beloved character. "But at that point," he observes, "you're thinking, 'There aren't going to be any more films, so I guess that's going to be okay.' Ricardo is a very good friend of ours and he was of Arthur's. They knew each other and were friends. We would have loved to have had another film with him in it, but the last film would have been further in the future and Armando wouldn't have been alive anyway. I hated to do him in, but if you don't have any characters you like die, it seems to lack importance."

February 9 and 10 saw production of scenes in which Caesar has been purchased by Breck himself, and is being indoctrinated, beginning with choosing his own name from a book of names. He makes his choice, leaving Breck—not realizing who or what he has in his possession—to muse, "Caesar . . . a king." On the eleventh, Thompson shot the auction itself which served as a strong encapsulation of the way in which apes in this society are moved as merchandise. The location of the auction scene was the University of California, Irvine.

Between February 14 and 16, the production shot scenes in which Caesar allows himself to be taken in to ape management after having hidden in a cage of

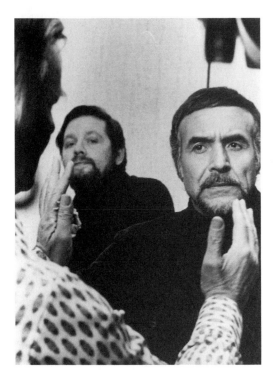

Director J. Lee Thompson frames a shot of Ricardo Montalban as Severn Darden looks on. Montalban's performance in *Conquest* remains highly underrated.

orangutans. Then they captured the few humorous moments in the film in which he goes through a training sequence of mopping, pouring water into a glass, and drying off his hands, all of which he does in a manner far superior to the rest of the apes and which McDowall practically highlights with a wink to the audience. Offers Capra, "I think that was a point where we could do a little bit of humor where there weren't many places to do that. Wherever you had the opportunity to do so, it was good to do it just to change the tone for a minute. It's a pretty unremitting film, as you know. We always felt that if we could find a place to do humor, either in the script or in the filming of it, we would do it."

February 17 and 18 were the days of the dramatic scene in which Breck has Caesar strapped to a shock table, and uses electricity to force the ape to speak. It is only through the secret intervention of MacDonald—who shuts off power to the table without anyone but Caesar noticing—that Caesar avoids being electrocuted. Reflects Capra, "Roddy had to really react to what was supposed to be happening. Of course his difficulty was the makeup and the appliances, which were attached to his face and neck with a sort of spirit gum adhesive so you could take it off at night. Sometimes sweat caused problems with it or excessive movement. It was pretty flexible, made of a kind of foam rubber and it was made to be as flexible as possible so facial expressions could be seen through it. At the same time, it wouldn't stand up to a lot of mistreatment. We had times where we had to repair makeup; where makeup would be beaten up in an action scene—like this shock table scene—and that took a lot of time."

Admitted McDowall, "That scene was very painful. It was very difficult because it meant arching the whole body, which was delicate to do because the wig could tear off when I arched my back, and it often had to be repaired."

In terms of production of *Conquest,* the apes finally began their revolt on February 21 in scenes taking place in ape management. The apes are killing their handlers, and the humans are desperately trying to coral the animals before they're forced to destroy this valuable property. Over the course of the next few days, the battle moved to the exterior of Century City for a number of night shoots in which the apes and human police officers engage in a violent and bloody battle that does, indeed, bare more than a passing resemblance to the Watts riots. Squeezed in during these shots was a scene

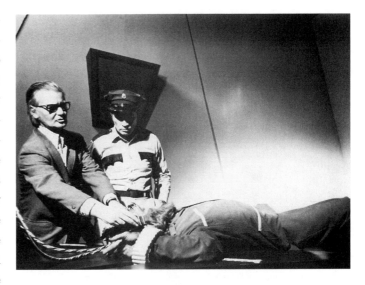

taking place earlier in the film in which Caesar, having learned of Armando's death, sees one of the circus posters in a storefront window and cries out in anguish, quickly clamping a hand over his mouth for fear of being overheard.

Filming on the battle sequences—which were quite literally modeled after footage of the real-life Watts riots—continued until March 1. "That was all shot at night in Century City," recalls Capra. "Night shooting is, generally speaking, more expensive than day shooting. It would be more expensive to film, but at the same time you could get away with a lot more at night in the shadows and so forth. So you could get away with a lot less made-up apes being fairly close to the camera. It

was not only for the dramatics of the scene—night is always more dramatic than daytime—but it was also for us, in terms of the production of the scenes. We were able to get away with more, because what you don't light you don't see. If we had done those scenes in daytime, first of all we would have had a lot more problems with passersby, pedestrians, and people in the mall, but at the same time, every little

thing would have been seen. So it was very conscious to make that a night scene. But shooting every night all night was very difficult.

"Daytime scenes with a lot of apes was tough," he adds. "To fill the screen with apes we had enough costumes and masks—pull-over-your-head masks—left over from the earlier pictures, but to do a lot of makeup was a different thing. That was

a much more difficult problem. You had to have a lot of apes in full makeup ready for an 8:30 shooting, and that meant a number of makeup and hairdressing people, because each one took between an hour and a half and two and a half hours. If you needed a lot of apes ready for camera early in the morning in a big scene so you could be close to them, that was difficult to do. We had to think about that in terms of scheduling and try to do it during the day so apes would be scheduled at different times. This way they wouldn't all have to be ready at the same time. Kind of a weakness of the film is you don't see many full made-up apes at one time, but on the other hand it's doing the best you can with what you've got. In *that* sense, the night scenes were easier."

The climactic sequence, shot between March 1 and 5, was probably one of the most controversial scenes in *Apes* film history. As such, it will be discussed a little further on.

On March 6, 1972, filming moved to a tunnel set in which Mr. MacDonald learns for the first time that not only can Caesar speak, but that he is also planning a revolution for the freedom of his kind. This sequence, as well as one in which Kolp and a pair of security officers are moving toward MacDonald's location, wrapped the following day. Between the eighth and the thirteenth, a number of pickup shots were filmed, serving as bridging moments between sequences, and so on.

Production wrapped on the thirteenth, and the film's producers began the usual postproduction process, including editing, looping, colorization, and music. Of the latter, due to budgetary limitations there would be no

Jerry Goldsmith or Leonard Rosenman this time, so the production had no choice but to turn to a relative newcomer.

"Music is always a roulette wheel," says J. Lee Thompson. "You can only discuss with the composer what you feel you would like. And then he goes away and composes it. And film being like it is, you can't hire an orchestra, ask the composer to play it for you, and say that you don't like it. The first time you hear it orchestrated is when he's going to record it, so it's a gambit. I mean, they will play you themes on a piano, but it is really not satisfactory. You do work closely with the musicians in as much as you run the film with them. You probably run it several times and discuss each scene and what you want the music to do for each scene. Sometimes it doesn't work out."

The composer of *Conquest* was Tom Scott, whose only previously produced credit was *The Culpepper Cattle Company*. His score, while still featuring the staccato, percussive march sound endemic to the earlier *Apes* scores, was scored for a much smaller group of players and often came off more as the work of a progressive jazz ensemble than a film score. The film receives extremely spare scoring throughout its first three quarters, with most scenes unscored until the beginnings of the climactic ape revolt. The cues that do occur before the action finale are few and far between, and often do little to accentuate the drama of the film's events. Particularly egregious is a circuslike cue for recorder and snare drums. One effective piece of spotting allows for the buildup to the climactic confrontation between the ape rebel army and the human riot police at Century City to play out unscored, while Scott's violent battle music is appropriately desperate and primitive-sounding, he allows comic effects to intrude even at this brutal juncture in the film. The inserted portion of Caesar's revolutionary speech was actually tracked with Jerry Goldsmith's "The Search" from the first *Apes* film.

At this point, everyone involved was extremely satisfied with the final results, confident that they had created an entry in the series that managed to stand apart from the rest but was nonetheless a significant part of the whole. As far as they were concerned, the film was complete. They were wrong.

As noted earlier, the conclusion of *Conquest* was among the most intense sequences ever shot for the film series. The city is in flames, humans are dying by the dozen, gorillas have brought the battered body of Governor Breck to lay before Caesar, and Man's fate is not . . . hopeful. To understand the power of the moment, it's necessary to quote directly from the shooting script:

REVERSE DOWN ANGLE
SHOOTING from between Caesar and Macdonald into the square. Below them the square explodes in cries of still unsurfeited vengeance as Breck's twitching body finally falls limp and motionless under the leash. The screeching of the angry apes grows louder as they lay about them with clubs and truncheons at the remaining humans in the square.

As written and shot, this climatic moment would have rivaled *anything* the series had done to date, but it just wasn't to be.

"*Conquest* was a really good, strong, political statement," offers director J. Lee Thompson. "In fact, the original film was so strong that it couldn't be shown. You know, we had to take it back into the editing room. We were getting complaints at the preview in Phoenix. It was a very violent ending and we had to change it around and make it a happy ending."

Elaborating, Thompson adds, "When the film was shown at a screening in Phoenix, we had some very bitter comments. Nobody wrote that it was too pro-black, but they wrote, 'How can you do this kind of thing?' I can't remember the actual quotes, but the inference was that it was very wrong to infer that whites could be so cruel to animals. In fact, that's the way they put it: 'Disgusting' was often a comment. Disgusting that humans should be portrayed hurting animals in this fashion. In other words, they were deliberately missing the whole point and were really getting angry about what was intended. The truth is, blacks loved the *Apes* films. I remember them standing up and cheering. In the film, in the end the apes took over. They loved it. If I remember correctly the apes were looked upon as the black people and the Nazi element was really the whites. So when the apes rebelled, I remember in the preview, which was in a black-oriented area, they really started cheering. We knew we had achieved what we set out to do."

Fox was pleased. There was great concern that not only would they be alienating family audiences, but that somehow the film would incite African-Americans to fight back against oppressive whites. Muses Frank Capra, "Somebody might have been a goody-two shoes and said, 'We have to be responsible about the ending,' but that would be a first, I believe. I don't see much responsibility coming around. If they thought they would make money from it, they wouldn't do it. In retrospect, somebody might have said, 'That's why we had to change it.' I think it was more than that. To end with the end of the human race was dissatisfying to us. It colored Caesar. Instead of being a flawed hero, he was a villain and you really didn't want that. That would have been the last image of him, screaming, 'That day is upon you now!' It was a pretty violent ending. J. Lee had shot the bejeezus out of it. When it was on the screen it was *scary*. It was just *too* strong, and it detracted from the film."

The solution was to fix the problem in the editing room. By recutting the existing footage, and dubbing in new dialogue, the producers opted for a more "upbeat" ending. The reality is that the change is *very* obvious, and fairly ineffective. In the final film, when Caesar proclaims, "That day is upon you now!" Lisa, the female chimpanzee, miraculously gains the power of speech when she looks at Caesar and says the word, "No." Suddenly, it's like the lightswitch has been thrown, and Caesar realizes that it's all been a mistake.

"Now we have passed through the night of the fires," says Caesar, "and those who were our masters are now our servants. And we who are not human, can afford to be humane. Destiny is the will of God, and if it is Man's destiny to be dominated, then it is God's will that he be dominated with compassion. And understanding. So, cast out your vengeance. Tonight, we have seen the birth . . . of the Planets of the Apes." Apes go wild, Breck is still alive, fade to black.

"The ending was watered down *a lot*," states J. Lee Thompson. "I was very unhappy, but had to do it. Arthur had to deliver a certain PG to Fox. It would have been an R rating because of the violence in the end. I had to water down all of the violence, too, and switch it and make it happier. Lots of things were cut. I remember the speech and he sort of suddenly changes his character. That was demanded by the distributors. That was a pity.

"By changing the ending," he continues, "I personally feel we were copping out,

because it wasn't the ending we intended. But I thought it was correct in terms of film entertainment to cop out, because I have no right to take an *Apes* film and really make it such a strong political platform. There's always been a political connotation in all the *Apes* films, and if it gets too strong and you're really beginning to upset people, then cool it. I was very happy to give it what we call a 'happy ending.' And a merciful ending, and in a way I think it was better and certainly sent people out happier. It was a copout, but it was one that I agreed with 100 percent."

Capra puts at least part of the blame for the ending's failure right at AP-JAC's front door. "Unfortunately," he admits, "we didn't do a very good job of fixing it. We were really under the gun and had to go out with it. The re-edit had to be done as fast as possible. We could have done it smoother given a little more time, maybe reshot a closeup of Roddy. The idea was that it was not satisfactory, not because it was going to give people ideas to go out and start a revolution, but it just didn't work for the character. It narrowed his greatness. I think it just made him and them revengeful. We were looking for something a little more. It should have originally been written and shot that way in the first place, which would have smoothed the transition and not made it seem so abrupt. We had to fix *so* much. To do it right we would have had to have rewritten it, reshot it, and have Caesar gradually come to this reflection. He'd become all the better for stopping the battle, but since it wasn't written that way, we didn't have anything we could do. So we had to use closeups and cut out his mouth and put a voiceover, which was not matching very well. I think we could have done much better if we had another week or two to fool with it, but we really didn't. We had to go. All the theaters were lined up."

Capra also believes that the "new" ending had further-reaching effects on the overall film. "Before we changed the ending," he says, "we were hoping that when Breck got killed, there would be some feeling of remorse from the audience. It's funny, but when you change one thing like that at the end of a picture, it touches so many other things that came before it. That's one of the problems with *Conquest* in that sense. When you abruptly do something differently, and it isn't characterized in the rest of the script, it's like a spider web. You pull one strand and you've affected a lot of others."

Naturally, the critics were quick to offer their views.

The Los Angeles Times: "Each film of the series has been so successful, it demanded still another installment, taxing the ingenuity of Jacobs's gifted writer, Paul Dehn. Every time, however, Dehn has met the challenge extraordinarily well. Indeed, No. 4 may well be the best since No. 1. *Conquest* is a self-contained allegory in which man's cruelty to beasts become symbolic to man's inhumanity to man.

The Village Voice: "With *Conquest,* unfortunately, the apes fantasy has finally worn itself out. Nothing marks its degeneration so much as the way its open-ended central conceit of man-like simians has been transformed into a simple-minded metaphor for racial conflict in America."

Variety: "Dehn's dramaturgy is perfect in that the violence to come is matched by the gross injustices being perpetrated. Thus, while the film is extremely rough toward the end, it is not offensive in this regard."

Cinefantastique: "The film so loads the dice against humanity, that the apes' bloodbath seems entirely justified. My complaint here is not a moral one really, but dramatically an aesthetic balance between the ape and human characters was desperately needed. It becomes a one-dimensional racial parable, perhaps unintentional, in which the death of one man seems enough reason for one ape to go crackers and kill every human in sight. It's not just a suspension of disbelief, but a semantic problem in storytelling that is never really conquered."

Herald-Examiner: "Round Four. Not quite a knockout, but a solid win. Starts in fine. Lots of action. Few neat quick jabs to the morals. Fair dose of spectacle. Nice sense of comic timing. Toward the end the nifty footwork gets a little tired and too much philosophical chat bogs down the pace. Paul Dehn's script displays sharp wit, but gets carried away by pulpit dialogue toward the end."

Evening Standard: "As usual, Paul Dehn's script is intelligent and at times witty, and he has left the ending at a pivotal point ready for another sequel."

One year later, APJAC would be addressing that challenge with *Battle for the Planet of the Apes.*

Makeup tests of a "half ape, half human" were made but ultimately discarded.

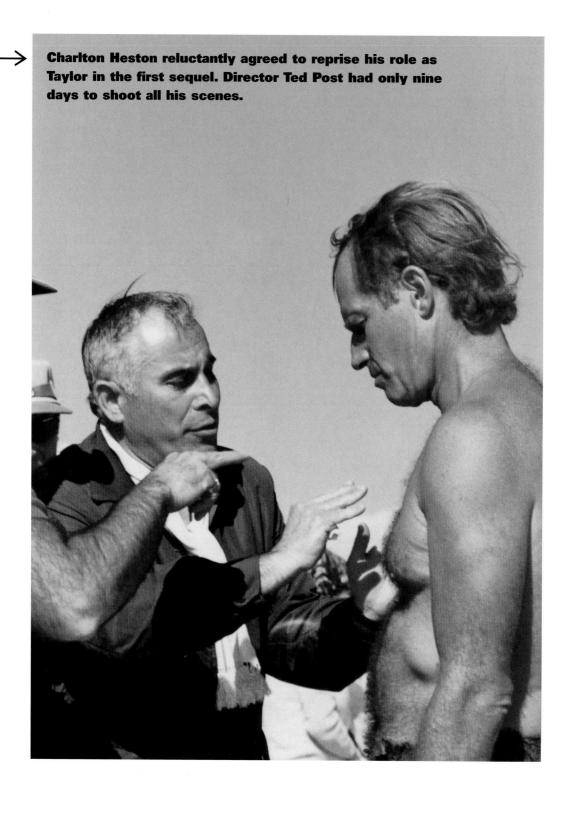

Charlton Heston reluctantly agreed to reprise his role as Taylor in the first sequel. Director Ted Post had only nine days to shoot all his scenes.

Makeup artist John Chambers receiving a star on Hollywood Boulevard.

Linda Harrison. PHOTO COURTESY OF JOE RUSSO

Natalie Trundy and Roddy McDowall. PHOTO COURTESY OF JOE RUSSO

Kim Hunter. PHOTO COURTESY OF JOE RUSSO

Conquest of the Planet of the Apes

Conquest of the Planet of the Apes (Released June 14, 1972). 88 Minutes. Produced by Arthur P. Jacobs. Associate Producer Frank Capra, Jr. Screenplay by Paul Dehn. Directed by J. Lee Thompson.

CAST
Caesar: Roddy McDowall; Breck: Don Murray; Armando: Ricardo Montalban; Lisa: Natalie Trundy; MacDonald: Hari Rhodes; Kolp: Severn Darden; Busboy: Lou Wagner; Commission Chairman: John Randolph; Mrs. Riley: Asa Maynor; Hoskyns: H. M. Wynant; Aldo: David Chow; Frank: Buck Kartalian; Policeman: John Dennis; Auctioneer: Gordon Jump; Announcer: Dick Spangler; Zelda: Joyce Harber; Ape with Chain: Hector Soucey; Second Policeman: Paul Comi; Stunt Coordinator: Paul Stader; Stuntmen included: Alan Gibbs, Dave Sharpe, George Robotham, Allen Pinson, George Wilbur, Larry Holt, Hubie Kerns, Victor Paul, Chuck and Bill Couch, Alex Sharp, Loren Janes, Chuck Waters, Ernie Robinson, and Henry Kingi.

PRODUCTION CREW
Music: Tom Scott; Director of Photography: Bruce Surtes; Film Editors: Marjorie Fowler, A.C.E., Alan Jaggs, A.C.E.; Creative Makeup Design: John Chambers; Unit Production Manager: William G. Eckhardt; Assistant Director: David "Buck" Hall; Sound: Herman Lewis, Don Bassman; Unit Publicist: Jack Hirshberg; Titles: Don Record; Art Director: Phillip Jefferies; Set Decorator: Norman Rockett; Makeup Supervision: Dan Striepeke; Makeup Artists: Joe DiBella, Jack Barron; Hair Stylist: Carol Pershing.

BATTLE FOR THE PLANET OF THE APES

6

The primary difference between shooting *Battle for the Planet of the Apes* and the series' previous sequels, is that at the outset everyone pretty much knew that this was the end of the line.

In London, screenwriter Paul Dehn admitted to journalists that he was beginning to run into a creative wall with the series. "The whole thing has become a very logical development in the form of a circle," he said of the last film's storyline. "I have a complete chronology of the time circle mapped out, and when I start a new script, I check every supposition I make against the chart to see if it is correct to use it. At the moment, I am starting on an outline treatment for the fifth film, which I am calling *Battle for the Planet of the Apes*. This will take us up to the point where Ape City, seen in the original film, is being built. After that, I

don't know. I am almost sixty years of age and I feel I've only got a couple more *Ape* films to give. Maybe these will give a new writer some ideas, and he will be able to take the saga off on a tangent, perhaps to another planet. Who knows?"

One thing Arthur Jacobs did know was that he had pretty much had enough of talking apes.

"Naturally, I'm fond of the apes," he told the Associated Press, "but it has become harder to find new plots that will work. Besides, I have other films I want to make. I don't want to keep turning out apes pictures like Charlie Chans or Tarzans. In both those cases, the first five or so of the series were excellent. Then, as the series fell into other hands, they became routine and not so good. I'd rather quit while we're ahead."

Associate producer Frank Capra, Jr. points out that while no one came right out and said there wouldn't be any additional sequels, "we felt it would be pretty challenging to try and do yet another. We all felt that," he says. "And as far as Arthur was concerned, I think he felt he had done enough *Apes*. He had done all five of them, and I think he was hoping to concentrate on other projects. He was also feeling pigeonholed at Fox, because all they wanted was *Apes* films. And our offices were at Fox. But for Paramount we made *Play it Again, Sam,* and for United Artists we did *Tom Sawyer* and *Huckleberry Finn*. He might have been having a hard time getting Fox to listen to any other ideas for films, but not other studios."

The first step in bringing *Battle* to life began in April and May of 1972, when negotiations began between APJAC and the newly incorporated Dehn Enterprises for Paul Dehn to write the film's script. Although there isn't a lot of information in terms of the creative aspect of the film that can be discerned through correspondence between the principals, it is obvious that money occupied a tremendous amount of time. Particularly the negotiations between Dehn's representative, Dennis van Thal, and APJAC. Based on an April twentieth letter, it's apparent that Jacobs had asked the writer to defer part of his salary so that the film could be made at a price. Thal didn't agree that Dehn should defer any of his fee, and he deflected this by pointing out that he was not asking for more money for Dehn—

despite the fact that he probably could. His suggestion was an immediate payment of $10,000, which would be non-returnable. If the film did, indeed, go into production, then that $10,000 would be applied toward a total fee of $100,000, which would be payable fifty percent on delivery of the script's first draft and the balance being paid out once the final draft had been handed in.

Haggling back and forth resulted in Dehn receiving $10,000 for the film's treatment, and the same deal he received on *Conquest,* which was $50,000 for the screenplay, $50,000 deferred and five percent of a hundred percent of the net profits. The $10,000 treatment fee would be applied against the $50,000 screenplay fee.

Dehn never got a chance to continue developing the treatment, and a series of delays culminated in August with his pulling out of the project. In a letter sent to Dennis van Thal, Dehn's doctor wrote on the seventh that Dehn was suffering from a condition that "can best be described as a tension-state" which, he claimed, was due to the fact that Dehn had been continually and feverishly at work for eighteen months without any kind of break. Dehn's doctor prescribed total rest for a period of at least one month.

The next week Dehn wrote to Jacobs, "I am so very sorry to have had to bother you with my health problems and fully appreciate that no director can be assigned until the outline is sufficiently complete for Fox to give us the green light. But if and when this comes to pass, it would be tremendously helpful if I could fly out for a week's story conferences and then come back here to write the screenplay under my doctor's eye . . ."

Despite hopes to the contrary, on August 17, Dehn pulled out of the project completely. "I know you were telephoned about my request to be taken off of *Battle,*" he wrote. "For me, this is a sad decision, but I'm sure that it's a correct one and fairest for all of us. You have a time problem and I have a pressure problem. I know that, until I've had the rest the doctor ordered, I couldn't produce work that was quick *and* good. I now enclose the completed outline, which I hope will be of use to the new writer. At least it ties up all the strands of a complex plot and still affords opportunity to build up sympathy for Caesar—struggling to retain his good intentions in the face of oncoming madness—and for his successor, Zeno . . ."

On August 22, Jacobs replied, "I received the last pages of *The Battle for the Planet of the Apes,* and I am most appreciative. I am truly sorry, as are all of us, that you won't be able to complete the job. We will miss you tremendously. I just want you to know that it has been a great pleasure working on the last three with you and I hope we will find some nonsimian project in the near future, or perhaps if they continue, another simian-project in the future . . ."

As journalist Abbie Bernstein reports, Dehn's treatment held within it a much more elaborate plot than any of the other *Apes* films. It addressed issues of betrayal between friends that final versions never took to such extremes; the outline also made a mighty effort to explain the origins of what we see in *Planet* and *Beneath*.

In Dehn's outline, Caesar has reigned for thirteen years. The city where *Conquest* took place is the center of his empire, still relatively intact (albeit with some innovations) following the riots, but there are several significant differences. Apes are in charge and all now possess the power of speech. While humans are not quite as bad off as the apes were in *Conquest,* their status is still basically that of slaves. Ninety percent of known territory is now under ape control, though there are still pockets of resistance in the north.

While Caesar is uncontested ruler, he is backed by a council of eight apes. The chimpanzee contingent is led by Pan, a pacifist who believes in giving humans equal rights with apes. On the opposite side is militaristic gorilla leader Aldo, who wants humans exterminated. Somewhere in the middle is orangutan spokesperson Zeno, who (though he doesn't know it yet) will some day become the fabled Lawgiver. MacDonald, Caesar's rescuer from *Conquest,* is the only human allowed to attend council meetings—and even he is not allowed a vote there.

The already volatile situation is thrown into chaos when a scout from the human rebels in the north is captured and brought in for questioning by Caesar's minions. The captive bears a threat: If Caesar does not set all humans free, the human rebel leader who calls himself Nimrod will use a plane to drop a bomb on Caesar's capital city. Caesar, recalling that humans did not willingly release their simian slaves, is reluctant to comply. When the captive turns out to be wired with listening devices, Caesar orders him shot.

As Nimrod and his cohorts prepare to fly in and drop their bomb, Caesar and his officials prepare for the deadly likelihood of nuclear attack. All apes are sent to bomb shelters; humans whose services are valuable to their simian masters are likewise welcomed into safety. Children and less essential human adults must make do with second-class shelters. The identity cards, proving who is and who is not allowed into the shelters, divide the humans into have and have-nots. Radio technician Frank murders a friend for his identity card; he is allowed into the bomb shelter while masquerading as a primate psychiatrist.

The city is indeed bombed from above by Nimrod. Humans caught outside the ape shelters either die or are hideously marred, prefiguring the mutants we see in *Beneath.* When the dust clears, the apes and healthy humans move on to uncontaminated land and begin building a new city—the one we see in *Planet*. The old, radioactive city is left to the irradiated human survivors.

Caesar is beginning to suffer from headaches. He puts cautious trust in the phony psychiatrist Frank, who faithfully radios secret reports back to Nimrod. Caesar's wife, Lisa, meanwhile, is pregnant with their first child. Detente seems on the upswing—Pan and Zeno override Aldo and persuade Caesar that the human children who survived the holocaust should be educated alongside juvenile apes.

Caesar, undergoing treatment for his incapacitating migraines, allows Frank to inject him with sodium pentathal. Under the drug's influence, he gives vent to his feelings of guilt about Armando's death and is unable to go to Lisa as she gives birth.

Lisa is severely weakened by the delivery of her son, whom Caesar names Cornelius Armando. Nevertheless, she accompanies Caesar as he presents the child to his assembled subjects, human and ape both. Unbeknownst to the kindly human Doc, Frank has switched around the syringes in the medical bag. When Doc gives Lisa an injection to help ease her postpartum discomfort, the dose is lethal and she dies.

During the ensuing confusion, baby Cornelius is stolen away by Frank. The rebel leaves the baby in the care of a human mutant couple, then waits to rendezvous with his leader Nimrod. (Note: About that name—remember, this was written in 1972 for 1973 release. "Nimrod" was not yet a synonym for "idiot.")

Caesar, enraged, now views all humans as potential traitors. Aldo presses his case for genocide. The chimpanzee Pan insists that Caesar has sworn an oath that there will be no more killing. Caesar, half out of his mind with grief and confusion, proposes that all humans be surgically made mute, which will presumably render them less able to conspire against him. Seeing that Caesar will not change his mind, MacDonald volunteers to be the first to undergo the operation.

The operation is scheduled to take place at the same time that Lisa's funeral is being held. The human coffin-maker has planted a transmitter in a metal ornament. When Caesar bends to bid Lisa a final farewell, he hears what he thinks is her voice (actually, one of Nimrod's female operatives, speaking into a far-off microphone) telling him that their child is safe but will be killed if one drop of human blood is shed.

Caesar bolts from the grave, announcing what he's heard, rushing to stop the surgery on MacDonald and ordering his people to set all humans free. Aldo and the orangutan leader Zeno, not having heard the transmitter's voice, think Caesar has gone insane (which, in a way, he has). Caesar arrives in time to save MacDonald from having his vocal cords severed, but Aldo wishes to assassinate his former hero. MacDonald sees Aldo take aim with his gun and leaps in front of Caesar, taking the bullet for him, but the reprieve lasts an instant. Aldo shoots Caesar as well; the dying ape leader begs the already-dead MacDonald for forgiveness.

With Caesar dead, all hell breaks loose. Nimrod's rebels launch an attack on Ape City, while Aldo and his soldiers try to slaughter every human in sight. Many of the human children in the city escape into the wilderness; Aldo's forces eventually chase Nimrod's men back to the radioactive old city. The apes are deterred from pressing onward by the threat of a device that will render them sterile. Aldo and the other apes retreat back to Ape City; Zeno declares the old city and the surrounding desert a "Forbidden Zone."

Nimrod reveals that his name is really Mendez (which makes him the forefather of the mutant leader Mendez XXVII in *Beneath*). The human children, still on their own in the wasteland, find little Cornelius and send him back toward Ape City.

Obviously, Dehn was moving into even darker territory than *Conquest* had, and this was most certainly not the direction that Jacobs, or Fox, wanted to go.

On August 22, Jacobs wrote to Fox's Marvin Birdt, "Attached herewith Paul Dehn's treatment for *Battle for the Planet of the Apes*. I believe the first act is quite close to being what we want, but the second act leaves a bit to be desired. . . . I wanted to inform you officially that Paul Dehn is unable to fulfill his contract, based on his doctor's orders that he must immediately take several months to rest. He has, of course, officially withdrawn from the contract which provided for the second step, whereby he would write the screenplay."

The production turned to other writers, and immediately contacted the team of John William Corrington and Joyce Corrington. The Corringtons both had come from careers in education when Hollywood beckoned.

"The script we had most recently written at the time," says Joyce Corrington, "was *The Omega Man,* which was a big Charlton Heston film. Even though we had never done science fiction before. Actually, we got into the movie business almost by accident. My [late] husband had been a legitimate Southern author and Roger Corman called him out of the blue one time, having read one of his books, and said, 'Wanna make a movie?' Bill had no particular respect for film, though it paid a lot of money. We were both in the academic world and even though Roger paid nothing for a script, it was as much as Bill earned for nine months of teaching. So he was like, 'Yeah, we'd like to do a movie.' So we did a few for Roger Corman. The ones that come to mind are *The Red Baron* and a film we called *The Arena,* but which Roger retitled *Naked Warriors.* It was in Roman times about the girls who supposedly were recruited to fight gladiator fights because the public had gotten jaded over male gladiators. Roger got us an agent and this agent hooked us into doing *The Omega Man*. Then we changed agents, but, because of *The Omega Man,* Hollywood, as it tends to do, characterized us as science fiction writers. They called us about *Apes* and Arthur Jacobs said he wanted to talk to us.

"They had done four at the time," she continues, "and we hadn't seen any of them. I began talking to people who *had* seen them to try and find out what their appeal was. I figured it out that the kids were relating to the apes like they were kids, and the humans were like the adult world. So the kids/apes were innocent. So we go out and talk to Arthur Jacobs, he sits us in a screening room and screens all four of the films. He hired us, although we were surprised he did because during our phone conversation he was such a flat personality, that when I hung up the phone I said, 'We'll never get that job.' There was no enthusiasm coming back about anything we said. But, surprise, surprise, he called us out, showed us all these *Apes* films, and hired us."

The Corringtons were fast writers, but their agent insisted that they send in no more than ten pages of script a week. John would fly out with those pages, meet with Jacobs, and fly home to New Orleans to write more pages.

"It was ridiculous," Joyce Corrington laughs. "Our agent wanted us to handle it this way, because we were getting paid relatively a lot of money and we were supposed to look like we were really sweating it out."

Before the writers began to map out their scenario, they were given Dehn's original treatment, which they quickly discarded. "The apes had gone from conquering the planet to Roman decadence. He had Caesar acting like Julius Caesar in a decadent society. We just totally ignored it, because it was irrelevant to what the audience wanted to see. Instead we went with the idea that the apes were totally inno-

cent. We did the Kane and Abel story—the first ape killing an ape. We deliberately picked up that mythology. We made them innocent. We put them in a Garden of Eden, we put them in tree houses. We tried to capture the innocence of childhood, but ultimately they had to face up to their own humanity, as it were, when ape killed ape."

Interestingly, the Corringtons segued over to a number of daytime soap operas, initiated by producers who were touched by the humanity of their apes.

When the Corringtons handed in their first draft treatment—dated September 4, 1972—it was obvious that they had followed their instructions and gone back to a more family-friendly adventure. A nuclear war has been waged, and Caesar leads the remnants of apes and humans to safety. Humans aren't exactly slaves, more like indentured servants. Caesar is pleased with the way things are going—with the exception of the attitude of his general, Aldo—but it is MacDonald who points out to him that Earth, particularly with simians in control, will have a finite lifespan. To prove his point, MacDonald leads Caesar and an orangutan named Virgil into what will ultimately becoming the Forbidden Zone to study the recorded words of Caesar's parents, Cornelius and Zira. While they're there, they attract the attention of survivors from the war, scarred from nuclear fallout, who

live among the ruins. Their leader is former Governor Breck, who, upon learning that his enemy is still alive, launches an attack on Ape City. The apes achieve victory—although in the process Caesar and Lisa's son, Cornelius, is killed by Aldo—and in the end Caesar finally relents, offering equality to humans.

This treatment was turned into a script that would be extremely similar to the final film. The primary differences are that the villain of the piece would eventually be Kolp, not Breck (Don Murray chose not to reprise his role); and MacDonald's brother (Austin Stoker, as Hari Rhodes wasn't available) would serve as Caesar's right-hand human. Unlike Dehn's treatment, the Corrington's Caesar is much more a benevolent despot from the outset and it doesn't take much to sway him to the side of egalitarianism, especially when he learns that the world will come to an end if apes and humans cannot get along. Also layered in this version is the fact that the mutants are the ancestors of those we would meet in *Beneath the Planet of the Apes,* and, in a scene that would ultimately only appear in the laser disc release of the film, that their reverence for the atomic bomb was begun here.

By mid-November of 1972, the Corringtons were more or less finished with their work on the film, and APJAC was not exercising its contractual option to have the writers revise their script. At that time, Paul Dehn, feeling sufficiently rested, came back on board and began the process of rewriting. One point he made was in terms of the death of Aldo at Caesar's hands (out of vengeance for the murder of Cornelius). "I would like to record my conviction," he wrote to Jacobs on December 13, "that after the death of Aldo the story should end much more briefly and briskly than in the Corrington script . . . I shall be redrafting and greatly shortening the action in the final pages . . ."

The following day, he wrote that "I now calculate I've rewritten about ninety-five percent of the dialogue; and though I don't want to press the matter, I wonder whether I shouldn't accept blame or (with luck!) praise for this in the credits. If, however, there is no WGA formula (other than split credits, which I don't want) on the lines you initially suggested—'Original story and dialogue by Paul Dehn'—then please forget it and just credit me with the original story . . ." In the end, the Writer's Guild would award him neither credit.

Dehn added one other significant difference to the Corrington draft. While both versions were framed by the orangutan Lawgiver preaching to ape and human children, the Corringtons ended their version with kids from each species fighting on a playground, while Dehn chose to go with the image of Caesar's grave, a statue of the chimpanzee having been built on that spot, and a lone tear falling slowly from its eye. Jacobs and company pushed for an alternative ending, but Dehn couldn't come up with one that, he felt, worked better. This image, he believed, supported his ultimately pessimistic view that the future could not be changed.

"I have given a lot of thought to a possible new end for the picture," he told Jacobs, "but have come up with nothing—chiefly because I am more than ever convinced that the present end is the right one for the last of the series. For the series to be linked consecutively in the form of a 'saga' (or even an epic!) we need to know that Caesar's good intentions failed—and the tear is both a necessary and moving forecast of Earth's destruction in *Beneath.* Naturally, if anyone should come up with a better idea for conveying this sense of Earth's final doom, I should be grateful for the opportunity of seeing and working on it."

Nobody did, and the ending stayed, much to the Corringtons' chagrin. "Wasn't

that stupid?" proclaims Joyce Corrington. "It turned our stomach when we saw it. We wanted to play up more of the bomb that destroyed the planet in the second episode, but I guess they didn't want to deal with that. I guess what the statue is trying to say is, 'Are you able to change history? Are you going to wind up with the first or second film where earth is destroyed? Is there a loop or are you able to deviate?' They were not able to deviate, so that's why the statue was crying, I guess."

Returning from *Conquest* was Roddy McDowall as Caesar, Natalie Trundy as Lisa and Severn Darden as Kolp. Gone were Murray and Rhodes, but there were several new additions to the cast.

Paul Williams was cast as Caesar's trusted aide, the orangutan Virgil. Born on September 23, 1940, in Omaha, Nebraska, Williams will undoubtedly be remembered more for his music than his acting stints. Although he has appeared in numerous television series and feature films, his music credits include the score for such films as *The Phantom of the Paradise* (1974), *Bugsy Malone* (1976), *The End* (1978), and *The Muppet Christmas Carol* (1992). Perhaps most enduring is his theme for TV's *The Love Boat*. "I could find a cure for cancer," he mused to one reporter, "but what they'll remember is that I wrote the theme for *The Love Boat*."

"The casting of Paul was Arthur's idea," says Frank Capra, Jr., "because knowing he had the music and the background of the music, and that he was kind of a small person, he would fit the character background as well. I think Arthur's idea was that we might be able to get some music out of him, too, thus having a crossover effect for the film. That was definitely Arthur's public relations background coming to the fore. There were no songs, unfortunately, but Paul turned out to be pretty good as an actor."

Bobby Porter made his acting debut in *Battle,* portraying Caesar and Lisa's son, Cornelius. His subsequent credits include such features as *Day of the Animals* (1977), *Every Which Way But Loose* (1978), *Under the Rainbow* (1981), *Night of the Comet* (1984), *Warriors of Virtue* (1997), and *Star Kid* (1997). He has also made a name for himself as a stuntman in films and on television.

Claude Akins was cast as Caesar's gorilla nemesis, Aldo. Born on May 25, 1926, Akins was an actor as comfortable on the big screen as he was on the small. He made his debut on *Dragnet* in 1952, guest starred in a number of classic television series, among them *Gunsmoke, Alfred Hitchcock Presents, I Love Lucy, Have Gun Will Travel, Perry Mason, Maverick,* and *The Rifleman*. His feature film credits include *From Here to Eternity* (1953), *Human Jungle* (1954), *The Caine Mutiny* (1954), *The Sharkfighters* (1956), *The Defiant Ones* (1958), *Return of the Seven* (1966), *The Devil's Brigade* (1968), *The Great Bank Robbery* (1969), and *Skyjacked* (1972). Numerous roles would

Claude Akins and Paul Williams at the wrap party.

Family portrait: Roddy McDowall, Natalie Trundy, and Bobby Porter.

follow *Battle,* including a starring stint on *B.J. and the Bear* and *The Misadventures of Sheriff Lobo* (both 1979). Akins died of cancer on January 27, 1994.

Unlike many of his predecessors, the late Akins developed his own physical take on the character. "I kind of came up with it myself," he said. "You throw your shoulders and arms forward, throw your fanny out the back and you pull your head back with the shoulders and arms forward, and let 'em hang. It's pretty easy to do walking, but damned difficult to do riding a horse while trying to keep that same posture."

Austin Stoker portrayed MacDonald's brother (as convoluted as that sounds). The actor made his motion picture debut in 1970's *The Aquarians. Battle* followed in 1973. Subsequent credits include *Sheba, Baby* (1975), *Riding with Death* (1976), *Victory at Entebbe* (1976), *Roots* (1977), *Time Walker* (1982), *Robert Kennedy and his Times* (1985), *A Girl to Kill For* (1990), and *Two Shades of Blue* (1998). Interestingly, Stoker would go on to voice one of the human astronauts in NBC's short-lived animated series, *Return to the Planet of the Apes* (1975).

Veteran actor Lew Ayres was cast in the role of Mandemus, the orangutan keeper of Ape City's armory as well as Caesar's conscience. Born on December 28, 1908, in Minneapolis, Minnesota, Ayres made his acting debut on the 1927 silent feature *The Flight Commander,* and he never stopped acting until his death on December 30, 1996. Although his film and television credits are far too numerous to mention, genre fans will undoubtedly remember him from such efforts as Gene Roddenberry's *The Questor Tapes, Battlestar*

Frank Capra, Jr. with Claude Akins and a chimpanzee extra.

Galactica (on which he played President Adar), *Damien: Omen II,* and Stephen King's *Salem's Lot.*

Frances Nuyen (born France Nguyen Vannga on July 31, 1939, in Marseille, France) portrayed the mutant Alma, who is left in charge of the atomic bomb at the end of *Battle;* the same atomic bomb that would ultimately destroy the earth if history stayed on its current course as represented in *Beneath.* Nuyen has portrayed many criti-

cally acclaimed roles on television and in film, but sci-fi fans will undoubtedly recognize her as Elaan in the "Elaan of Troyius" episode of the original *Star Trek.* Other shows she has appeared on include *The Man from U.N.C.L.E.* in 1965, *Columbo: Murder Under Glass* in 1977, *Magnum, PI* in 1980, a starring role on *St. Elsewhere* from 1986–1988, and Tom Clancy's *Op Center.*

A real coup to the production was the addition of veteran actor/director John Huston, who was signed to play the Lawgiver—the famed orangutan credited in the original *Planet of the Apes* for laying down the scriptures of ape society.

Huston was born on August 5, 1906. His acting career spanned from 1929's *Shakedown* to 1986's *Momo.* He undoubtedly achieved his greatest success as the director of, among many others, *The Maltese Falcon* (1941), *Across the Pacific* (1942), *The Treasure of the Sierra Madre* (1948), *Key Largo* (1948), *The Asphalt Jungle* (1950), *The Red Badge of Courage* (1951), *The African Queen* (1951), *Moby Dick* (1956), *The Night of the Iguana* (1964), *Reflections in a Golden Eye* (1967), *The Life and Times of Judge Roy Bean* (1972), *The Mackintosh Man* (1973), *The Man Who Would Be King* (1975), *Victory* (1981), *Annie* (1982), *Under the Volcano* (1984), *Prizzi's Honor* (1985), and *The Dead* (1987). He passed away on August 28, 1987.

"John Huston was a real trooper," says Capra. "I remember being on the set with him on the first day. I think he had a little concern about the makeup until they put it on him. But you don't end up coming in on the very first day never having tried the makeup on. What you have is makeup fittings. They fit the appliances, so you get a little feel for what it's going to be like by what the appliances, which are being fit to your own face, feel like. Then they make up a whole series of

John Huston.

them. That's what gives it its distinction. Deep down, it really looks like the actor. So he had to come in for that, and had little knowledge of it. He looked great and how can you beat that voice?"

According to returning director J. Lee Thompson (incidentally, the only person to direct more than one entry in the series), he was the one responsible for getting Huston to agree to do the film. "He was probably hard up for a little bit of gambling money or something," he says. "He was also a good friend of Arthur's. But we tried other people first. We tried Rex Harrison, but Rex got very angry at the thought of being considered to play an ape."

Battle for the Planet of the Apes was a fairly uneventful production. Considering that the film shot between January 2 and February 14, 1973, there really wasn't a lot of time for much to happen. The film was brought in on time and on budget (a measly $1.2 million), but everyone pretty much knew that, creatively, the film was lacking the power of its predecessors.

"I think we kind of ran out of steam there," admits Capra. "We didn't have much money for it and we had to do what we could with what we

John Huston as the Lawgiver.

had. I'm impressed that we were able to pull off what we did, but I kind of knew that would be the end of it for a while. We tried to get as much on the screen as we could, of course, but we lost the continuity of the writer. It also lost the continuity a little bit of where we were going with it. We didn't get to build a lot of great sets or use the Century City locations. That's something you can really do at a studio well: You get craftspeople and, if you know how to do it, you can achieve a great visual look. The films had created a visual look in the past that we didn't have. The others all had set pieces that were pretty strong, and a visually interesting production design. *Conquest* had Century City, and we had tree houses. There was a feeling that we had done our thing and probably gotten the most out of it that we could. I'm sure Arthur felt that way."

For his part, J. Lee Thompson wasn't too pleased with the film, either. "It was the fifth film and it wasn't very good," he says matter-of-factly. "We never really got a good screenplay. It just didn't work and like a lot of films, you have a date to start and you can't pull back. There are certain factors that dictate that you must make that film on that starting date. That happens all the time. We had to start shooting in January and the script was not in a good shape. I worked with the Corringtons a little bit, but there was always something not quite jelling with it. It was a patchwork job. We had a lame script, which wasn't awfully good, but if I had Paul working on it, we could have got it better. We were all to blame. I'm not blaming the script people. It just went wrong. While you're making the film, you try to patch it together and improve it and we couldn't. It was enjoyed by the audience and made money, but it wasn't a good film. It's not one that I loved. I regret, in a way, having made it. It's cartoony. As such, that's the only thing I had to hang on to.

"I was never happy with it," Thompson continues, "and we were struggling the whole time. Probably in the editing room we continued that struggle—juggle some scenes, cut some others too ruthlessly. Then we found we had a short film and I think we started to build up the beginning by going over other thoughts. I consider it a mess. I was very upset. And it was a cheap film. It wasn't like *Star Wars* or like James Bond. James Bond grew in takes. The *Apes* didn't. The *Apes* went down. The first picture grossed the most money, the second less and so on. So the budgets were correspondingly cut on a law of averages. The third film will do such a percentage of the second, therefore the budget has got to be less for the third film in order for us, on average, to make any money. And we had *such* a low budget for *Battle*. It was made on Twentieth Century Fox farmland."

Considering his disappointment, one has to question why Thompson took the

assignment in the first place. "Arthur came to me and said, 'We're going to do another one. Would you like to direct?' and I wasn't doing anything at the time, so I took it," he says. "You care about *every* film, but I came in before the script was finished. So I take responsibility, too. I had the attitude, 'Okay, we'll get it right.' But we never did."

Despite the obvious budgetary limitations that hobbled *Battle,* the producers once again sprang for Leonard Rosenman and a full orchestra. As he had on the first film, Rosenman was forced to rescore sequences from films he hadn't written music for in the first place, as *Battle* opened its scant eighty-five-minute running time with a lengthy rehash of sequences from *Escape* and *Conquest*. Rosenman scored these flashbacks with a percussive opening cue that hints at the material he would use in his *Battle* title march, an offbeat and heraldic march that was far more tuneful and catchy than Rosenman's more abstract *Beneath* music. He stuck to this more tonal path throughout much of the

Roddy McDowall during a dialogue looping session.

film's scoring, writing particularly reflective, almost lyrical cues for the death of Caesar's son, Cornelius, and other moments between Caesar and his wife. Rosenman saved his avant garde stylings for sequences in which Caesar and a scouting party infiltrate a wrecked human city and are eventually threatened by what will apparently eventually become the mutants of *Beneath,* although these mutants are wearing much more cost-effective makeup effects. Rosenman's strident ape music was employed in several scenes

of power-hungry gorilla Aldo and his struggles with Caesar. The composer also provided several lengthy pieces of battle music and did all he could to lend some scope and drama to the film's undernourished climactic confrontations between apes, humans, and mutants.

Battle for the Planet of the Apes was released on May 2, 1973, and managed to earn its production cost back, but it seemed that not only had the filmmakers run out of creative steam, but the critics had grown tired of the whole thing as well.

Among the negative comments:

Roger Ebert: "*Battle for the Planet of the Apes* is the fifth and, merciful God, the last of the Apes movies."

Los Angeles Times: "*Battle* brings to a fitting, effective close Arthur P. Jacobs' s phenomenally successful *Apes* series. Although it is launched from a more thinly contrived premise than any of its predecessors, it becomes just as involving as they were. *Battle* ends appropriately on a note of reconciliation between man and ape. But we can't help remember that in *Beneath the Planet of the Apes,* set much further into the future, they eventually destroyed the world."

Washington Post: "Somewhere along the path leading away from the *Planet of the Apes,* the expedition has gone astray. Now, the fourth sequel in the series ends it all with more a thud than a bang, prolonging the concept but, again, failing to extend the idea."

New Orleans Today: "Perhaps it is for the best that *Battle* is the last chapter in the popular series. The gimmick of apes behaving like men has become very worn, and the listless script sounds like something from a grade-B science fiction quickie of the fifties, with lumps of dialogue that stick in the ear like oatmeal. But for all that, *Battle* is a lot of fun, and even if it comes nowhere near approaching the quality of the best of the series, the familiar melodramatics still strike a responsive chord in this fan."

New York Times: "*Battle for the Planet of the Apes* is not great, but it is appealing and a bit sad. I am told that the plot more or less brings the story back to the start of the original *Planet of the Apes,* though I can no longer be sure. J. Lee Thompson will not win any award for *Battle,* but the film's simplicity defuses criticism. The chimpanzee and orangutan makeup remains remarkable, and the lines are occasionally bright and funny. There are far worse ways of wasting time."

And with *Battle* the *Planet of the Apes* finally came to an end as a feature film franchise. Of course, it wasn't quite the end of *Apes,* with Jacobs selling his interest in the property to Fox, which wanted to launch a weekly television series in 1974. Jacobs desperately wanted to move on to fresher pastures.

"Let me tell you something," says Andy Knight, a longtime friend to Jacobs, "there's a bottom line to everything, and Arthur had certain plans and certain projects lined up. APJAC Productions he sold to Fox, then he formed APJAC International, which had certain production plans over the next five years, amongst them *Dune, Journey of the Oceanauts, Oliver Twist,* and all kinds of things. All of which requires capital. And you are in a much better position as a producer if you can come up with a certain amount of money on your own. So now he's done *Apes,* they've already brought him a lucrative income, and Fox was willing to give him, at that particular time, a fabulous amount of money to buy all his rights outright. He said, 'Good, now I can start with a clean sheet. I've got the money and I can do my own thing.'"

Unfortunately, he never got a chance to achieve those goals. In 1973, he had scored a success with a musical version of *Tom Sawyer,* and he decided to tap into

Mark Twain territory again with *Huckleberry Finn*. But he never lived to see the end of production. Arthur P. Jacobs died of a heart attack on June 27, 1973. He was only 51.

"Arthur was showing signs for some time," says J. Lee Thompson, who was helming the film. "We were all very worried about him. Arthur would always insist he had indigestion, but we knew it was heart trouble. I was with him once when we were coming back from London after a discussion with Paul Dehn. And at London Airport, Arthur suddenly had this terrible attack. He was put in a wheelchair and taken onto the plane in a wheelchair and taken off in a wheelchair in LA. He wouldn't stay behind for treatment. He just said it was an attack of indigestion. Of course, it was a minor heart attack. He went right back to work. When he was in London making *Doctor Dolittle,* he spent a lot of time in bed at the Savoy Hotel. He had had a major heart attack, and ever since he was not a well man."

Andy Knight remembers June 27 well as he was the one who found Jacobs's lifeless body. "Arthur's doctor, Charlie Kimowitz, had been at the house the night before," he explains. "Arthur didn't feel very well, y'know. He had terrible, awful indigestion. Charlie left about two in the morning and Arthur was fine—he was okay, the heartburn had gone away. I got in usually between eight and eight-thirty A.M. Arthur had left a message with Miss Julia, who was the housekeeper at the time, that he wanted breakfast at eight-thirty. She buzzed him and he didn't answer. When I came in she said, 'Mr. Jacobs doesn't answer the buzzing.' So I said, 'Well, I better go up and wake him. Maybe he's sleeping.' And when I came in, he was dead."

Jacobs's wife, Natalie Trundy, was in the midst of filming *Huckleberry Finn* when she received the news. "He used to call me every morning on the set," she says, "but that morning someone else called. I picked up the phone and I said, 'Good morning.' It was Andy Knight, and he told me that Arthur was dead. I cannot explain to you the feeling. Have you ever felt your whole body go to a piece of rubber? Where everything is not just shaking, but you can't feel anything? That's what happened to me."

News of Jacobs's death made its way quickly through newspapers around the world, a generation of *Planet of the Apes* fans probably discovered for the first time just who it was that had brought them the franchise that had touched their imagination.

Arthur P. Jacobs left behind a legacy that has spanned over thirty years; a legacy that will continue with an all-new version of *Planet of the Apes* directed by Tim Burton and produced by Richard Zanuck, the man who had the courage and

Natalie Trundy and Arthur Jacobs.

belief in Jacobs to greenlight the original film.

"It's such a unique concept," offers Frank Capra, Jr. regarding the films' continuing popularity, "and the concept that it is Earth in the future is what really makes it work. That's surely of interest. There's all of this talk about the descent of Man, evolution, where do we come from? Where are we going? I think it's just a startling kind of a concept that Man *devolves* and another creature *evolves*. It's got psychological implications, physical implications, metaphysical implications. It has a lot of values in the inherent story that go beyond the action and the adventure. All of that tends to make it very unique, and when something is unique, it gets a lot of attention."

And it captures the imagination of several generations, who have embraced and will continue to embrace the vision of a man with a dream.

Battle for the Planet of the Apes

Battle for the Planet of the Apes (Released June 13, 1973), 86 minutes. Produced by Arthur P. Jacobs. Associate Producer Frank Capra, Jr. Story by Paul Dehn. Screenplay by John William Corrington and Joyce Hooper Corrington. Directed by J. Lee Thompson.

CAST

Caesar: Roddy McDowall; Aldo: Claude Akins; Lisa: Natalie Trundy; Kolp: Severn Darden; Mandemus: Lew Ayres; Virgil: Paul Williams; The Lawgiver: John Huston; MacDonald: Austin Stoker; Teacher: Noah Keen; Mutant Captain: Richard Eastham; Alma: France Nuyen; Mendez: Paul Stevens; Doctor: Heather Lowe; Cornelius: Bobby Porter; Jake: Michael Sterns; Soldier: Cal Wilson; Young Chimp: Pat Cardi; Jake's Friend: John Landis; Mutant on Motorcycle: Andy Knight.

PRODUCTION CREW

Music: Leonard Rosenman; Director of Photography: Richard H. Kline, A.S.C.; Film Editors: Alan L. Jaggs, A.C.E, John C. Horger; Art Director: Dale Hennesy; Set Decorator: Robert de Vestel; Special Mechanical Effects: Gerald Endler; Creative Makeup Design: John Chambers; Makeup Supervision: Jo DiBella; Makeup Artists: Jack Barron, Werner Keppler; Hair Stylist: Carol Pershing; Unit Production Manager: Michael S. Glick; Assistant Director: Ric Rondell; Second Assistant Director: Barry Stern; Sound: Herman Lewis, Don Bassman; Casting: Ross Brown; Title Design: Don Record.

Television Goes Ape

7

By the time that *Battle for the Planet of the Apes* had gone into production it was pretty much decided that it would be the last entry in the lucrative series. The bottom line is that everyone involved felt that, creatively, they had little more to offer on the big screen. Television, however, was a different story.

There had been some talk of turning the film franchise into a weekly television series as early as 1971, but those discussions never went very far as long as the features were in production. By the time of *Battle*'s release, Arthur Jacobs had allowed Fox to buy the rights he owned to the property, and the studio immediately began looking into the idea of creating a weekly version, inspired, no doubt, by the phenomenal ratings that *Planet, Beneath,* and *Escape* had garnered in their recent broadcast debuts on CBS.

Stan Hough, a production executive at Fox who represented the studio on each of the *Apes* features, was signed on as executive producer, and it was his job to bring the show to life. His first move was to hire Rod Serling to pen the "bible" for the show as well as the first two scripts. What Serling offered was a concept in which astronauts Virdon and Kovak (the latter a medical officer), trying to find the missing Colonel George Taylor, land on Earth in the future. They ultimately find themselves aligned with a chimpanzee named Galen, who believes that gorilla general Ursus and orangutan leader Dr. Zaius are wrong in their desire to exterminate humanity. The trio end up on the run, trying to escape Ursus and his soldiers and, hopefully, finding a new life for themselves.

"This is a My-God-what-could-be-over-the-next-hill show," Serling said at the time. "Always coming at you, always attacking the visual senses. We are constantly on the move. Escape, survival is the name of the game . . . Point of fact. Unlike the feature, our planet will not be limited just to animal-like humans and sophisticated apes. In the infinite variety of isolated subworlds that exist here, humans will be found in every stage of development, from the primitive of the first feature to the passive, illusion-creating superhumans of the second. But overriding all these subworlds will be the dominant figure of the ape. The power, the physical weapons, the organization will be theirs. And with it, they hold the balance of terror in their hairy fists . . .

"Over the next hill," continued Serling, "can be as wildly imaginative an alien civilization as *Star Trek*'s *Enterprise* ever encountered in outer space. With one difference. A major difference—they will not consist of intellectually obscure lifeforms that only the fanatic sci-fi buff can relate to—the ape counterculture is rooted in simple, recognizable basics. That's important. What we see will be a fascinating, terrifying, yet still recognizable world. It's the flip side of ours."

The writer emphasized that the show would nonetheless be an entertainment-oriented one. "We can safely pledge," he said, "that when we see a primitive girl racing sure-footed across the alien landscape, she will be at least as long-legged as Linda Harrison and hopefully as impressive as a spear-carrying Raquel Welch stepping out of the poster in her *One Million B.C.* fur-and-leather bikini. Fantastic. Who wouldn't love it? And maybe the overlay on it is that she is pursued by a mounted hunt club of red-coated apes in full cry. But hold it. That's a natural. We know that the visual excitement, the look of the show is all there—how about the story drive? What's its attack on a week-by-week basis? Glad you asked. I feel what we're dealing with here is unique. The first-time wedding of two classic forms, the Western and the science fiction-adventure. The union is made in heaven. Both forms deal in one solid Dramatic Basis: the isolated, totally self-contained world cut off from everything else. It could be an alien overlord controlling his planet or a Western cattle baron dominating his town—a pacifist race of superintellects incapable of defending their planet or an isolated band of Quaker farmers—either way, the central story thrust is the same."

Serling proposed that since the Western half was the more familiar basic, everyone involved should take a shorthand look at a few feature films of the time to see if they fit the format. "Off the top," he said, "any Indian picture like a *Broken Arrow* has to work because it deals with the conflict of two different worlds. Let's pass those and move on. Take *The Magnificent Seven,* cut it down to the magnificent three and we have our leads saving a small farming community of humans from a marauding band of gorilla terrorists. *Skin Game* is another natural. Galen leads Virdon into an ape community at the end of a chain, has him perform a few simple tricks and sells him. Maybe for money, maybe for supplies. At any rate, the plan calls for them to rendezvous that night, but it doesn't work and Virdon suddenly finds himself trapped as an ape family pet. Escape, etc., and in the finale, they go over the next hill into a new world and the roles are reversed with Galen at the end of the chain. I can even see a *Butch Cassidy and the Sundance Kid* moment when Virdon and Galen take the leap off the cliff together to escape the super posse of gorillas. But it's more than just Westerns. This is a world beyond time or labels. It can be as raw and savage as a *Deliverance* as our three escape down an uncharted river. Or it can be as imaginative as a *Flight of the Phoenix* with Virdon trying to build a primitive plane out of stretched skins and a huge rubber cable. It's the whole framework of adventure, made larger-than-life with everything turned thirty-degrees off center for a look we've never seen before.

"Just what is the threat?" Serling elaborated. "What is the dark at the top? The ape power structure bestrides our planet, overshadowing everything. It is a house divided—belligerent hawklike gorillas pitted against chimpanzee doves. But in the end, as always, it is the war lovers who are dominant. Chief among them is Ursus, chief of the Secret Police, complete with metal-studded leather tunic and the steadfast belief that the only good human is a dead human. Working in conjunction with him is Dr. Zaius, the Maurice Evans chimpanzee [sic] out of the first two features. The highly learned President of the Ape Scientific Academy, he knows the astronauts came from Earth as it once was and is determined to destroy them before they can breed a race of humans that would once again send the world to the brink of destruction. He's an interesting, complex key character—not a fanatic like Ursus, but a rational, dedicated scientist. He isn't happy about the morality of what he's doing, but he's committed to it. Galen, if caught, is to be tried and quickly executed as a traitor. But the secret orders on Virdon and Kovak are to kill them on sight. What they know of the past is too dangerous. They cannot be allowed to speak. They must not be heard."

At the same time, Serling noted that the key relationship on which the show would be based would be Virdon and Galen—man and ape. "Every moment they're head and head on screen," he detailed, "locks us back into our basic premise. Wherever we are, even in those rare moments of respite, Galen's presence will always remind us that we are on the *Planet of the Apes.* Their relationship is going to be very special, close, deeply supportive and yet, at the same time, highly competitive. Galen is not a copout. In any given situation, he is going to try to explain and defend the ape culture using all the precise logic of *Star Trek*'s Mr. Spock. Meanwhile, at the opposite pole, Virdon tries to explain the way it used to be. How superior it was, and why it should go back that way. In the final analysis, the edge is to Galen. He has the words and his world is all around them. For Virdon, it's tougher. His moments don't come that easily. [For instance], once, when they are deep in mysterious caves beneath the Planet of the Apes searching for a lost community of humans, Virdon uncovers a tile wall embedded in the rock. He scrapes the rubble away and reads the words marked on the tile: IRT SUBWAY—QUEENSBORO PLAZA. It's his moment, but somehow he can't find the words. How do you explain all that to a 200-pound monkey with an IQ higher than yours?"

Taking a cue from the David Janssen series *The Fugitive,* and predating a slew of seventies sci-fi series that used the same format (*Logan's Run, Fantastic Journey, Battlestar Galactica,* among others) Serling noted that there "must be an Emerald City. There must be a goal in all this. Somewhere out in the vast reaches of the Planet of the Apes, there is rumored to be a city; a Camelot of sorts, untouched by catastrophe, where ape and man contentedly coexist, sharing their heritages. Not just a better world than this nightmare, but perhaps a better world than our own. A hope, a dream. And yet conceivably it does exist out there. Will-o'-the-wisp clues are found along the way and they keep us going. There is an indication that Taylor, the last astronaut who had gone before, had made it to this safe haven. A primitive mute girl is found with his dog tags but cannot tell how she got them. In a remote village they find an old wise man whose grandfather saw the city and told of the wondrous things there. Virdon listens, identifying them as from the world he knew. And Virdon pushes on. It's out there somewhere. Maybe over the next hill, maybe the next mountain and over a rainbow, but it's there. It has to be."

It's no surprise that Serling's characters are a bit more mature and reflective than the final versions of the chimpanzee Galen (Roddy McDowall), his human astronaut associates Alan Virdon (Ron Harper) and Pete Burke (James Naughton), and their nemesis, the orangutan Dr. Zaius (Boothe Colman). Serling's first proposed script hews much more closely to the original film, even invoking the names of Taylor and Zira. Both characters have already (albeit recently) died when Serling's script begins, though they have met different fates here than they did in the feature film series. In Taylor's case, it could hardly be otherwise, since his death in *Beneath the Planet of the Apes* triggered the destruction of the planet Earth—not only the bleakest ending ever for a G-rated feature, but also really difficult to use as a point of continuation.

Intriguing though the Serling script is, the *Planet of the Apes* TV series opener is one of those instances where most of the revisions improved the final product. It's hard to imagine *any* TV series episode opening with two pages (roughly, two screen minutes) of expository voiceover with no accompanying physical action. We don't meet an ape until the end of Act 1; he doesn't actually speak until the start of Act 3.

In contrast, Art Wallace's (who along with Anthony Wilson is credited with developing the series) final draft, dated July 3, 1974, introduces us to a talking ape—the adolescent chimp Arno—on page two. The astronauts find an old book with a picture of New York City in Act 2, figure out where they are and get on with the story. To be fair, none of the scripts or final versions of the films or the TV series ever address the universal-translator question, i.e., why isn't it immediately obvious to the astronauts where they are as soon as they hear English words being spoken by species they've seen on Earth? Still, since the TV audience knows perfectly well that a series entitled *Planet of the Apes* is going to feature talking simians and be set on a future Earth, it seems counterproductive to prolong the "suspense."

Then there's the era in which the series takes place. The aired series is set between *Battle for the Planet of the Apes* and the original *Planet:* there is mention of a team of astronauts who preceded Virdon and Burke, but they remain unnamed. The film timeline is never directly contradicted (with the exception of the presence of dogs, which goes against what we know about the extinction of canines from *Conquest*). The Serling draft is trying to tie in to the films directly by mentioning Taylor and Zira. However, the humans in the series are not the inarticulate, uncivilized creatures of the first two films; they are more like the timid underclass seen in *Battle.* Further, anybody who remembers Taylor is also going to remember that he's not buried in a grave—there's not enough left to bury and nobody left to wield the shovel—and that Zira was not killed at the same time as Taylor.

One can see why Serling's concept of Zaius didn't make it into the series. For starters, since his version of Galen is considerably better informed on ancient history than the character finally was, having a second knowledgeable ape sympathetic to the twentieth-century humans seems redundant. It's almost as though Serling had seen *Beneath* and recalled the antagonism between Zaius and Ursus, but misunderstood the reason for it. While the film Zaius had contempt for the gorillas' hear-no-evil ignorance, his objection to Ursus's war-mongering was not based in anything resembling respect for human life. Instead, the orangutan (rightly) feared that his own kind could prove just as destructive as homo sapiens, given means and opportunity. What Zaius does get to do in the Serling draft is give unbridled vent to the writer's passionate anticensorship sentiments. Even Zira, the most truth-loving, xenophilic character in the entire *Ape* series, might balk at risking wholesale takeover of her world by humans. In *Planet,* Zira and Cornelius persist in their quest for information precisely because they don't understand the stakes. Cornelius is willing to back off at a word from his superior Zaius—never mind the threat of imprisonment, he's in line for a promotion and he doesn't want Taylor gumming up the works.

Zira has more backbone, but her insistence on helping Taylor the individual and her belief in reverse Darwinism are still a far cry from Serling's TV Zaius, who threatens Ursus: "I'll make the arrival of the spaceships common knowledge and I will document the nature of the men who came here and why it is you have this anxiety to place them into the ground without being seen or heard." When Ursus counters that "It is a planet full [of humans] . . . who could . . . place us into the ground," Zaius retorts, "Even with that certain knowledge." Indeed, Serling's Zaius is less like *any* ape in the film series than he is like the human Armando (played by Ricardo Montalban in *Escape from the Planet of the Apes* and *Conquest of the Planet of the Apes*), who is so fed up with man's inhumanity to beasts that he knowingly lays the groundwork for the initial shift in power from humans to apes. Even then, Armando is guided partly by friendship for Zira and Cornelius and love for their offspring, Caesar. Serling's Zaius hasn't even met the astronauts when he takes his stand—he's operating on pure principle. In realistic character terms, it doesn't quite make sense, but it's easy to understand the satisfaction Serling might have felt in writing the role: The image of Dr. Zaius confronting the House of Un-American Activities Committee with some of those speeches is irresistible.

Galen's attitude in the final version is also much more pragmatic and dimensional. In Serling's draft, the chimpanzee is almost saintly. He encounters these human monsters he's heard so much about, who shoot him while he's unarmed, and he *still* is entirely helpful and trusting. The Galen we see in the TV series is fairly ethical, with a healthy streak of curiosity, but he doesn't intentionally give up freedom and safety just because it's the right thing to do. Instead he's forced into going on the run with the astronauts because he winds up accidentally shooting a soldier—all he *intended* to do was talk to the two strange humans in their jail cell. While subtlety wasn't one of the series' most dominant traits, there's a thoughtful moment at the finale of the opening episode, entitled "Escape From Tomorrow," in which Burke realizes that Galen is thoroughly depressed. When the human asks the ape what's wrong, Galen responds, "I had family. I had friends." Burke realizes that while Galen is not as far from home as his human companions, his life has still been completely wrecked by their association. "You still have friends," the astronaut offers awkwardly. Serling's script takes the ape's aid for granted. Wallace's version acknowledges that the human characters must earn goodwill; it is not theirs by divine right. This is the kind of detail that made the *Planet of the Apes* TV series endearing.

On the other hand, while the differences are again not huge, it's a pity the series didn't get Serling's Ursus. He's more articulate, a better strategist, and simply better motivated than Urko. Urko seems to be operating out of sheer racism against these uppity humans, whereas Ursus fears them for good reason—his arguments to Zaius on the threat they pose is based on logic.

Serling did accomplish quite a lot with his draft. For all the differences in specifics, the structure he created is the one that was used: Two astronauts emerge from crashed spaceship, meet the curious Galen, are captured, discover they're back on an Earth semidestroyed by human warfare, get free, find their ship destroyed, and begin their wanderings. The quality in Serling's script that is most noticeably lacking from the final version is his trademark sense of wonder: Virdon and Kovak both take time out to let themselves marvel at the sheer strangeness of it all. The series, selling itself as science-fiction/action, felt obliged to plunge ahead with running, jumping, and plot schematics, whereas Serling's characters—human and ape—stop and smell the conundrums. The ruminative speeches might not be acceptable on a weekly basis even now on most science fiction episodics, but they remind us of Serling's far-reaching influence on present-day TV and why he is still missed. Indeed, all one has to do is look at his "Episode Two" script as further evidence of this.

The scenario has Virdon, Kovak, and Galen go underground in New York City, where they encounter a race of (nonmutant) humans who have captured Ursus's son, Zonda, and are planning on executing him. In fact, once our heroes arrive, Galen is put on their hit list as well, until both Kovak and Galen address the gathered assembly. Says Galen, "What is it you accuse us of? Is it murder? I don't think so. Not just murder. Neither of us has ever taken a life. But we stand guilty of something else. Because what we're accused of is being apes—and we have no defense. We're accused of being animals—and how can we deny that we're animals? Hear me now, for I ask a very simple thing. I ask that you put me to death . . . in place of [Zonda]. All that's needed here is proof of man's superiority. All right. Won't one death of one ape suffice? Let *me* die—and let this young one go. You will then have your ape victim . . . you will have your proof of the sovereignty of man . . . and you will also have demonstrated that not only can man reason, he can be compassionate. And what more proof of superiority is there than that?"

And *then,* Kovak begins quoting from Shakespeare's *The Merchant of Venice,* discussing the nature of mercy. Even more amazingly, Galen joins in, quoting from the same source and for a magical moment managing to bridge the centuries that separate man and ape.

The fact that their argument is successful is almost beside the point. One only has to sit back and relish in the very notion of Shakespeare being quoted in a proposed episode of *Planet of the Apes.* While it was necessary to alter much of Serling's approach in actually creating the television series, one can't help but miss the sheer literacy his efforts would have brought to the show. In the end, unfortunately, the powers that were at CBS decided it would be necessary to "dumb down" the show, gearing it for children and virtually ignoring any adults who had made the original film such a hit.

So what, exactly, did television audiences get in September 1974? Well, the premise of the weekly *Planet of the Apes* put astronauts Alan Virdon and Pete Burke crashlanding on earth's simian-infested future, and immediately put on the run along with chimpanzee sympathizer, Galen, in an effort to elude gorilla general Urko and the power of the ape society as represented by Dr. Zaius. Virdon is driven by the hope that somewhere on earth there will be a computer that will provide a means of using data from their spacecraft to return him and Burke home, so that he can be reunited with his wife and daughter. Burke is more practical, accepting when and where they are and willing to learn to adapt to their surroundings; the pessimist to Virdon's optimist. Galen initially doesn't believe the claims of the humans that they come from another time in the planet's history, where man was the dominant species. When he discovers that their statements are true, Galen feels betrayed and lied to by the people—or apes—that he believed in most. Then, as noted before, when Urko's soldiers plan a trip to execute the humans despite Zaius's orders to the contrary, Galen inadvertently kills a gorilla and finds himself a fugitive as well. The trio set off on the road, getting involved in adventures in different ape and human villages, all the while being pursued by Urko and his soldiers.

In description it sounds like an interesting series, but in execution the series was a classic example of repetition; the majority of the fourteen episodes produced felt like remakes of each other.

As to how the series came together, in the pages of the *Planet of the Apes* magazine published by Marvel Comics, casting director Marvin Paige noted that CBS had seriously planned on producing the series in 1973 rather than 1974. "I was out at Fox the previous year," he said. "They'd made a deal with me to cast pilots and a couple of Movies of the Week. As a matter of fact, we started on a presentation for *Planet of the Apes* at that point. And then the network, I think, had to decide whether they were going to put *Planet of the Apes* on that season or *Perry Mason.* They decided to go ahead with *Perry Mason,* which unfortunately didn't make it. Or, fortunately, depending on how you look at it. Then they ran the films on television to see what the ratings would be. And the ratings were so tremendous that they decided to go for the series. And that was the beginning of *Planet of the Apes.*"

Also at the beginning was the fact that Roddy McDowall was interested in starring. Paige admitted that he and just about everyone else involved was surprised that he agreed to be on the show. "With anything," he said, "you want to make sure that your people are going to be fellows who catch on. Now, as far as the chimp, we had begun looking at actors for that role, never feeling that Roddy would be interested at that point or that a feasible situation could be worked out. Then Roddy, kind of through his representatives, approached us and indicated that he would certainly be interested in discussing the situation, and we finally did get it all worked out. I think he's a tremendous asset to the series. And he's playing a character that's really different from the other characters he's played in the features. In other words, on the features he played several different roles. In the various different features it wasn't always the same part. And Roddy now stars as a young chimp that's sort of broken away from his mold and become a friend of the astronauts."

Despite Fox's preconceptions of his interest level, McDowall was actually thrilled with the idea in the series—regardless of the fact that it would forever link him with the franchise. "For years," he said, "I've been fighting being typecast as an Englishman and dog's best friend. I made four pictures with animals, actually, and scads of them with humans, but somehow I'm remembered for the four *Apes* films because they are such gigantic successes. Galen was a characterization I was fascinated with. The possibilities were immense when you think of the philosophy involved. We were hoping that the audience would draw their own conclusions about the important humanistic attitudes admired by civilization of the day, which the show attempted to symbolize. We must assume that Galen is a courageous chimpanzee who possesses some of the taboos of his civilization, but is open-minded and receptive to the humans. During my involvement with *Apes,* I played three different characters, and ultimately the character I liked to play the most was Galen, and for a specific reason. Caesar was very interesting to play, but Galen was larky. He had a wonderful sense of humor and a great sense of the childlike. So that character I enjoyed playing the most.

"I loved the total of the man. 'The man,'" he mused with a laugh. "He was bright. He was witty. He was inventive. He was caring, compassionate, an enormous sense of innocence about him, very good-natured. He was a wonderful character. Really lovely."

Amazingly, at the time McDowall had had his face insured for $100,000 due to the rigors of makeup, particularly on a series that was at least *designed* to be on the air for a minimum of five years. "In some ways," he explained, "the series was, in a sense, easier to do than the features because I had a cutoff point. When I started the series, I told them that I could not work longer than a twelve-hour day. Whereas on the films . . . well, one time it was twenty-one hours. I think it was the first. Kim [Hunter] and I spent nineteen to twenty-one hours in the makeup. And on the *last* film, I would tell [director] J. Lee Thompson when I was totally exhausted, because the hours were dreadful. But on the TV series, if I went in at 4:30 in the morning, then I was through at 12:30 in the afternoon. Also, it had never been tried before. Every third or fourth day, if it was possible, I didn't work in the makeup. Except for once, that was respected. Because the skin begins to deteriorate and you could never get it back, so every third or fourth day it could not be put on. That sort of worked, so I enjoyed the TV series."

With Rod Serling out of the picture, Fox turned to producer Herbert Hirschman, who at the time was working at GE on a variety of television projects. He was asked by then CBS entertainment president Fred Silverman to take over the series. "The truth is that I would spend only half a day at Fox," says Hirschman, "and then spend the rest of my day doing GE work. I was probably very active on the show for its first ten episodes or so. CBS and Freddy Silverman thought the show was a shoo-in. Freddy *loved* the pilot. He thought it was the greatest thing since Pepsi-Cola."

One of Hirschman's early challenges was to cast the series. While Mark Lenard, best known to genre fans as Mr. Spock's father, Sarek, and Boothe Coleman were cast as, respectively, Urko and Dr. Zaius, the tough decision was who to hire in the roles of Virdon and Burke (which would eventually go to Ron Harper and James Naughton). "The astronauts were obviously very important to us," he says, "and we wanted to keep hope alive for them. That's why we did the business of Virdon going back for the disc from the ship in the hopes that someday they would get home, otherwise they'd have to accept living in the world that they were in. We wanted to give some reason for their moving around instead of just settling down some place; to keep searching for something. I think we were aware pretty early in the game that we had to give them some hope, with one guy figuring that they would never get home and the other guy hoping that they would be able to. But finding the actors to play them gave us a lot of trouble. I know with Ron Harper's role, in particular, we did an awful lot of testing before we settled on him. We even tested Bruce Jenner for the role, I believe. James Naughton, I think, was cast before Ron Harper, because he got approval early on. One of the people we tested was Marc Singer, who went on to star in *V* and the *Beastmaster* movies. We flew him down to test, but he didn't get a part as the astronaut. We did cast him as the young man in the episode 'The Gladiator,' and eventually he went on to bigger and better things. But he had no reputation in television at the time, and Ron Harper had done *Garrison's Gorillas*."

Truth be told, despite the phenomenon that had preceded it, *Planet of the Apes* simply did not work on television. Extremely expensive, the show never garnered enough in the way of ratings to secure its position, losing the battle—and badly—to the NBC powerhouse combination of the time, *Sanford and Son* and *Chico and the Man*. "Even the first show, with all the publicity, didn't get any ratings," Hirschman points out. "There just wasn't an appetite for it. Ordinarily, if there's a smell about a show that the audience senses—whether it's the prepublicity or little blurbs in *TV Guide*—they decide whether or not they want to see it. For this show, people just didn't want to see it. It wasn't as if it started with a good rating and ratings went down because the shows were lousy. It *never* had an audience. It was never sampled in adequate numbers for it to build a loyal audience."

Things weren't helped, he adds, by the decidedly childish approach that was eventually taken, aided in no small part by Fred Silverman's hiring of Ken Ruby and Joe Spears—kings of Saturday morning television—as story editors. "My interest," says Hirschman, "was making the show for adults and hopefully the kids would enjoy it, too. But the focus changed. Freddy was concerned we weren't doing so well. He thought the scripts were too sophisticated. You know how these things go. When he saw the first script, he thought it was absolutely fantastic. When the ratings didn't come in, he started complaining that we were too sophisticated, and that the villains should be all black-hats and the heroes should be all white-hats. I think the scripts did become more simpleminded, for lack of another term."

Naturally, everyone has their own theories as to why the show didn't succeed.

Actor Ron Harper notes, "I don't think the writing was good enough. It's just not interesting. The basic plot was one of us would be captured by the apes and the other two would rescue him. We took turns week after week seeing who was captured, who was rescued. After fourteen repetitions of that, it was no longer fresh or interesting. They needed some more imaginative writers to go some other direction, give us more of a scope. Also, as originally conceived, the Pete Burke character was more or less a comic foil to Alan Virdon, who was the straight hero—theoretically. Jim is a very fine actor, but he doesn't have a light touch. So instead of having something we could have bounced off of each other, it was really like two heroes and it was less interesting. Pete Burke when he was originally conceived was a very reluctant hero. He didn't want to risk his life for anybody, including apes. He just wanted to get back into his spacecraft and get back to Earth and leave the heroics to somebody else. Pete Burke as it evolved was very heroic and I think we missed some opportunity to take some lighter touches. I always try to find humor in drama and drama in humor."

During the show's production, the late Mark Lenard offered his feelings about the series and where he would have liked to have seen it go. "My feeling has always been that the apes are the interesting ones," he detailed. "When I saw the first movie, I liked that the humans were mute. I accepted the fact that in a series you've got to have more latitude and that you're playing for younger kids, so you've got to tone some things down. I would like to see them investigate the apes culture more, the apes character, and abandon this whole idea of the astronauts saving the poor apes with their technology and their wiliness and more advanced scientific knowledge and what-not. The apes *do* have a fear of humans and their science; that's been expressed, because of mankind's violent nature, but it's not really been too consistent . . . I would like to see more of the mystery of being on a strange planet brought into it—the relationship between the humans and the apes. And as I said, much more about the ape culture, investigating what a planet would be, how animals like that have evolved in a very short time, what they would have taken from the humans and what they would bring from their own native beings into their own native society."

To a large degree, McDowall agreed with Lenard's assessment. "I think the show was ill conceived," he admitted. "They had absolutely cut-and-dry proof of why the material worked through five previous films. An enormous audience appeal. And when it first started, the reason the *Apes* [film] series worked was because the audiences were primarily interested in the behavior of the apes and the chimpanzees, not in the humans. That had been proven. But the problem with the TV series to begin with was that it was centered initially on the humans, the astronauts. By the time that switched around—and the shows *were* getting better— it had run out of steam. We only did fourteen and I think everybody copped out. You have to remember that television is not a medium of support, really. Everything is put on the air to kill something else. *Planet of the Apes* was put on opposite *Sanford and Son* in its second year with the idea that it could knock it off the air. Now that's ridiculous. It had audience appeal. *Apes* was on at the wrong time and when it didn't prove itself immediately, it was deserted. *Now* the network would say that they didn't do that.

"One of the problems," he continued, "was Bill Self, a lame duck president of Twentieth Television, who was a lovely man. But right after the series started, he said he was going to leave Twentieth and Jack Haley was coming in. But as I remember, Bill was there until January, before Haley came in, but he was a lame duck president and the series got the squeeze. And it *was* very expensive. In fact, it was the most expensive series on the air. Twentieth, I felt, should have absorbed the cost and gone on making them. I think they were very shortsighted, because *Apes* merchandise was also the most profitable merchandising ever up until *Star Wars*. It was gigantic; staggering. I tried to express my opinions, but it doesn't mean anything. Just like the guys in *Star Trek*. If the studio doesn't want to do something, everybody has an excuse of why it isn't going to work. There are charts and there are demographics telling you why it isn't working. What are you going to do?"

If you're *Planet of the Apes,* you leave the air, presumably forever. But NBC, deciding that there was still life left in the franchise, decided to take a chance and gave the order for an animated version of the films. Titled *Return to the Planet of the Apes,* the series debuted on the network in September of 1975. The premise of the show had astronauts Bill Hudson, Judy Franklin, and Jeff Carter arriving in earth's future, and finding themselves almost immediately on the run from the simians. Unlike the features or even the live-action show, the apes in this society are technologically superior to their predecessors, armed with a variety of weapons, driving around in vehicles and taking to the sky in planes—much as the apes in Boulle's original novel.

Producer/director Doug Wildey, the creator of *Jonny Quest,* had his own struggles with the network, whose concern that the show reach the proper kid audience often took its toll on the dramatic flow of the stories. "In the Pierre Boulle novel," he says, "there was always an underlying kind of sense of violence. He didn't really overdo it, but it was there and it was part of the general concept in the way the man wrote his book. There was plenty of violence in the actual films. On the show, it became very tough to make an interesting story out of something that they would feel would work, but didn't. I'll give you an example. I wrote the premise for each show, from one to thirteen, and I wanted to get titles for each show. So I had stuff like, 'Episode One: Flames of Doom.' I then came up with 'Highway to Death.' I got a call from NBC and they said, 'You can't use death in the title.' I said, 'Death is a perfectly good five-letter word.' 'We don't want death. We don't want kids to be reminded of death.' So you've got people creating their own little worlds for kids, and it got kind of sticky there because I didn't really feel that many of the criticisms were valid at all. Not even criticisms, they were orders. That kind of a thing became a situation where every time you would try and build to some kind of a climax, it had to be diluted. I had one show where the ape army is advancing on the astronauts and they're on a cliff. They have an automobile on top of a cliff and there's a narrow path leading up that the apes will be taking. So they push the car over the cliff to land on the narrow cliff to hold back the invading ape army. The network got into the *sound* of the episode. I had had them push the car over, it bounces off the side of the cliff and lands on the pathway. NBC came down on me at that, saying the sound of the car crashing was too realistic, so we had to mute all that. I never understood why they took this kind of subject matter as the basis for a show. It wound up to be a lot of chases and things like that, but each time you did something to create an illusion of excitement, you had to cut back on it. Once you get into this kind of a thinking process, it becomes pretty insane."

Truth be told, despite these limitations—and the God-awful animation utilized on the show—*Return to the Planet of the Apes* was intriguing in that it actually allowed for evolvement of the characters and, indeed, the relationship between apes and humans.

"When I first mapped out the show," Wildey explains, "I took the astronauts and kept them separate as much as I could from the other humans through the first three or four shows. At that point, I got them involved with the other humans up to a point. So the original idea was they were astronauts arriving on the Planet of the Apes, they're fugitives, and mainly they keep hiding to figure out what the hell they're going to do. I put the stories together from one to thirteen in the sense that at the end of thirteen, the humans are almost as powerful as the apes. At the beginning, though, they're like mice running around, hoping not to get trapped. That's the simplified philosophy behind it. I wanted the humans to progress somewhere in each episode. In other words, if you look at it the other way, where the humans are simply animals, it would crush any kind of an idea process. They would be there, but like animals under the iron hand of the apes. There had to be some sort of an outlook from the beginning of this show to the end of this show, to show that at least the humans progress. My idea was they would be animals at the beginning and slowly evolve into a crude civilized bunch of people from the standpoint that they might be more organized."

The show only lasted thirteen episodes, but NBC had mulled over the possibility of producing three more episodes for the second season to wrap up the storyline. Although never produced, Wildey had mapped out a direction for those three shows.

"In episode thirteen," he details, "the humans finally get to the point where they can actually attack something as an organized force. Show fourteen would have them organizing to hit the apes where it hurts, which is the munition dumps and airplane fuel tanks. Show number fifteen was where there would be a big fight—how the hell I would have done it, I don't know because you couldn't hurt anybody—and the final episode was the one where they blow up the ammunition dumps, the gas, and the whole thing. I basically brought it to the point where there was an uneasy truce between apes and humans where they set up in the Forbidden Zone; this kind of truce thing where the two leaders meet and we wrap the show up. Maybe, just maybe, they could learn from each other."

In many respects, *Return to the Planet of the Apes* was more ambitious than its live-action predecessor the previous season, but like that show, the animated spinoff didn't make its mark in the ratings. Despite its phenomenal success as a franchise, *Planet of the Apes* simply faded away in an unheralded manner, never to return.

Maybe.

Planet of the Apes Episode Guide

EPISODE ONE
"Escape From Tomorrow"
Original Airdate: 9/13/74
Written by Art Wallace
Directed by Don Weis
Guest starring: Royal Deno (Farrow), Bobby Porter (Arno), Woodrow Parfrey (Veska), Biff Elliot (Ullman), Herome Thor (Proto), William Beckley (Grundig)

Hurled eons into the future by a time warp, two astronauts become fugitives from a race of intelligent apes that have come to control earth.

EPISODE TWO
"The Gladiators"
Original Airdate: 9/20/74
Written by Art Wallace
Directed by Don McDougall
Guest Starring: John Hoyt (Barlow), Marc Singer (Dalton), William Smith (Tolar), Pat Renella (Jason), Mark Lenard (Urko), Eddie Fontaine (Gorilla Sergeant)

The astronauts are captured in a village of humans ruled by an ape. Believing that men are violent-natured, the simian encourages them to participate in grisly sports similar to those of ancient Rome.

EPISODE THREE
"The Trap"
Original Airdate: 9/27/74
Written by Edward J. Lasko
Directed by Arnold Laven
Guest Starring: Norman Alden (Zako), John Milford (Miller), Eldon Burke (Olam), Ron Stein (Mema), Cindy Eilbacher (Lisa Miller), Wallace Earl (Mary Miller), Mickey Leclair (Jick Miller)

Burke and his arch enemy, the gorilla Urko, must work together to survive when an earthquake traps them in the ancient ruins of a subway station.

EPISODE FOUR
"The Good Seeds"

Original Airdate: 10/4/74

Written by Robert W. Lenski

Directed by Don Weis

Guest Starring: Geoffry Deuel (Anto), Lonny Chapman (Polar), Bobby Porter (Remus), Jacqueline Scott (Zantes)

   Galen and the astronauts seek shelter at the farm of a peasant ape whose son believes that the humans have put a curse on their one precious possession—a cow.

EPISODE FIVE
"The Legacy"

Original Airdate: 10/11/74

Written by Robert Hamner

Directed by Bernard McEveety

Guest Starring: Zina Bethune (Arn), Jackie Earle Haley (Kraik), Robert Phillips (Gorilla Captain), Wayne Foster (Gorilla Sergeant)

   In a ruined city, the astronauts find a filmed message from scientists of their own era. If they can elude gorilla pursuers long enough to repair the ancient projector, the film will tell them why their world was destroyed.

EPISODE SIX
"Tomorrow's Tide"

Original Airdate: 10/18/74

Written and Directed by Robert W. Lenski

Guest Starring: Roscoe Lee Brown (Hurton), Jay Robinson (Bandor), Kathleen Bracken (Soma), Jim Storm (Roma), John McLaim (Gahto)

   When the astronauts are captured in a fishing village employing human slave labor, they must prove their worth as fishermen or be sacrificed to the gods of the sea.

EPISODE SEVEN

"The Surgeon"

Original Airdate: 10/25/74

Written by Barry Oringer

Directed by Arnold Laven

Guest Starring: Jacqueline Scott (Kira), Martin Brooks (Leander), Jamie Smith Jackson (Girl), Michael Strong (Travin)

After Virdon is seriously injured in an escape from gorilla soldiers, Galen enlists the reluctant aid of a chimpanzee surgeon who was once his sweetheart.

EPISODE EIGHT

"The Deception"

Original Airdate: 11/1/74

Story by Anthony Lawrence

Teleplay by Anthony Lawrence and Ken Spears & Joe Ruby

Directed by Don McDougall

Guest Starring: Jane Actman (Fauna), John Milford (Sestus), Baynes Barron (Perdix), Pat Renella (Zon), Eldon Burke (Chilot), Tom McDonough (Macor)

While hunting a band of murderous ape dragoons, Burke inadvertently wins the heart of a blind female chimpanzee who is unaware that he is human.

EPISODE NINE

"The Horse Race"

Original Airdate: 11/8/74

Written by David P. Lewis and Booker Bradshaw

Directed by Jack Starrett

Guest Starring: John Hoyt (Barlow), Meegan King (Greger), Morgan Woodward (Martin)

In exchange for a condemned human's freedom, Virdon agrees to ride a chimpanzee prefect's horse in a match race, only to learn his opponent is Urko.

EPISODE TEN

"The Interrogation"

Original Airdate: 11/15/74

Written by Richard Collins

Directed by Alf Kjellian

Guest Starring: Anne Seymour (Ann), Beverly Garland (Wanda), Normann Burton (Yalu), Harry Townes (Dr. Malthus), Eldon Burke (Peasant), Lynn Denesch (Nora)

Captured by simian pursuers, Burke faces two equally menacing possibilities: The gorilla, Urko, wants to kill him, and the orangutan ruler Dr. Zaius wants to use him in a brainwashing experiment.

EPISODE ELEVEN

"The Tyrant"

Original Airdate: 11/22/74

Written by Walter Black

Directed by Ralph Senensky

Guest Starring: Percy Rodrigues (Aboro), Joseph Ruskin (Daku), Michael Conrad (Janor), Tom Troupe (Augustus), James Daughton (Mikal), Gary Combs (Gorilla Driver), Arlen Stewart (Gola), Ron Stein (Gorilla Guard)

The fugitives are trying to foil the plans of a tyrannical ape, who is using bribery to gain total control over a district of human farmers.

EPISODE TWELVE

"The Cure"

Original Airdate: 11/29/74

Written by Edward J. Lasko

Directed by Alf Kjellian

Guest Starring: David Sheiner (Zoran), Sondra Lock (Amy), Eldon Burke (Inta), Ron Soble (Kava), George Wallace (Talbert), Albert Cole (Mason), Ron Stein (Nessa)

When an outbreak of malaria sweeps through a village of humans, the astronauts must convince a suspicious chimpanzee doctor to accept their superior methods of fighting the disease.

EPISODE THIRTEEN

"The Liberator"

Original Airdate: 12/6/74

Written by Howard Dimsdale

Directed by Arnold Laven

Guest Starring: John Ireland (Brun), Ben Andrews (Miro), Peter G. Skinner (Clim), Jennifer Ashley (Talia)

Galen and the astronauts expose a plan by a group of humans to use a mine and poisonous gas to kill a great number of apes.

EPISODE FOURTEEN

"Up Above the World So High"

Original Airdate: 12/20/74

Story by S. Bar David

Teleplay by S. Bar David and Arthur Browne, Jr.

Directed by John Meredyth Lucas

Guest Starring: Joanna Barnes (Carsia), Frank Aletter (Leuric), Martin Brooks (Konag), William Beckley (Council Orangutan), Glen Wilde (Human Driver)

Galen's flight on a hang glider highlights this story about the fugitives' attempts to help a human who is determined to learn the secret of flying.

Return to the Planet of the Apes Episode Guide

EPISODE ONE

"Flames of Doom"

Original Airdate: 9/6/75

Written by Larry Spiegel

Directed by Doug Wildey

A trio of astronauts thrusted forward in time crashlands on the Planet of the Apes, and immediately find themselves fugitives.

EPISODE TWO
"Escape from Ape City"
Original Airdate: 9/13/75
Written by Larry Spiegel
Directed by Don Wildey

After nearly dying in an attack on the humanoids' caves by General Urko's gorilla army, Jeff is able to hide with Nova and escape capture.

EPISODE THREE
"Lagoon of Peril"
Original Airdate: 9/20/75
Written by J. C. Strong
Directed by Doug Wildey

The Simian Senate is holding a top-secret session to debate the rumors of intelligent humans begun after one of Urko's soldiers returns delirious from the Forbidden Zone.

EPISODE FOUR
"Tunnel of Fear"
Original Airdate: 9/27/75
Written by Larry Spiegel
Directed by Doug Wildey

Bill and Jeff move the humans from the path of Urko and his army.

EPISODE FIVE
"The Unearthly Prophesy"
Original Airdate: 10/4/75
Written by Jack Kaplan and John Barrett

Urko and his army are searching the desert for the entrance to the Underdwellers caverns.

EPISODE SIX
"Screaming Wings"

Original Airdate: 10/11/75

Written by Jack Kaplan and John Barrett

Directed by Doug Wildey

Bill, Jeff, and Judy are heading for the human settlement across the plain between the mountain ranges when they spot what looks like humans far below.

EPISODE SEVEN
"Trail to the Unknown"

Original Airdate: 10/18/75

Written by Larry Spiegel

Directed by Doug Wildey

Bill, Jeff, and Judy begin building rafts to help the human tribe reach New Valley on the river and escape Urko's patrols.

EPISODE EIGHT
"Attack From the Clouds"

Original Airdate: 10/25/75

Written by Larry Spiegel

Directed by Doug Wildey

During the night, Ape City is awakened by the sounds of huge flying objects overhead.

EPISODE NINE
"Mission of Mercy"

Original Airdate: 11/1/75

Written by Larry Spiegel

Directed by Doug Wildey

As a result of the dog fight with the flying monster, most of the plane's fuel is gone, leaving only a two- to three-hour supply.

EPISODE TEN
"Invasion of the Underdwellers"
Original Airdate: 11/8/75

Written by J. C. Strong

Directed by Doug Wildey

Reports begin coming in to the police that burglars are striking all over Ape City.

EPISODE ELEVEN
"Battle of the Titans"
Original Airdate: 11/15/75

Written by Bruce Shelley

Directed by Doug Wildey

Urko has been relieved of his duties for three months because of his recent negligence involving his leadership and the failed attempts at capturing Blue Eyes and the rest of the humans.

EPISODE TWELVE
"Terror on Ice Mountain"
Original Airdate: 11/22/75

Written by Bruce Shelley

Directed by Doug Wildey

During an archeological dig, Cornelius uncovers an ancient, human book called *A Day at the Zoo.*

EPISODE THIRTEEN
"River of Flames"
Original Airdate: 11/29/75

Written by Jack Kaplan and John Barrett

Directed by Doug Wildey

Bill and Jeff are discussing the best means of eluding Urko's troops when Judy insists they use the laser they rescued from the ship to help in their escape.

Remaking the
PLANET OF THE APES

8

Go Ape!

That was Twentieth Century Fox's demand when, in 1974, they reissued the *Planet of the Apes* film series to neighborhood theaters and drive-ins around the country. In an unprecedented move, the studio allowed theaters to play any configuration of the series that they chose to, with the vast majority electing to feature all five films in a single day!

While on the surface this may have seemed like an effort to milk every last dollar out of the franchise that the studio could—and undoubtedly that was, indeed, the plan—at the same time it re-infused the franchise with a great deal of energy and is, in fact, the way that many people today remember being introduced to *Apes* for the first time.

Even beyond box office, the "Go Ape!" program also had the side benefit of selling a great deal of *Planet of the Apes* merchandise to moviegoers who couldn't get enough, from model kits to action figures and beyond. Essentially this went a long way in proving that there was still a great deal of interest in the *Apes* saga, but at that point Twentieth Century Fox wasn't willing to invest the necessary funds to create a sixth feature film. Additionally, as *Battle* had proven, creatively the behind-the-scenes crew had pretty much run out of ideas.

The bottom line is that interest in *Planet of the Apes*—despite the failure of both the live-action and animated television series—never really faded away. Admittedly the original film series essentially became an icon of nostalgia for a generation, but there have been rumblings of a return to that simian world for a number of years. Malibu Comics even went so far as to launch a short-lived series that didn't last long due more to execution than for a lack of interest. The premiere issue, though, broke records for the company.

Director J. Lee Thompson, who helmed the fourth and fifth entries in the original series (*Conquest* and *Battle*) attempted, in the mid-1980s, to interest Cannon Films in acquiring the rights from Fox, but Fox for its part wasn't particularly motivated in parting with those rights. Perhaps they saw what Cannon—an exploitation house that, for a time, made the big time—had done with *Superman IV: The Quest for Peace,* and felt *Apes* would be better served as a fondly-remembered memory rather than a cheap exploitation effort. Then, writer/director Adam Rifkin wrote (on spec) a script for a potential film that focused exclusively on warring ape factions, but this never got the greenlight from the studio.

The first time that it became apparent that Fox was truly interested in an all-new *Planet of the Apes* came in December of 1993—twenty years from the time of *Battle*'s release—when director Oliver Stone expressed an interest in producing the film. Considering Stone's box office success with, among others, *Platoon, Wall Street,* and *JFK,* the idea seemed like an inspired one. That same month, screenwriter Terry Hayes was given the assignment of figuring out what the approach should be. It made sense, with Hayes seeming to be a perfect fit as he had scripted Mel Gibson's *The Road Warrior.* That sci-fi action/adventure which, like *Apes,* was told against a post-apocalyptic background, suggested that he was the right man for the job. While Hayes set about writing the script, Stone piqued Arnold Schwarzenegger's interest in starring in the film several months later. The idea appealed to Schwarzenegger, particularly Hayes's story in which a genetic manipulation of humanity from the dawn of time is endangering the human race. A scientist (presumably Arnold) develops a means of projecting himself backward in time, and upon his arrival he finds a race of intelligent apes that are plotting man's downfall.

In January of 1995, Schwarzenegger reportedly approached director Philip Noyce, who had scored so successfully with the Tom Clancy adaptations of *Patriot Games* and *A Clear and Present Danger*. Although Noyce was interested, he opted instead to shoot *The Saint,* starring Val Kilmer. From there, the project fell into the hands of director Chris Columbus, best known for the first two *Home Alone* features and a director represented on screens in 2001 with his adaptation of *Harry Potter and the Sorcerer's Stone*. Columbus—a long-time comic book and sci-fi fan—felt a real connection with the material, and brought in screenwriter Sam Hamm (who had adapted *Batman* in 1989 for Tim Burton) to rewrite the script. Unfortunately, the results were fairly disastrous with a semi-campy adventure that takes place on another planet. It begins seriously enough with a spacecraft splashing down in New York harbor and the dying pilot—an ape!—unleashing a virus that spreads immediately and results in human fetuses being still-born. Left unchecked, this virus threatens the future of the entire human race.

An astronaut is sent to an alien planet to find a cure, and is shocked to learn, that this world is populated by intelligent apes and that their leader, Dr. Zaius, has been receiving satellite transmissions from earth. Zaius has used these to more or less duplicate our society but with a decidedly simian twist. Hamm's script was pretty much rejected right away.

By November of 1997, there hadn't been much progress on the new *Planet of the Apes,* until James Cameron agreed to climb on board, though exactly what his role would be wasn't clear. Apparently Fox wasn't too concerned as the filmmaker's creations continued to smash records and expectations from the time he helmed *Aliens* to *Terminator 2: Judgment Day, The Abyss,* and *True Lies*. No matter how seemingly insane his budget or schedule was, his touch was golden. This point was driven home over the next few months when *Titanic* was released and began smashing records. Prior to release, everyone thought that the film—which had cost a record-breaking $200 million to make—would sink Fox. Ultimately, though, Cameron had the last laugh when the film went on to gross $1.6 *billion* at the global box office, obliterating all films that had come before it.

By the beginning of 1998, Cameron (who was also trying to get Sony's *Spider-Man: The Movie* off the ground) announced to the trades that he would be writing and producing the new *Apes* film, but in all likelihood wouldn't direct.

During this period, rumors began circulating that Arnold, despite his frequent collaborations with Cameron, had passed on the project so that he could shoot the

Charlton Heston and Linda Harrison reunited during the 30th Anniversary showing of *Planet of the Apes* in Los Angeles. Credit: Mark Ragonese

Natalie Trundy-Jacobs meets up with some of LA's most enthusiastic *Apes* fans. Credit: Mark Ragonese

John Chambers with some of his "creations" during a surprise party thrown for him by a legion of fans and fellow make-up artists whom he had discovered and inspired during his 40+ year career.
Credit: Mark Ragonese

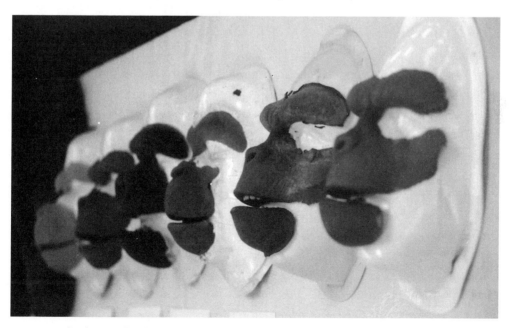

A private collection of original ape make-up appliances. Credit: Mark Ragonese

Roddy McDowall and Linda Harrison at a promotional event for the documentary *Behind the Planet of the Apes,* July 1998. Courtesy of American Movie Classics

still unfilmed *SWAT,* based on the '70s television series of the same name. Other name actors were bandied about, including Harrison Ford and Kevin Costner, though representatives for both were pretty quick to dismiss those rumors. Meanwhile, Cameron revealed, *"Planet of the Apes* is definitely somewhere in my future." In June at a Toronto press conference he added vaguely, "I haven't really made a decision. I'm developing a few things. I'm sort of not eager to jump back into it."

In the July 6, 1998, edition of *Entertainment Weekly,* director Michael Bay *(The Rock, Armageddon, Pearl Harbor)* revealed in an interview that he was talking to Cameron about directing *Apes* under Cameron's production banner.

On July 9, an *Apes* fan reported on the Internet: "It makes perfect sense for Cameron to make *Planet of the Apes* as a continuation of the original series. The last series installment, *Battle for the Planet of the Apes,* set the stage for astronaut Taylor to return to a much altered 'planet of the apes.'" In the rest of the described scenario, the story flashes forward thirty years when five new astronauts arrive on the planet and learn that an elderly Taylor has sired a community of intelligent humans that will fight for equality with the apes. It should be noted that this was the *only* summary of Cameron's supposed story that was ever offered to the public.

Toward the end of July, the original films were brought back into the public spotlight in order to celebrate the thirtieth anniversary of *Planet*. To commemorate that anniversary, the AMC cable network broadcast the original documentary, *Back to the Planet of the Apes*. In many ways, that two-hour special—which was hosted by Roddy McDowall—serves as an unofficial companion to this book; a visual behind-the-scenes guide to the film and television series featuring a wide variety of interviews with cast and crew members. The special also heralded the video reissue of all five films in a deluxe slip-case (all of which would precede the 2000 DVD release of the film series). The most interesting thing to note about the special is that it resulted in a tremendous amount of media interest, all of which must have proved reassuring to the collective corporate marketing minds at Fox as to whether or not an adventure on a planet of talking apes could still be relevant.

On September 2, in an interview with *TV Guide Online,* McDowall was asked his opinion as to whether or not a remake of the first film should be undertaken. "I don't see any reason to remake them," said Roddy. "Why? They're there, and they're as potent as ever. On the other hand, I've always thought it would be very sensible to continue the canon and I can't imagine why nobody's done so." He was also asked whether or not he would appear in a new film. "Well," he mused, "it depends on what it is. I wouldn't do it just for the sake of doing it."

Unfortunately, McDowall would never have the opportunity to ponder the question. On October 3, 1998, he passed away after a bout with cancer. Offered his friend Dennis Osborne, "It was very peaceful. It was just as he wanted it. It was exactly the way he planned."

People around the world were in shock. McDowall, who had actively promoted the thirtieth anniversary of *Planet of the Apes* through a number of interviews, gave no sign at all that he was ill. Right until the end he moved forward, living life to the fullest, expressing his life-long love for film and his craft, and exiting peacefully. The Roddy McDowall story remained incredible, right to the very end.

During the press conference for *Behind the Planet of the Apes,* McDowall had demonstrated, again, the love he had felt for a series that had played so significant a role in his life.

"As an actor," he said, "I think at a certain point one takes the project a little bit differently. I was very fortunate, because in the span of five films and the thirteen television segments, I played three different characters. So that's a great gymnasium to be in, and strangely enough, the television series was the most rewarding from the acting point of view. That's because inside the character of Galen, I played a lot of different characters, so that was just terrific. And I loved playing the role of Caesar in the fourth and fifth films. Caesar's a great, great character and really took an immense amount of imagination and stamina to play, because he grew to be such a monster. Sort of like Richard III, in a sense. They were wonderful characters, so I never thought, 'Oh, this is better or worse than the one before.'

"Also," he continued, "an unfortunate thing that goes along with gigantic success and repetition of that success is that people get jaded about what has been done, and I don't mean the people inside it, but the idea, 'Well, this won't be commercial . . .' I always thought it was a mistake that each of the subsequent films were so bound by restrictions of budget. The amount spent on the last two films was appalling by comparison. Not only in comparison to the amounts of money that had been spent on the first two, but to the level of monetary return, which was phenomenal."

During that same press conference, Charlton Heston paid McDowall high praise indeed: "I really want to say that Roddy was superb in all the different interpretations. He did an extraordinary piece of creative acting in taking, as he said, the diminishing budgets with the feeling that people had seen much of it before, but he made his various characters extraordinarily different and extraordinarily believable." And it was that ability that will allow the memory of McDowall—both on and off the *Planet of the Apes*—to live on.

In December of 1998, James Cameron announced that he *would not* remain involved with the new *Planet of the Apes*. No explanation was given, but the impression was that the success of *Titanic* had convinced the director to only work on projects which he created himself.

On January 31, 1999, rumors hit the Net proclaiming that Andrew Kevin Walker, the writer of *8mm* and *Seven,* had submitted an *Apes* story to Fox. Noted the Internet poster going by the name of Ma-Gog, "Walker has taken the saga in a dramatic new direction, something different than anything we've seen before . . ." The plot apparently involved a journey to the center of the earth in search of an energy supply resulting in the discovery of an underground society of intelligent apes that are plotting to take over the surface world. Needless to say, this scenario never came to pass either.

In February of 1999, director Michael Bay was interviewed for the DVD Review website, where he revealed the following: "Twentieth Century Fox called me up some time ago. They want me to do a new version of *Planet of the Apes*. That's a project I would really like to do. It's a big challenge." Apparently too big, as he would eventually drop out.

The next big step in the project's development occurred on March 12, when Fox announced that screenwriter William F. Broyles was being brought on to take a swing at the script. Broyles's first writing credit was for the critically acclaimed television series *China Beach* in 1988. He followed with the 1993 miniseries *JFK: Restless Youth,* 1995's *Apollo 13,* 1999's *Entrapment,* 2000's *Castaway,* 2001's (of course) *Planet of the Apes,* and 2002's *The Unfaithful.*

A little less than a year later—in February of 2000—Fox made it pretty clear that they were thrilled with the script that Broyles had handed in. The story, taking place about fifty years in our future, has an astronaut inadvertently traveling through a wormhole to an alien world on which intelligent apes rule—despite the fact that the primitive (though not, it's important to note, savage) humans outnumber them by a vast majority. What follows is a conflict between ape and man, and within various ape factions.

Almost immediately, a project that had been bandied about since 1993, was suddenly put on the fast track for production, with Fox announcing that the film would reach theaters in the summer of 2001. Almost immediately, Tim Burton was signed as director and the production quickly began snapping up actors and creative behind-the-scenes personnel for various roles.

"For whatever reason," muses Ralph Winter, who was signed to the film as a producer, "all the elements came together, from Tim to the cast, and the truth is, it's being released as a summer movie to make back the investment of whatever it was going to cost. I think you really want to make it a summer movie to get all the audiences who want to see it. So there's definitely been a push to sort of get it out in the summertime. And when you do all the math and figure it out, it's just less time than you'd like. I read the script in December of 1999 when I was with *X-Men.* I met Tim in March. We started in April. We were going to start photography in October, but that got pushed and we started November 6. So we have a shorter post-production than I'd like, but we don't have five hundred visual effects shots like *X-Men,* because all of the visual effects you see are in front of the camera. It's all in apes. It's all in the makeups that take so much time and effort to put on— we're filming those every day. So we have a hundred, a hundred and twenty-five effects shots which is sort of the normal in today's movies. But we're doing more with the camera than you'd think on a big special effects science fiction movie."

Since 1984's *Star Trek III: The Search for Spock,* Winter's credit has appeared on a variety of motion pictures as either a producer or executive producer, many of them in the sci-fi genre. "That's the way it's turned out, but not necessarily out of design," he says. "But I am attracted to the science fiction material. It's fun. It's enjoyable to create those other worlds. And *Star Trek, X-Men,* all this other stuff—it's been fun. Science fiction has more of a following. You know, those hardcore science fiction fans want to see science fiction movies, and it's kind of fun to make movies for those people." Beyond finding Spock, Winter's credits include 1986's *Star Trek IV: The Voyage Home;* 1989's *Star Trek V: The Final Frontier;* 1991's *Star Trek VI: The Undiscovered Country;* 1992's *Captain Ron;* 1993's *Hocus Pocus;* 1994's *The Puppet Masters;* 1995's *Hackers;* 1996's *High Incident;* 1997's *The Spittin' Image;* 1998's *Mighty Joe Young;* 1999's *Inspector Gadget* and *Opie Gone Mad;* 2000's aforementioned *X-Men, Left Behind: The Movie,* and *Shoot or Be Shot.* One can only assume that Winter will be involved with sequels to both *X-Men* and *Planet of the Apes.*

Naturally it was the addition of Burton to the project that caused the most buzz, automatically suggesting a take on the material that would be quite different from anything that had come before. *"Planet of the Apes* is basically about reversals," says Burton. "I don't want it to be a sequel, I don't want it to be a remake. But there's something about the material of *Planet of the Apes* that's very strong. The idea of sort of reimagining this mythology and coming at it from different way, and looking at it from a different way, was very exciting to me. It's a way to see the humanity in ourselves but from a different perspective. We want to take the essence of the material and revisit this amazing planet of the apes."

Burton, of course, is well known for his off-kilter views of the universe. Born on August 25, 1958, he began his career as an animator at Walt Disney, where he worked on such projects as 1981's *The Fox and the Hound,* 1982's *Tron* and 1985's *The Black Cauldron.* That same year he also animated the "Family Dog" episode of Steven Spielberg's *Amazing Stories.* His television directorial efforts include 1982's *Hansel and Gretel,* 1984's *Aladdin and His Wonderful Lamp,* and 1985's *Alfred Hitchcock Presents.* In between he helmed the short films *Vincent* (1982) and *Frankenweenie* (1984). In 1985, he helmed his first feature film, *Pee Wee's Big Adventure,* which he followed with 1988's *Beetlejuice,* 1989's phenomenally successful *Batman,* 1990's *Edward Scissorhands,* 1992's *Batman Returns,* 1994's *Ed Wood,* 1996's *Mars Attacks!,* and 1999's *Sleepy Hollow.* Between that film and *Planet of the Apes* he spent nearly a year on Warner Bros.' aborted *Superman Lives,* which was supposed to star Nicolas Cage as the Man of Steel. He also produced a television series pilot called *Lost in Oz,* which failed to materialize due to creative differences with the studio, Sony. In the case of both *Superman* and *Oz,* the respective studios essentially hired Burton but wouldn't allow him to be Tim Burton.

Additional Burton credits include his serving as producer of the 1989 animated *Beetlejuice* series, the short-lived 1993 series version of *Family Dog,* 1993's *The Nightmare Before Christmas,* 1994's *Cabin Boy,* and 1996's *James and the Giant Peach.*

Also adding instant credibility to the project was that Richard Zanuck had come aboard as producer. While Zanuck has an incredible résumé in its own right, most important to *Apes* fans is the fact that he's the one who gave the original film the greenlight as well as its first sequel, *Beneath the Planet of the Apes.*

Says Fox's Tom Rothman, "This is a big film with a very, very significant director. Richard Zanuck is a pro's pro and there's the karmic unity of the fact he was here when the series started. There's a certain poetry to that."

Adds Zanuck, "Strange is probably not the right word. I feel like I'm in my own time warp in many ways. I just feel like I'm revisiting my younger self when we were going through the early stages of the first picture. I initially put this into production when I was at Fox thirty-some years ago. The idea was so intriguing to me then, and I think we can do better now because technology will allow us to improve the look and articulation of the apes.

"In those days," he elaborates, "of course, there were a few things that aren't true today. Certainly the cost of making films was so reduced. The first one was just a fraction of what we're doing now, and that was considered heavyweight at the time. There was great uncertainty as to whether this would work. Here we were with talking apes speaking perfect English, and there was always the fear that within the first thirty seconds we could be laughed off the screen. It seems simple now, but at that time it was very uncharted ground. We were trying to do more than science fiction. We were trying to say a little something by this role reversal. We didn't know whether that would get through or whether this whole thing might be considered laughable. This time out, the challenge is different. First of all, we have the past to live up to and we have many fans around the world who know that title and there are great *Planet of the Apes* cults all over the place, not just in this country but all over the world. But when you say *Planet of the Apes* and Tim Burton, that idea is kind of explosive—just the idea of him being on that film. The pressure is that we have to live up to it. We have to deliver something.

"I think that Tim brings to any film a tremendous sense of imagination,"

Rick Baker. Credit: Al Ortega

Zanuck enthuses. "All you have to do is look at his films and see that they are all highly imaginative and highly visual. He's a visual director. He hits things a bit off center, which is what this needs—this film doesn't need to be done by the numbers. Actually what interested me in this whole re-envisioning of this world was Tim Burton. That's what attracted me to the project. As soon as I heard that Tim Burton was involved, I wanted to be involved, because I just thought that his vision and imagination and creativity was just the kind of freshness that this needed. We didn't need to do *Planet of the Apes* in a routine way. We needed to do it in a highly visual and inventive way and something that would be fresh for today's audience. The important thing for people to know is that this isn't a remake at all. There's a common falsity out there that this is a remake. This has nothing whatsoever to do with the first picture or any of the pictures. The similarity is a role-reversal where apes are in charge. That's the similarity. It's not a remake of the original *Planet of the Apes*. It's an entirely different and new story."

In attempting to highlight some of the differences, Ralph Winter notes that the original *Planet of the Apes* was mostly desert-set, while much of the new version takes place in jungle settings.

"Remember, Ape City in the first one was more of a desert enclave," he points out, "and this is the total opposite of that. Lake Powell is rock and water and no vegetation. A lot of their trekking around from place to place is mostly just sand, rock, barren—how do you live off the land here? But in the place where the apes live now, in the jungle, it's very lush, very green, and very much what you'd sort of expect. The humans are sort of pushed out into all those other areas." Winter notes that another difference is the fact that in the original, humanity was nearly extinct, whereas in Burton's take on the *Apes* universe, humans are more plentiful. Says the producer, "In the mythology of what we're putting together, the humans outnumber the apes ten to one, and so that's why they sort of oppress them and keep them under their thumb, to keep them away."

The cost of producing a new *Planet of the Apes* is quite different than it was back in the mid-1960s. Whereas that film had a budget of a little more than $5 million, the new version reportedly is costing an incredible $160 million!

"The costs are very high," Zanuck concurs. "Just the whole ape appliance makeup and outfits are just staggering in what they cost. And people are much more critical now. Obviously the makeup people have made giants strides in what we did in those days to what they can do today. The apes will be much more articulated in their facial movements and look like real apes. We have a little ape school going on so our actors can learn how to behave. We did that on the original, though much more briefly. These apes just kind of loped along. Here we're really trying to have our actors get into a kind of rhythm of ape movement."

Originally brought in to handle the makeup chores on the film, was creature creator Stan Winston, whose long line of credits include the Alien Queen from *Aliens,* the Terminator, the dinosaurs that filled the *Jurassic Park* trilogy, and the robots of Steven Spielberg's *A.I.*

"It's a bittersweet feeling," says Winston. "*Planet of the Apes* was something I wanted to do very, very badly. I had actually developed concepts on it for over a year. At the same time, I would like to say that there could never be a negative of anybody going with Rick Baker to do anything. The guy is as good as anyone out there. No one has more respect for Rick Baker than I do. I know that he's done something fabulous. I'm envious that I did not have a chance to do it. It's a double-edged sword. It was happening at the same time as *A.I.* and *Jurassic Park III.* We were in the middle of production. I did talk to Tim Burton about it, I would have loved to have done it, but I think if I had been Tim Burton, and knowing the workload I was under at that particular time, I probably would have gone with Rick Baker. That's because it would not have had 100 percent of my attention. I would have given it everything I could give, but I would also have to give to *A.I.* and

Jurassic Park. I think the artistic and creative choice Tim Burton made in going with Rick Baker is something that I would have made myself.

Baker joined the project on May 3, and it would seem that no one knows more about movie apes than he does. Born on December 8, 1950, he also happened to be the first recipient of the first annual makeup Oscar for his work on *An American Werewolf in London*. Although he has worked in special effects and costuming, his makeup credits alone are astounding. It began with 1971's *Schlock* and continued with 1974's *The Autobiography of Miss Jane Pittman* and *It's Alive!;* 1976's *Zebra Force;* the remake of *King Kong* and *Squirm;* 1977's *Star Wars* and *The Incredible Melting Man;* 1978's *The Fury* and *It Lives Again;* 1980's *The Howling; The Incredible Shrinking Woman,* and *The Funhouse;* 1981's *American Werewolf in London;* Michael Jackson's 1983 *Thriller* video; 1984's *Greystoke: The Legend of Tarzan, Lord of the Apes;* 1986's *Ratboy* and *Captain Eo;* 1987's *Harry and the Hendersons;* 1988's *Something is Out There; Coming to America; Missing Link;* and *Gorillas in the Mist,* 1991's *The Rocketeer;* 1993's *Body Bags;* 1994's *Ed Wood* and *Wolf;* 1995's *Batman Forever;* 1996's *The Nutty Professor, The Freighteners,* and *John Carpenter's Escape From LA;* 1997's *Men in Black* and *Critical Care;* 1998's *Mighty Joe Young;* 1999's *Life;* and 2000's *Nutty Professor II: The Klumps* and *How the Grinch Stole Christmas.* Despite all this, however, *Planet of the Apes* could very well prove to be his biggest challenge.

"I have to admit," Baker laughs, "that the ape thing didn't have the charm it once did for me. I really did think that *Gorillas in the Mist* was going to be my last apes thing, but I couldn't turn down *Mighty Joe Young,* and I couldn't turn *Planet of the Apes* down either. It is different, it's not real gorillas. It was such an important makeup movie. In this digital age, when people seem to think makeup is a dying art, I think *The Grinch* helped show that makeup is still going to be very cool. I think this will as well."

Reflects Baker, "After *How the Grinch Stole Christmas* and *Nutty Professor II,* I wanted to take some time off, because it was really hard work and I'd lost my mother during the course of that fairly long period, and I wanted to reconnect with my family. So I actually closed up my shop and got rid of people I'd had for a bunch of years, and kind of locked it up. I wanted to paint and do some stuff, and then Tim calls me and ruined all of those plans. He said, 'I don't know if you heard, I'm doing *Planet of the Apes* and I want to talk to you about it.' I went, 'Okay.' He came to my office, we talked and I got real excited, just the fact that it was *Planet of the*

Apes and it's Tim Burton. Well, I guess I can take ten months off after. I had a real hard time turning it down. If I hadn't had the experience with *Grinch,* I probably would have turned it down, because he talked me into it. It was right before the Academy Awards last year, and they were ready to start up, so it'd be like so much time until we had actors, and all of our main apes were the actors to be cast. And, as always happens on these things, they cast like three weeks before we started filming. We concentrated first on doing background, generic. Most of the work was done in four months. I would've asked for a year.

"Early on," he says, "I was working day and night doing this stuff, and I was de-signing and making up charac-ters all over the place, because I didn't have a clue what was in the movie. None of those re-ally applied pretty much to what we ended up doing, be-cause when I got a script, it was, 'Oh, I see what it's like.' I did one character that was this kind of sleazy orangutan that I always visualized as kind of a Peter Lorre character. I experi-mented with a lot of different things. Before Michael Clarke Duncan was cast, I did a gorilla and I thought that maybe some of them would shave, like a shave-head one that had kind of naked hair. A lot of different things. We also experimented. I thought it would be cool to ex-plore the whole primate king-dom and maybe have baboons that were like the first wave of guys they sent out, more ex-pendable in the whole caste

Mark Wahlberg. Credit: Al Ortega

system. There's so many cool things in the primate kingdom you could do. It turned out that there just wasn't a place for it. Maybe the next one."

As a result of conversations with Burton, Baker truly attempted to differentiate the different species of ape. "My initial conversation with Tim was about the fact that chimps are the crazy ones in the ape family," he reflects. "The gorillas are the biggest and scariest looking, but in fact they're very passive. I've been close to gorillas in the wild and felt no fear whatsoever, but I wouldn't want to be around chimps. I kind of talked to him about the fact that chimps are insane. They really flip out and they do this cool stuff. He was talking about battles, and it would be really cool to see this bunch of insane chimps just swinging their arms around and jumping all over the place, pulling somebody with his foot and pounding on this guy over here. Thade was originally in the script a gorilla in charge of the gorilla army, and Tim decided to make him a chimp because of that insanity factor. So you'll see him hopping all over the place. Crazy chimps!

Tim Roth. Credit: Al Ortega

"I was originally approached about this when Oliver Stone was attached six years ago," continues Baker, "and I thought to myself, 'What is *Planet of the Apes* this many years later? We can't do the same thing,' even though I liked it at the time. I thought, 'Wow, these are cool, but it'd be nice to see their teeth and it'd be nice to see a little more expression and individuality.' The only reason I think they looked different is they had a design for the gorillas and the chimps and the orangutans, and they pretty much did the same makeup on everybody. The sculptures are basically the same. The wrinkles are in the same place, it's just the proportions of the face that they put it on were different. I really wanted to make them individual characters as much as possible and give them more mobility."

One of the makeup challenges of the original films was the fact that it was virtually impossible to get the actors to articulate their lips around the teeth. "Well," Baker offers, "in the old films, it was a big thick chunk of foam that had rubber teeth stuck into it. The actors' real teeth were buried behind about an inch of rubber. I thought about this for a long time, because when they first approached me six years ago, I thought, well, we can do animatronic gorillas that look ab-

Michael Clarke Duncan. Credit: Al Ortega

solutely real, we've done that, but that's not *Planet of the Apes*. Part of the charm of the first film was an actor-motivated ape. So I think we really have to do makeups, and I think we need to be able to show the teeth, so let's just make some big-assed dentures, as big dentures as we can, push the muzzle out as much as we can with the teeth, and have as little amount of foam as possible. So that's what we have, a big set of teeth and a thin piece of foam. The problem there is speaking with the teeth in. It takes some doing—it takes some practice. We made practice teeth for everybody, told them to take these home, read the newspaper, say and do whatever you have to do to get used to speaking with them. First you're going to

Helena Bonham Carter. Credit: Al Ortega

think it's impossible, but you'll find out you can do it. Some people are much better than others. One of the problems is saying p's, because you have to put your lips together. In fact, there was a really funny scene that was supposed to be a dramatic scene with Thade saying, 'Apart from my father.' But he kept saying, 'A fart from my father.' I think they're going to have to loop that. The truth is, we've got these makeups that are much more expressive and we're doing all this stuff, but there's no real innovation here. It's the same material as, basically, they used in the first film. It's just applied differently."

In early June 2000, Burton began looking at possible locations for the film in Hawaii. Interviewed by the *Honolulu Star-Bulletin,* Burton explained, "My films are not shot in the most beautiful locations. This is really an uneasy feeling. But honestly, we're just looking around. The stage we're in right now with this film is to think and dream and look. Once you get going on a film, you don't get a chance ever to sit and appreciate a place."

On June 22, 2000, Mark Wahlberg was signed to star in the film as the astronaut who arrives on a planet of apes. "People tell me I'm pretty simian," he mused, "but I think Tim Burton wants me to be the Charlton Heston role. Tim is the kind of guy where I just say yes to anything he wants me to do. I did say, 'What kind of ape do you want me to play?' and Tim said, 'You're the human.'"

In *Planet of the Apes,* Wahlberg portrays astronaut Leo Davidson, who inadvertently finds himself on an alien planet where simians reign supreme. Wahlberg was born on June 5, 1971, in Dorchester, Massachusetts. He made his movie debut in *The Substitute* (1993) and followed with 1994's *Renaissance Man,* 1995's *The Basketball Diaries,* 1996's *Fear,* 1997's *Traveler* and *Boogie Nights* (the film which really put him on the road to superstardom), 1998's *The Big Hit,* 1999's *The Corruptor* and *Three Kings,* 2000's *The Yards* and *The Perfect Storm,* and, in 2001, *The Truth About Charlie* in addition to *Planet of the Apes.*

Tim Roth, born in England on May 14, 1961, was then cast as Thade, the film's chimpanzee antagonist. Like many British actors, Roth has had no problem segueing back and forth between motion pictures and British television. His extensive credits include 1981's *Meantime;* 1982's *Made in Britain;* 1984's *The Hit;* 1985's *Murder with Mirrors* and *Return to Waterloo;* 1987's *Metamorphosis;* 1988's *To Kill a Priest, A World Apart,* and *The Modern World: Ten Great Writers;* 1989's *The Cook, the Thief, His Wife & Her Lover;* 1990's *Yellowbacks, Vincent & Theo, Rosencrantz and Guildenstern Are Dead,* and *Farendj;* 1991's *Backsliding;* 1992's *Common Pursuit, Reservoir Dogs,* and *The Perfect Husband;* 1993's *Murder in the Heartland* and *Bodies, Rest & Motion;* 1994's *Heart of Darkness, Pulp Fiction, Captives,* and *Who Do You Think You're Fooling?;* 1995's *Rob Roy* and *Four Rooms;* 1996's *Everyone Says I Love You* and *Mocking the Cosmos;* 1997's *No Way Home, Gridlock'd, Hoodlum, Deceivers,* and *Animals;* 1998's *The Legend of the Pianist on the Ocean,* 2000's *Vatel, Bread and Roses, Lucky Numbers,* and *Invincible,* and in 2001 is featured in—besides *Planet of the Apes—Inside Job* and *D'Artagnan.*

Portraying the orangutan Limbo is Paul Giamatti, born on June 6, 1967, in England. Beyond television appearances in the critically acclaimed *NYPD Blue* and *Homicide: Life on the Street,* he starred in 1990's *She'll Take Romance;* 1992's *Singles* and *Past Midnight;* 1995's *Mighty Aphrodite* and *Sabrina;* 1996's *Breathing Room, Ripper,* and *A Further Gesture;* 1997's *Donnie Brasco, Private Parts, My Best Friend's Wedding,* and *Deconstructing Harry;* 1998's *Tourist Trap, The Truman Show, Doctor Dolittle, Saving Private Ryan, The Negotiator, Safe Men,* and *Winchell;* 1999's *The Cradle Will Rock* and *Man on the Moon;* 2000's *If These Walls Could Talk 2; Big Momma's House, Duets,* and *In the Boom Boom Room;* and, in addition to *Apes,* the so-called *Untitled Todd Solondz Project.*

Michael Clarke Duncan, born on December 10, 1957, portrays the imposing gorilla warrior Attar. Although he appeared on such television shows as *Married . . . With Children, The Jamie Foxx Show, Sparks,* and *Built to Last,* Duncan has made his biggest impression in such features as 1995's *Friday;* 1997's *Back in Business;* 1998's *The Player's Club, Bulworth, Armageddon,* and *A Night* at the Roxbury; 1999's *Breakfast of Champions, The Green Mile,* and *The Underground Comedy Movie;* 2000's *The Whole Nine Yards* and *Soldier of Fortune,* and 2001's *See Spot Run, They Call Me Sirr, Return of the Mummy,* and, naturally, *Planet of the Apes.*

Mark Wahlberg's leading "lady" in *Planet of the Apes* is the chimpanzee Ari, who is portrayed by Helena Bonham Carter. Born on May 26, 1966, in London, Carter's career has spanned both television and film. In 1984 she burst on to the American scene with several appearances on Michael Mann's *Miami Vice.* Her features include 1986's *Lady Jane* and *A Room With a View;* 1987's *The Vision* and *Maurice;* 1988's *The Mask;* 1989's *Francesco;* 1990's *Hamlet;* 1991's *Where Angels Fear to Tread;* 1992's *Howard's End;* 1993's *Dancing Queen* and *Fatal Deception: Mrs. Lee Harvey Oswald;* 1994's *Mary Shelley's Frankenstein, A Dark Adapted Eye,* and *Butter;* 1995's *Mighty Aphrodite* and *Margaret's Museum;* 1996's *Twelfth Night: Or What You Will, Portraits of Chinois,* and *The Great War;* 1997's *The Wings of the Dove, Keep the Aspidistra Flying,* and *The Petticoat Expeditions;* 1998's *Merlin, The Revengers' Comedies,* and *The Theory of Flight;* 1999's *Fight Club, Women Talking Dirty, The Nearly Complete and Utter History of Everything,* and *Carnivale;* and, moving beyond *POTA,* 2001's *Till Human Voices Wake Us* and *Novocaine.*

In describing the character of Ari, Carter says, "She's basically a human rights activist who's a chimp. She was sort of an upper-class chimp and a princess, but they demoted me. I don't know why. They wooed me with the idea that, 'She's a princess, she's got all their courtiers and she's very powerful and smart,' and then it all vanished. Suddenly I just became an upper-class chimp. I don't have a crown—nothing, no courtiers. But I'm just this human rights activist who's disgruntled with the state of affairs on the planet vis-à-vis how humans are treated, and I strongly believe that humans are sort of savages and slaves, but I believe that they have potential. They have souls and they can be taught to live with us as equals. And I see in Mark's character, who's this human who has come from a different planet, the potential and a sense that he likes me and has a rebellious quality. Actually, that we can change and help make change, as he promises, the situation."

For Carter, perhaps the most humiliating part of performing in *Planet of the Apes* is the fact that she flunked right out of Ape School.

"Ape attention deficit disorder," she explains. "*Major* ape attention deficit disorder. I lacked *everything.* But then I buckled down and I was told to concentrate and I did develop, I think. You know, it's not easy being an ape and discovering you're an ape. It's much more challenging than I thought it was at first. It requires a strange kind of concentration. But we learned all sorts of things at Ape School. First, about how to move, how to walk. They explained that we have different anatomy to humans. We're essentially a quadruped. Then, that we have much shorter legs so we had to sort of develop this walk. Apes—chimps, anyway—have no sort of forward leg/hip movement, so you have to sort of develop a . . . well, it's not exactly a waddle, but we had to keep that in mind. Also, we've got much longer arms. The other essential thing, too, is that they've got a grace and an economy of movement. That's quite useful as an actor, which you can sort of implement as an actor, in that you don't move unless you have to move. And a grace and a fluidity and a coordination which I lack anyway in normal life. It was very interesting and it was like a real bonus to have four weeks of ape training. It makes you much more focused and centered. We did a lot of breathing. It was taken very seriously.

"But at the same time," Carter adds, "it's quite difficult to keep a serious face, particularly when you look around. I think that's one of the hardest things—it takes a major suspension of disbelief, this job, more than most because you look around and everyone's got ape heads on. The other thing is that we're heavily disabled, because we're wearing teeth which makes it difficult to talk and we've got ears on so it makes it difficult to hear or listen. And so it is very hilarious when you've got a load of apes because we can't hear a word we're saying, and so we're always going, 'What? What are you saying?' And we're all incomprehensible. So it's very diverting."

She also finds it liberating to play an ape in the film, much more so than if she had played a human role. "It's a real liberation; a sort of license," Carter notes. "The mask is a sort of license to completely misbehave. Because apes are much more tactile, I can sort of get away with screwing people up and being naughty, really. And, you know, you can be rude and disrespect people. They're much more sensual as well, so that's pretty fun. Exhaustion is another factor of the job, because you have to wake up quite early to get ready by the time they shoot. I'm in five hours of makeup, so one is always working on a sort of deprivation of sleep. But what keeps me going is the absurdity of it all and there's always a constant source of humor and hilarity and absurdity that's always present, so that keeps me awake."

Some of that hilarity was supplied by Rick Baker, who continuously tried to demonstrate how the actors could make the makeup work for them and become more expressive. "There was one day of dailies," Baker says, sounding a lot like Roddy McDowall who also discovered three decades earlier that it was necessary to keep all facial muscles twitching, "where I ran into Tim Roth and I said, 'You're not moving your face enough.' I did a cameo thing and did a test a few weeks before that, walking around the stage, goofing off basically. Helena said, 'You can really move this! How come you can move it so much more than we can?' I said, 'Because I'm moving my face underneath it and I'm not afraid of making an ass of myself, basically.' Most actors are afraid of overacting. You really have to in this kind of stuff. I was doing all this chimp stuff and she kept saying, 'I'm going to steal some of this from you.' I said, 'Please, please steal—watch me a lot and do it.' She picked up a lot. She's really good at being a chimp.

"But the females are the biggest problems," he adds, assuming talking about female apes rather than the gender as a whole. "When Tim first spoke to me about it, he wanted this kind of sexual tension between the human astronaut character and the female ape, and wanted her to be kind of sexually attractive to men. That's a tough one, 'cause I like apes a lot, but I've never really wanted to do it with one. Her makeup takes closer to four hours. Part of it is you're doing a smoother, prettier one and you've got to be really careful. You're doing an appliance makeup and then you're doing a beauty makeup on top of that. It's about two-and-a-half to four hours. She looks good, actually. It was quite a battle, but Tiffani Smith, who's a runner at my shop, and I started doing tests. I said to Tiffany, 'Hey, c'mere, let's take a cast of you.' We did some really hideous females to begin with and were saying, 'Oh God, this is not going to work.' We actually ended up using Tiffani in the movie. She looks real pretty. We solved the problem through trial and error. Some of the initial ideas were maybe humanizing a little bit, and it actually made it more grotesque. I mean, it just looked like a freak human. It's funny, but I'm so used to Helena as Ari that she looks odd to me now without the makeup."

For the actress, a genuine appeal of the project was the opportunity that it presented to work with Tim Burton. "He's fantastic," Carter enthuses. "He's a really good person and he's so funny himself. He's so energetic. He's certainly a visionary. I mean, he has such a strong vision and every single film of his has his stamp and signature on it. Yet to work with him is unbelievably collaborative and open and non-controlling and non-dictatorial. I don't quite know how he manages that. He does a perpetual sort of juggling act, so he's always listening to your ideas, but obviously at the end of the day I know this picture will be inimitably his. But he's all intuition and instant heart, and it's all about feeling. He never finishes a sentence, but somehow he'll come up and give you a note and he's probably said about three words and none of them have much relation to each other, but somehow you understand exactly what he means. He's great fun, very dynamic and very pleasant. And thank God, because, frankly, this wouldn't be tolerable if he wasn't."

As Rick Baker explains, it was extremely important for the film to make sure that the actors would not be claustrophobic, as had been the case with a number of actors on the original film series. "I made a real big point about that," says Baker. "I said that we had to make sure that these guys understand what they're getting into. When you're casting, casting is real important. In the way I'm doing the makeup, the person has to have the right kind of face for this to work, first of all. I actually gave them life casts—I said, 'This is a bad life cast, this is a good life cast. I wanted them to see what made a bad face, which would be a nose kind of like mine—a big nose, and a short upper lip. So they started out worrying about it, but they completely forgot, because they cast Tim Roth in one of the most important parts. He has a bigger nose than I have. When they said Tim Roth was a possibility to play Thade, I was going, 'What part of this big nose thing did you not understand? Good life cast, bad life cast. Here's Tim Roth.' They said, 'But he's a really good actor.' I said, 'I know he is, but . . .' It turned out to be really cool-looking; I think it's really interesting. He's a great villain. It worked out really nicely. I spent time with everybody before we were taking the life casts, telling them what it is. I showed them the dentures they had to wear, I showed them some video of makeup tests. I said every day, every morning, some joker will put glue on your face.'"

Real excitement for cast and crew was Charlton Heston's agreeing to have a cameo in the film—this time as an ape! The veteran actor portrays Thade's father in a pivotal scene. "My cameo was not a very difficult day's work but it was a rather weird experience," Heston explains. "Dick Zanuck said, 'I need you to do a scene—not a scene really but a shot.' It's a very short piece but I think it will work very usefully."

On getting into Rick Baker's grueling ape appliances and experiencing the flip side of the evolutionary chain, Heston confides, 'This was one of the most uncomfortable makeups I've ever worn and that's saying a great deal. It was a brute but I knew that going in. I don't wonder that Roddy McDowall and those guys had such a hard time. Anyway, we got it done and the make-up was marvelous."

Also agreeing to a cameo in Burton's reinvention was another original cast member, Linda Harrison, who played the savage mute Nova. Once again, she plays a role similar to her previous incarnation. "Isn't it ironic that Richard would be asked to produce the new *Planet of the Apes,*" she muses, "and Heston and I are back on screen but in different roles?"

In October of 2000—just weeks before production was to begin—the writing team of Lawrence Konner and Mark Rosenthal was brought in to finesse Broyles's script. Konner and Rosenthal were first represented on screen in 1985's *The Jewel of the Nile* (sequel to the Michael Douglas/Kathleen Turner starrer *Romancing the Stone*) and *The Legend of Billie Jean.* In 1987 they co-wrote *Superman IV: The Quest for Peace,* followed a year later by *The In Crowd.* Next was 1990's *Desperate Hours,* the 1991 television miniseries *Sometimes They Come Back,* and they received story credit for that year's *Star Trek VI: The Undiscovered Country,* 1993's *The Beverly Hillbillies* and *For Love or Money,* 1998's Bruce Willis thriller *Mercury Rising* and the remake of *Mighty Joe Young,* 2001's *Planet of the Apes* and the feature film version of the classic sci-fi television series, *The Prisoner.*

"The script needed another revision," explains Konner, "more work done, and some high-up decision was made that we should be the guys to do it. It's a big mystery to me why these things happen; how they're decided."

A highlight for both writers was just the opportunity to work with Burton. Konner opines, "I can describe him in the way he works with writers as a director. His imagination is a fantastic thing, as you might guess. I don't want this to be too corny-sounding, but, really, it's supposed to feel like an opportunity to get into his mind a little, and that seems to be a real opportunity. You know, he doesn't work in a linear fashion. He tends to have an idea for X-moment and it might be the kind of feeling he wants to get at a certain line, and we try to write that and get back to him, then do changes and it's a very kind of back and forth process, and continues to be.

"Story-wise," he continues, trying to convey the nature of working with Burton, "you have to keep it moving. Real characters create motion, and I don't mean just physical motion, although, certainly, there's a lot of physical motion in this, but kind of dramatic motion. Tim has cross-out pen strikes at the place where things stop for too long, holds for too long, or when he wants to keep the story driven. I think that's a very good thing. It's collaborative. Lots of times it's him making suggestions, it's us making suggestions, it's Dick Zanuck. Somebody was asking me the other day about screenwriting in general. I think screenwriting, unlike some other things, is a real problem-solving occupation, and almost all the time you don't have lined pages with nothing to do. You have something you have to accomplish next. If it's a love story, then, okay, how do they meet? So you've gotta get them to meet. So now there's this problem you need to solve. Well in this particular case, we not only had sort of the standard writing kind of problems to solve, but problems such as production problems and idiosyncratic notions of that. In a sense, every day we were presented with a new problem that we had to go back and solve, present the solution back to Tim, and say, 'What do you think of this way of getting the story . . . ?' and he would either like it or not like it. But, you know, you drop a pebble in a pond and you're the pebble and the ripples—I don't know if this is a good image or not—but Tim's genius is those ripples. His genius is the next idea and the next idea and the next idea, on top of more of the genius you thought you were. But you walk and he has now spun into something that is very unconventional and you sort of sit there and think, 'Well, it's Tim Burton.' He's a genuine artist, and what's remarkable is that he is a genuine artist who manages time and again to connect to the biggest possible world-wide audience. You know, it's an amazing thing. I don't think there's anybody else in the business who can say this. Tim Burton makes the biggest international, huge, entertaining, satisfying movies, and yet every one of them has a stamp. It's individual and very different from the rest of the pack. I think you know you're in a Tim Burton movie when you're in a theater. It may not be perfect every time, but it's always exciting and always interesting."

Mark Rosenthal emphasizes, "This will definitely be a Tim Burton movie. He's definitely putting his stamp on it. The studio has been extremely stoked and it's going to be a very different version. It's going to be Tim Burton's *Planet of the Apes* just like he created Tim Burton's version of *Batman*. He has done some very cool things with the apes. This is *not* just guys walking around in rubber ape masks. No matter how you slice the first one, they still, unfortunately, have two-legged actors standing around in rubber ape masks. This is actually rethinking how apes really would evolve into more intelligent than human creatures."

Impressive to Rosenthal was the previously mentioned ape school that was designed to teach the actors how to move more ape-like. "All of their movements are all based on how you would imagine apes who became intelligent would move. They go from sort of human-like to when they get very emotional, where they quickly rely on much more ape-like movements. It's all integrated in. I don't know if you've ever seen an ape charge, but they charge on all fours; they charge on their front knuckles. So a character will come running up on his knuckles and suddenly stand up and start speaking in an English accent. That is *very* cool. Or in a romantic thing, they will go from dialogue to flashing their fangs. Pretty amazing stuff!"

Producer Ralph Winter admits that he's pretty impressed with Burton as a filmmaker. "I actually was going to work with Tim on *Mars Attacks!,* but that didn't work out," he says. "And I've been looking forward to this and it's been even better than I thought. You see Tim and you think he's a little eccentric, and his vision of his movies is certainly a little more offbeat than what a lot of directors are.

But what you don't expect and what you see here is that this guy is buttoned down. This guy is organized. He knows what he's doing. Nothing gets by this guy in terms of how the story gets told and the details. Certainly the visual details and the story details. And he's a nice guy to boot. This is a guy who says please and thank you, and for some reason that's become rare in our business. He's genuinely a nice guy, and the crew knows that. They respect that and they work hard for this guy. They work hard because he's nice to them, but they also work hard because he's creating a vision and creating something spectacular. And we think it's cinematic history. It's pretty amazing to work on this project with Tim Burton and *Planet of the Apes*."

One of the challenges facing the filmmakers is the Internet, and the way that details about the film—some true, most false—make their ways into fans' hands far earlier than the creative team wants. One such instance was the furor over rumors that the film would face an interspecies love story between Leo and Ari. "That's absolutely insane," says Zanuck. "No truth to it. I almost got into it to respond back and say this is a lot of hogwash. I didn't because I didn't want to get dragged into it. There's nothing about that at all. There's as much going on between the Mark Wahlberg character and the Helena Bonham Carter character as there was between Heston and Kim Hunter's characters. It's absolutely tame. They like each other, but there's nothing sexual there. There's no kiss or anything like that. We have no intention of doing anything like that. Even if we did, which would be crazy and unimaginable, this has to be a PG-13. It's not that kind of picture. I was actually very annoyed when I saw such fabrication take place."

"We're protective," adds Ralph Winter. "We're very protective about the script. It's numbered and if you're a member of the crew, your name is on every page. You sign a non-disclosure being a member of the crew. And so we're trying to contain that and you only get a script if you really need it. Even the revision pages go out with your name on it. It's a logistical nightmare for the office, but it helps keep control of that stuff. When we're downtown (at Fox), it's pretty easy because we own sort of the whole lot. We don't have a lot of non-combatants on our stages. Here it's probably the most open where we've used black curtains at times where we have so many apes outside. We just don't want photographs of that coming out too soon. And we use little airport shuttle buses with dark windows and all that kind of stuff. I think we're so far out in the desert while on location that you've gotta be a real die-hard to trek seven miles from the road to find us. But you want to keep the lid on the pot until it's time to eat, and, unfortunately, you can't control it all. I hope they feel good about themselves taking third-rate pictures and putting them on the Net. You know, I almost want to release pictures that are the good ones. I want to show you what Rick Baker looks like in makeup. He does a cameo in the movie. Don't judge me by the third-rate pictures that are on the Net. And it's like, 'Do you want to spoil the ending? Do you want to read the last chapter of the book before you read the first part?' You're not going to appreciate it. You need to see what it's about. So we're trying to tell a story. We're trying to have fun. We're trying to build it in such a way that it'll be enjoyable for everybody. Unfortunately, we have to sort of be a little tight about all the rest of the stuff and kind of keep the lid on the pot for everybody."

On November 6, 2000, filming on the first new *Planet of the Apes* adventure in nearly thirty years officially commenced, with that extravaganza reaching theaters on July 27, 2001.

Amazingly, when Arthur P. Jacobs first became captivated by Pierre Boulle's original novel in 1963, there was no *Star Trek,* no *2001: Space Odyssey,* and no *Star Wars.* In fact, with the exception of *Forbidden Planet* and *The Day the Earth Stood Still,* there had barely been *any* intelligent science fiction films that attempted to deal with issues affecting humanity within a genre backdrop. Creatively, the Hollywood community thought that sci-fi was a dead end, a sure-fire way to lose money at the box office.

But Jacobs believed, and that belief turned the Hollywood community and its limited vision on its ear. *Planet of the Apes* was deemed an instant classic. Additionally, as the first science-fiction film series with direct continuity from one entry to the next, and which gave birth to a wide number of merchandise tie-ins, in many ways *Apes* paved the road for *Star Wars.* It proved that the audience *wanted* to be challenged; that they would be willing to journey to an upside down world provided they were given characters to identify with and a story that could somehow provide reflection and illumination of their own lives.

Amazingly, as Burton's reinterpretation of the material has proven, Jacobs's dream is still very much alive nearly forty years later. Then and now, *Planet of the Apes* serves as the quintessential motion picture classic that has more than withstood the passage of time. It has touched the imagination of two generations and will move on to a third in the years to come.

Apes rule, indeed!

INDEX